MW00445900

Martin Luther King

THE LIBRARY OF AFRICAN AMERICAN BIOGRAPHY

General Editor, John David Smith
Charles H. Stone Distinguished Professor of American History
University of North Carolina at Charlotte

The Library of African American Biography aims to provide concise, readable, and up-to-date lives of leading black figures in American history, in widely varying fields of accomplishment. The books are written by accomplished scholars and writers and reflect the most recent historical research and critical interpretation. Illustrated with photographs, they are designed for general informed readers as well as for students.

Martin Luther King: A Religious Life, Paul Harvey (2021)

Madam C. J. Walker: The Making of an American Icon, Erica L. Ball (2021)

Fannie Lou Hamer: America's Freedom Fighting Woman, Maegan Parker Brooks (2020)

Jackie Robinson: An Integrated Life, J. Christopher Schutz (2016)

W. E. B. Du Bois: An American Intellectual and Activist, Shawn Leigh Alexander (2015)

Paul Robeson: A Life of Activism and Art, Lindsey R. Swindall (2013)

Ella Baker: Community Organizer of the Civil Rights Movement, J. Todd Moye (2013)

Booker T. Washington: Black Leadership in the Age of Jim Crow, Raymond W. Smock (2010)

Walter White: The Dilemma of Black Identity in America, Thomas Dyja (2010)

Richard Wright: From Black Boy to World Citizen, Jennifer Jensen Wallach (2010)

Louis Armstrong: The Soundtrack of the American Experience, David Stricklin (2010)

Martin Luther King

A Religious Life

Paul Harvey

ROWMAN & LITTLEFIELD
Lanham • Boulder • New York • London

Published by Rowman & Littlefield
An imprint of The Rowman & Littlefield Publishing Group, Inc.
4501 Forbes Boulevard, Suite 200, Lanham, Maryland 20706
www.rowman.com

86-90 Paul Street, London EC2A 4NE, United Kingdom

British Library Cataloguing in Publication Information Available

Library of Congress Cataloging-in-Publication Data
Names: Harvey, Paul, 1961– author.
Title: Martin Luther King : a religious life / Paul Harvey.
Description: Lanham : Rowman & Littlefield, [2021] | Series: Library of African
    American biography | Includes bibliographical references and index. |
    Summary: "In the first biography of Martin Luther King to look at his life
    through the prism of his evolving faith, distinguished historian Paul Harvey
    examines Martin Luther King's life through his complex, emerging, religious
    lives. Harvey's concise biography will allow readers to see King anew in the
    context of his time and today"— Provided by publisher.
Identifiers: LCCN 2021019984 (print) | LCCN 2021019985 (ebook) | ISBN
    9781538115923 (cloth) | ISBN 9781538115930 (ebook)
Subjects: LCSH: King, Martin Luther, Jr., 1929–1968. | King, Martin Luther,
    Jr., 1929–1968—Religion. | Civil rights workers—United States—Biography.
    | Baptists—United States—Clergy—Biography. | African Americans—
    Biography. | African American clergy—Biography.
Classification: LCC E185.97.K5 H315 2021 (print) | LCC E185.97.K5 (ebook) |
    DDC 323.092 [B]—dc23
LC record available at https://lccn.loc.gov/2021019984
LC ebook record available at https://lccn.loc.gov/2021019985

To
Maria Varela,
An Inspirational Friend,
and
The Reverend William Barber,
Keeper of the Flame

The end is reconciliation; the end is redemption; the end is the creation of a beloved community.

—Martin Luther King Jr., 1956

There's something wrong with a religion that has nothing to say about the oppressive realities that exist in life. God is the God of the oppressed.

—Reverend William Barber
Interview from *The Black Church: This Is Our Story, This Is Our Song*
PBS documentary film, 2021

Contents

Acknowledgments

My deepest thanks to the folks at Rowman & Littlefield, especially Jon Sisk and John David Smith, for their faith in this project and great patience in waiting for it as I completed another work in line ahead of it. My thanks also to my friend and fellow biographer of Howard Thurman, Peter Eisenstadt, for his careful reading of the manuscript and numerous suggestions, corrections, and critiques of it, and to my friend and colleague Jeff Scholes, for years of conversations on this and many other subjects in American religious history. Susan Nishida likewise scoured the manuscript with her unerring eye for unnecessary words and phrases and her insistence on getting to the point. Finally, a scholarly note of thanks and gratitude to the numerous scholars and other biographers whose work I have drawn on extensively here and to all over the years who have worked with the Martin Luther King, Jr. Papers Project; all scholars of twentieth-century American history are in their debt.

Introduction

The Redemptive Power of
Martin Luther King Jr.

I am a profound advocate of the social gospel.

—Martin Luther King Jr., paper at Crozer Theological Seminary, 1948

Speaking at Stanford University in 1967 on "The Other America," Martin Luther King Jr. analyzed the urban conflagrations then raging throughout the United States. His words were reprinted in May and June 2020 as Black Lives Matter (BLM) protests in the midst of a pandemic and political turmoil grabbed the attention of Americans. The 2020 uprisings arose from the same complex of causes that King had tried to explain to the nation in the 1960s—most especially the reality of police brutality and of a justice system singularly focused on policing, arresting, and incarcerating black people. Much the same was the case in 2020 following the death of George Floyd, a young black man in Minneapolis, from the force of a policeman pinning him to the ground until his life literally was extinguished. Protests ensued, and so did acts of rage. In 1967, in the midst of similar urban unrest, King explained his position:

> Let me say as I've always said, and I will always continue to say, that riots are socially destructive and self-defeating. . . . But in the final analysis, a riot is the language of the unheard. And what is it that America has failed to hear? It has failed to hear that the plight of the Negro poor has worsened over the last few years. It has failed to hear that the promises of freedom and justice have not been met. And it has failed to hear that large segments of white society are more concerned about tranquility and the status quo than about justice, equality, and humanity. And so in a real sense our nation's summers of riots are caused by our nation's winters of delay. And as long

as America postpones justice, we stand in the position of having these recurrences of violence and riots over and over again.

King entered the later years of his life a troubled, harried person. He stayed constantly on the move but was consumed with a desire for stillness and downtime. He led a movement of great social power but was plagued by doubts about its efficacy and infighting; he kept his faith in an America that he increasingly saw as hopelessly racist; he symbolized for many the moral strength of a movement for justice while he himself sought escape from it in private bouts of binge drinking and compulsive philandering. His magnificent oratorical voice had been taxed by overuse and smoking. Public opinion polls showed him to be widely unpopular among whites, in part because of an FBI-directed campaign to undermine him; meanwhile, some African Americans suspected him of being too beholden to nonviolence to understand the role of self-defense. He lived a very public life but privately was constantly surveilled by the FBI and other government agencies. He was exhausted from years of constant turmoil and infighting with civil rights organizations. He yearned for some time to step aside from the rush of events and meditate on the best path forward. He never got it.

King had become the spokesman for a true interracial social democracy: a radical idea that challenged centuries of white supremacist rule. This involved far more than desegregating buses or being able to sit at a hamburger counter or shop unmolested at a department store. Rather, it demanded a radical restructuring of society, a redistribution of wealth, and a full acknowledgment of the systemic racism that defined and controlled the lives of African Americans and other minorities.

King was imbued with a vision of brotherhood. He also preached a radical political message of justice and equality economically. This is the apostle of justice pretty well known to scholars but one generally unfamiliar to most general readers. Around his birthday each year, Americans are treated to a few of his greatest hits—the dream, the content of our character, nonviolence, and others—shorn of context and missing many of the most fundamental themes of King's message. The brief two-minute life of King presented each year in January is not completely false. He did have a dream, and he did believe in a universal brotherhood of humanity. But stripped from the context of his ever-evolving life and the social radicalism of his views, King's message remains blurred and incomplete. This work, by contrast, presents a King who consistently pursued a religiously based vision of social democracy, one that required a transformation of American society.

Any biographer taking on a familiar subject faces a challenge. Why is another biography necessary? The reason, I believe, is that the richness of the scholarly literature on King has yet to reach a more general audience. One central aim of this text is to provide a short, readable study of the religious lives and visions of Martin Luther King Jr., one emphasizing his role as a religious figure and moral philosopher.

This work draws from and incorporates a generation and more of study on King and his life. Included at the end is an extensive bibliographic essay discussing that literature and pointing out the works on which I have relied the most. Nor is this a complete narrative of his life or of the civil rights movement of those years. Other extensively detailed and brilliantly accomplished studies of that sort exist. They give blow-by-blow accounts of huge events in civil rights history and provide close and powerfully reasoned arguments about the sources of and influences on King's thought.

Rather, this short and synthetic study offers students and general readers a chance to reflect on Martin Luther King Jr. as a *minister*, a *master orator*, a *movement leader and strategist*, a *moral philosopher and prophet*, a *morally and personally conflicted man*, and a *misunderstood martyr* in his afterlives. These categories will frame a discussion that tries to capture Martin Luther King Jr. through the lens of his religious visions for a moral transformation in American society. Obviously, important details of his life, narratives of key moments in civil rights history, and other staples of King biographies are present here. But they are deployed in the service of what I hope is less of a conventional "life and times" book and more of an interpretive essay on King.

In brief: King is the single most important figure in modern American religious history, far more so than many of the usual suspects often granted that status. And while he did not "cause" it, he became the symbol for the most important social movement of twentieth-century American history.

This book features parts of King's life that best match these themes. Its focus is on his religious lives, messages, conflicts, and philosophies. It portrays him as a figure who interpreted and foresaw the dilemmas, then and now, of racial inequality in the United States and abroad. I seek to avoid romanticizing King. He was almost morbidly aware of his own failures and weaknesses. I also resist reducing his complex and evolving message to a quick and easily digestible message. Instead, the book centers King's radical message of hope amid tragedy and suffering, of moral courage in the face of state-sanctioned evil, of clear-eyed critique in the face of romanticized pabulum, and of common humanity in an age of a fractious divisiveness and social rage.

King was a prophet in the full biblical sense. He was not a saint or a model easily adaptable for the current agendas of many who try to claim him. Rather, he was a radical truth-teller, speaking about the roots and expression of the social evil of racism, and the moral means to overcome that, to a society organized on the constantly reproduced lies of white supremacy. And like a prophet he called his nation to holiness and redemption. King's vision was far from realized at the time of his death, of course, and he was far from certain that it was realizable. He wondered whether Malcolm X had been right—that the dream was really a nightmare from which one could not awaken.

But the failure to reckon fully with King's critique and vision left a gaping hole that recently has become more publicly focused. King's full linking of racial reconciliation and brotherhood *together* with economic justice and moral accountability for systemic inequalities has yet to be well comprehended. Beyond that, King's evolution as a thinker requires a better understanding. He held firm to certain core radical convictions expressed very early in his life and fully developed later. He also underwent a constant process of thinking over and through those convictions. As he did, he came to a clearer (albeit darker) vision of the insidiously evil history and nature of American racism and the moral and practical complexities of promoting human brotherhood within a system that deliberately and systematically thwarted achieving it. King was never overcome by pessimism. But he acknowledged a growing understanding over time of what we would now call systemic racism.

A major question facing any biographer of King is whether he effectively stood for the same thing during these years, or whether he fundamentally changed his mind on key issues. Or, for that matter, whether he even saw America as a land of hope or only invoked that language to appeal to a mass white audience. Some scholars and biographers have portrayed King as a man of the left throughout his adult life, a democratic socialist more willing to announce those views in public as time went by. Hemmed in by McCarthyism in the 1950s, King kept his more radical views discreetly under wraps—but they were there. And when the opportunity rose to express those views more publicly and articulately, he did so. And he paid a heavy price for doing so.

King's deepest religious visions derived from his synthesis of his immersion in the black church from childhood with theologies and ideas he gained from academic and personal study. From his youngest writings, even in unpublished personal correspondence while courting Coretta Scott, he expressed three of the principles and queries that would drive his religious philosophical development in the future. *First* was his profound sense of human evil. King's "dream" is often portrayed as a positive forecast of the days of human brotherhood to come. Such a view omits all the struggle against evil human institutions that would be required even to catch a distant glimpse of the promised land. The prophetic rage that King expressed most pronouncedly in the last three years before his assassination came in part from his sense of the intensity of the struggle against human evil. King portrayed this understanding as having come from his studies of neoorthodoxy and Reinhold Niebuhr. Certainly they gave him a certain language of description. But he saw and knew evil that those theologians could not have known, on a personal basis. Evil had a bitter personal pungency for him; he had lived with it his whole life, and while academic theology gave him a certain language to describe it, his personal experience of it drove his rage against it.

A second was his sense, at first skeptical and incomplete and later wholeheartedly philosophical, that nonviolence was not just the means but itself the message. Over time, too, that message grew more radical, as King confronted the challenges of Malcolm X and younger black radicals in the 1960s. King established close personal relations with some (such as Stokely Carmichael) and a kind of distant respect for others (Malcolm X). He learned from them. He then did with their ideas what he did with everything else he learned: he digested them, assimilated their central insights, and wove those into his own addresses and sermons. King was not an original thinker so much as a master assimilator and synthesizer of groupings of ideas he derived from multiple sources. He took from anything so he could give it everything. But he did so in service of his central idea: the moral message of nonviolence, the most powerful force in hopes of transforming the world. He preached that philosophy clearly and unfailingly, no matter what challenges he received for doing it.

A third was King's dream of social democracy. From his youngest juvenile writings, he described himself as a "profound advocator of the social gospel." But he took *social gospel*, a term describing an earlier twentieth-century movement aimed at applying the gospel to social conditions of life, and morphed it into *social democracy*. A state that consciously worked toward greater equality, toward the elimination of poverty and injustice, toward the equitable distribution of wealth, toward protecting jobs and livelihoods: that was central to King's dream—more so, even, than the parts about the content of character counting above color of skin, because that vision could come only with the transformations brought about by a movement toward social democracy.

Through his life King was an advocate of a European-style social democracy. He derived that from the black social gospel tradition into which he had been trained and from his everyday observations about how inequality worked in American society. He was more reluctant in the 1950s than toward the end of his life in fully expressing that vision. Hemmed in by McCarthyism and concerned about the movement being tarred as too radical, he invoked instead the language of American civil religion. The movement, he stated repeatedly, wanted to "save the soul of America"—that is, to make it realize the dreams of its founders for equality, to make it possible for African Americans to be part of the American dream instead of the American nightmare.

King expressed these points much more self-consciously and clearly later in his life. Many of his later addresses involve surprisingly detailed proposals for dealing with problems such as the automation of jobs, police brutality, an inegalitarian tax system, systemic discrimination in housing and employment, and the growing alliance of southern white supremacist forces with national conservatives interested in defending "states rights" and western civilization. As scholar Brandon Terry writes, King's focus on the systemic structuring of injustice "does not inflate 'racism' to make it explain *all* racial disparities, but understands that such inequalities are outcomes of many phenomena that interact with racism, *yet cannot be* reduced to only racism. These include technology, political economy, and cultural patterns." King's stance against the Vietnam War, articulated more brilliantly and memorably in New York exactly one year before his death, was not just against the war. Rather, it explored how unjust and unnecessary wars drained the very lifeblood from any hope of an egalitarian social democracy in the United States.

While he modulated for public audiences his most radical rhetoric during the height of McCarthyism and the early years of his involvement in the civil rights movement, he often gave such messages straightforwardly to black audiences. The magnificent scholarship represented in the current seven volumes (later to be fourteen) of *The Papers of Martin Luther King, Jr.*, as well as the outstanding work of other scholars who have gone through unpublished audio recordings of King's addresses, allow us to see King as someone who strategically chose his themes according to audience—not that he preached different messages fundamentally, but the emphases shifted by audience. The moral philosophy behind nonviolent civil disobedience; the yearning for a brotherhood beyond race which would allow men and women to live in harmony; the blistering words directed toward racist reactionaries but even more so toward "moderates" who prized order over justice; and the profoundly Christian message of God's love for all, the very love that allowed for brotherhood—he preached all of these consistently, through his entire life. To black and international audiences, in particular, he put more in the foreground a critique of imperialism and colonialism, a vision of economic justice made possible by a more egalitarian distribution of wealth, and a prophetic critique of the systemic racism that had empowered white supremacy in America since the arrival of slaves in the early seventeenth century. Eventually, over the last three years of his life, those became the primary themes of his public addresses. Long before then, he had articulated them frequently and with explosive power before his congregants in Montgomery and Atlanta, and to black church and civil rights audiences across the nation.

King's radicalism had deep roots. The black religious tradition informed him through its history of protest and proclamation. He drew from its critique of injustice and his envisioning of divine reality, its sense of suffering and hope for the beloved community. King also came from a long history of the black social gospel. Its history only recently has been uncovered and rewritten by scholars. His fundamental ideas were those of a radical social gospel bent on bending the moral arc of the world toward justice. He refined and tweaked his vision, and his language of presenting it, over time, but this always led him toward a radical vision of social equality.

It prepared him to adopt the language and concepts of social democracy. Through his studies and distillation of Hegel and other philosophers, he found a social diagnosis and theory of social change. He was no Marxist in any classical sense and frequently explained why Soviet-style communism stifled human freedom just like segregation in southern society—but with the important difference that in the United States, one had the right to protest for rights. One scholar has put it this way: "His was a social democratic sensibility through the social gospel of Walter Rauschenbusch, modified by the Christian realism of Reinhold Niebuhr, and governed by the basic philosophical categories of personalist idealism." More deeply, it was inspired by the sensibilities and spirit of the black religious tradition, particularly the black social gospel tradition of Howard Thurman, Benjamin Mays, and many others. King lived out and expanded the ideas that came from a black social gospel dating from the nineteenth century to the 1960s.

The historian and theologian Gary Dorrien has best captured this aspect of King's life and thought in his survey of the long tradition of the black social gospel. In *Breaking White Supremacy*, he writes, "King modified his conception of the classic social gospel with a dose of Christian realism and, thus, expanded the social message of Christ to its broadest, most inclusive, most radical extensions." King remained, in Dorrien's estimation, a "steadfast proponent of a radical social gospel for the world" and a "radical within a religious context. . . . His application of universal values makes him both a benchmark figure within a continuous radical tradition and an historical agent working within the unique contingencies of a particular time and place."

It's that combination—universal values set within the "unique contingencies" of the Jim Crow South—that drove King forward. This way of thinking about King foregrounds the historical trajectory of his radical religious ethos. As King once wrote, "While I saw neo-orthodoxy as a helpful corrective for a sentimental liberalism, I felt that it did not provide an adequate answer to basic questions." Finally he found an answer in a "realistic pacifism." True pacifism was a "courageous confrontation of evil by the power of love."

In the process, he learned from Gandhi. Put more precisely, he learned Gandhi as he did other theologians and thinkers, secondhand via the works of others. Like most black Americans, he took from Gandhi those parts that were most relevant to the black American experience (in particular, the technique of nonviolent civil disobedience) and shed other aspects of Gandhi that simply made no sense in an American context. And then he deliberately Christianized Gandhi, particularly in his first book *Stride Toward Freedom*. For King, Gandhi was the practitioner *par excellence* of a Christian love ethic combined with a powerful mode of resistance to evil. And in many cases, that ethos emerged as much from the practical experience of being thrust into the position as a symbolic leader of a movement, as from his theological study. "Many of the things I had not cleared up intellectually concerning nonviolence were now solved in the sphere of practical action." King worked out in his own mind an organic social gospel that found expression in actions of ordinary people who had never heard of the theologians but who empowered themselves as moral agents of change. His was a multiethnic mission of racial liberation.

King was a personalist, by his own description. It was a philosophy he had encountered in graduate school; more important, its emphasis on the dignity and worth of human personality inherently appealed to him. Personalism holds that personality of God and humans, infinite and finite, is the ultimate reality. The black church ethos that he grew up in was steeped in those same concepts, shorn of the fancy philosophical language. "The Kingdom of God is neither the thesis of individual enterprise nor the antithesis of collective enterprise, but a synthesis which reconciles both," King preached. In King's view, the oppressed were agents of their own destiny. The dispossessed had it within themselves to move against their own dispossession, with the unconquerable power of love and nonviolence transforming both themselves and their oppressors.

RELIGION AND THE MOVEMENT

In the mid-twentieth century, visionary social activists set out to instill in a mass movement a faith in nonviolence as the most powerful form of active resistance to injustice. The ideas of nonviolent civil disobedience first had to make their way from the confines of radical and pacifist thought into African American religious culture. This was the work of the generation before the civil rights movement of the 1950s and 1960s. A legacy of radical ideas stirred women and men from Pauli Murray and Ella Baker to Walter White, Charles Johnson, and Bayard Rustin. Black humanists, atheists, freethinkers, and skeptics transmitted ideas of nonviolent civil disobedience to a skeptical audience of gun-toting churchgoers and blasted the ways in which conventional southern Protestantism stultified social movements for change.

Because of the prominence of Martin Luther King Jr. and other ministers, many have interpreted the freedom struggle as a religious movement at its core. More recently, scholars have highlighted the politically radical and secular roots of the struggle in the political black Left (especially the Communist Party) of the Depression. Moreover, the argument goes, the movement's Christian morality and dependence on dramatizing the immorality of segregation through acts of nonviolent civil disobedience fell short when forced to confront deeper and more structurally built-in inequalities in American society. To those stuck in poverty, the right to eat a hamburger at a lunch counter was not particularly meaningful. Further, as the 1960s progressed, more rhetorically radical leaders emerged. Often, they distrusted black Christian institutions, seeing them as too complicit with larger power structures.

But this view minimizes and trivializes what the civil rights movement tried to accomplish, which was certainly more than a hamburger. And it remains impossible to conceive of the civil rights movement without placing black Christianity at its center, for that is what empowered the rank and file who made the movement *move*. And when it moved, major legal and legislative changes occurred. Martin King Jr.'s deep vision of justice, moreover, increasingly moved toward addressing issues of structural racial inequality. As the 1960s progressed, his moral critique of economic stratification, white colonialism, and the Vietnam War drew him harsh criticism from many whites. It also made him the target of a relentless surveillance apparatus at federal, state, and local levels.

Activists in the 1960s held a more chastened view about religion's role. For example, the institutional conservatism of Martin Luther King Jr.'s own denomination, the National Baptist Convention, forced King and a splinter group of followers to form the Progressive National Baptist Convention, a denomination more avowedly tied to civil rights. At local levels, indifference, theological conservatism, economic coercion, and sometimes threats of violence repressed the majority of black churches. Student volunteers from across the country, often coming with their own forms of religious skepticism, witnessed how often churches hindered rather than motivated a southern revolution. Further, activists often encountered the view that humans could do little to move the forces of history.

There was nothing inherent in "religion" in the South that either justified or blocked social justice struggles. The southern freedom struggle redefined how the central images and metaphors of black southern religious history could be deployed most effectively to mobilize a mass democratic movement. It also vividly illustrated the emotionally compelling power latent in the oral and musical artistry developed over centuries of religious expression, from the spirituals and gospel to sermonic and communal storytelling traditions.

To transform the region so dramatically, southern activists wove a version of their own history of social justice struggles out of a complicated tangle of threads. To do so, they engaged in narrative acts that allowed people to see themselves as part of a longrunning tradition of protest. They revivified part of the history of black southern Christianity. They did not have to invent a tradition, but they needed to make it a coherent narrative.

Nothing else could have kept the mass movement going through years of state-sponsored coercion, constant harassment, and acts of terrorism. The historically racist grounding of whiteness as dominant, blackness as inferior was radically overturned in part through a reimagination of the same Christian thought that was part of creating it in the first place. Many perceived it as a miraculous moment in time and sanctified its heroes. But that moment arose slowly and only after decades of preparation and struggle.

The connection between religion, civil rights, and social justice in everyday life found an especially powerful connection in the "local people" who did much of the actual work of the civil rights movement. In some ways, the southern-based freedom struggle in the 1960s began not with Montgomery but with an earlier boycott led by black Baptist pastor T. J. Jemison in Baton Rouge, Louisiana, in 1953, an action that set the stage for mass mobilizations to come. In lesser-known locales such as Baton Rouge, Tallahassee, and a variety of other small cities, black citizens organized protests and began to experiment with the methods of nonviolent civil disobedience. Those lessons would be imparted to Martin Luther King Jr., who put them to skillful use in Montgomery during a boycott of buses in Alabama's capital city that stretched for more than a year and resulted in a complete victory for the movement. In Montgomery, the churches played a central role, and the success there led to the formation of the Southern Christian Leadership Conference, King's organization for the remainder of his life.

Because of his epic 1963 piece "Letter from a Birmingham Jail," King is remembered now for his excoriation of "moderates" in the South. But for much of the 1950s, King still perceived that white southern ministers could provide moral leadership. Speaking at Vanderbilt in 1957, he professed his belief that "there are in the white South more open-minded moderates than appears on the surface. These people are silent today because of fear of social, political, and economic reprisals." He urged them to lead the region through its necessary transition to equal treatment for black citizens and reassured all that the aim of the movement was not to "defeat or humiliate the white man, but to win his friendship and understanding."

Part of the galvanizing effect of the movement in the early 1960s was a maturation in King's own vision. During the Birmingham campaign in April 1963, he issued a masterful public letter explaining the motivations behind the movement. The contrast with his hopeful 1957 sermon is striking. His "Letter from a Birmingham Jail" responded to a newspaper advertisement from eight local religious leaders. Reasoning that an imminent change of city government would soon take power out of the hands of Bull Connor and into a more reasonable city council, they suggested that the protests were "ill-timed." Noting that he had never been engaged in a campaign that had been deemed well timed, King chastised those willing to settle for "order" over justice. Oppressors never voluntarily gave up freedom to the oppressed; it always had to be demanded by "extremists for justice." He had lost the faith he had expressed in 1957 in a rising of white moderates.

That faith came under its crucial test late that summer. In August 1963, King found his public voice in the March on Washington, in one of the epic speeches of American history. Just three weeks later, a dynamite blast destroyed part of the Sixteenth Street Baptist Church in Birmingham, blowing out all but one of the stained-glass windows. The surviving window frame had featured a stained-glass rendering of a visually white Jesus. While the frame and structure of the window miraculously survived, the window itself sustained powerfully symbolic damage: the face of Jesus had been blown off. In a gruesome parallel, one of the girls killed in the attack had been decapitated by bricks that fell into the basement where the children had been dressing for church.

The reality of beatings, bombings, and murders shook the faith of believers in nonviolence. For many it had turned too passive. Perhaps, some thought, nonviolence caved into whites' desire for the thrill of dominance through a violence directed against the sacred. Just a few weeks after the Birmingham bombing, comedian Dick Gregory's angry satire captured a crowd uncertain of the future of the movement. He urged an audience to "look at that window there because that is one of the greatest pieces of artwork that exists on the face of the earth. Because it took 100 years of hate to produce an artist that could produce that picture the way it looks now. . . . There's a heck of a price they had to pay to produce an artist that can produce a masterpiece."

King kept the faith. In his eulogy for the murdered girls delivered later that month, he explored how suffering could be "redemptive," provided that its response remained one of active nonviolent resistance. The girls were the "martyred heroines of a holy crusade for freedom and human dignity." Their murders condemned every minister who had "remained silent behind the safe security of stained-glass windows." Comprehending the girls' deaths meant understanding the entire system which had produced the murderers. Congregations such as the Sixteenth Street Baptist Church embodied a movement for justice. Radical segregationists understood this. Precisely for that reason, they torched church buildings and harassed (or murdered) black Christians active in the struggle.

Civil rights demonstrators could never win at the game of violent confrontation, but they could beat their oppressors through love and nonviolence. These were forces their enemies could not understand or defeat. Over time, King applied the same philosophy to attack economic inequalities. And he did so fully recognizing that even nonviolence could involve coercion, for it became clear that shaming oppressors into recognizing their complicity in injustice would not suffice. Economic, legal, and political coercion would be necessary. And, as social philosopher Brandon Terry has explained, "King thought only mass civil disobedience would create, shape, and sustain such transformative goals" as attacking the most fundamental economic injustices built into the structure of American society. As Terry explains, King amplified his philosophy in unexpected ways later in his career, as he reached to contact more with the classes of American society most unaffected by the initial gains of the movement:

> Developing a richer understanding of King's commitments helps us to better appreciate his departures from conventional markers of respectability. . . . Transgressing the norms of a Southern Baptist preacher, King recruited gang affiliates in pool halls and street corners, and even invited them into his home, engaging them in long debates and training them in nonviolent methods. Such efforts, which have been obscured in King's legacy, sit provocatively alongside the work of the Black Panthers and Nation of Islam, and anticipate efforts of present-day organizers in Baltimore, St. Louis, and elsewhere.

Ultimately, this was the key to King's redemptive power, and hence the title of this book. Redemption has many meanings, of course. In the classical Christian sense, it means being cleansed from sin. In American history, "Redemption" (ironically) refers to the period in the 1870s and 1880s during which white southerners "redeemed" the South from an alleged tyranny of "Negro rule"—in effect, it was the redemption of white supremacy from the loss it had suffered during the Civil War. For many social gospelers, redemption meant both the cleansing of the individual soul from sin and the extirpation of sin from the social order. Redemption, in short, was personal as well as structural. That had long been the message of the black social gospel, and it was King's message as well.

King used it much in that sense but gave it added layers of complexity and meaning. King wanted to redeem white people from their enslavement to and corruption by the same system that had degraded and oppressed African Americans. He hoped to redeem the United States from its legacy of white supremacist rule and support for such regimes abroad. He looked to redeem the South, the section of the country most identified with American's original sin, slavery. And he sought to redeem himself from his own internal struggles as a movement leader and moral failings as a person. The guilt he carried from the latter seemed to push him ever more strongly, even desperately, toward enlarging his vision, at the exact moment that agents of the government pursued him so viciously in hopes of destroying him. In the end, King was not so sure that America's soul could be saved—or that there was a soul to save in the first place.

And, of course, King could not save the soul of America. The "soul" metaphor, applied to a nation-state that exercised a global hegemonic power, is inherently inapt. Ultimately, nation-states have interests, not souls. But "nation" in the sense that King used it came from the deep idea of an American civic nation, the constellation of ideas associated with freedom, liberty, and democracy. The hypocrisy of those ideas in contrast with the white supremacist nature of the workings of American governance empowered the moral force of the movement.

King served as a symbol and one spokesperson for that movement. The movement long predated him, and the local movements across the country, from Montgomery to Albany, Georgia, to Birmingham, Chicago, Selma, and Memphis, grew from the activities of local people. King knew that; he understood that he had been thrust to a position of leadership that he never could have anticipated. That made him uncomfortable and guilty, but it also allowed him to exercise the great gifts of his oratory. He often spoke of "dramatizing" the evils of segregation and oppression, and he was a master of that. He could only do so when there was a mass movement in the first place. He was no master of creating that, but, when it arose, he understood how to speak for it and exploit it in ways that drew international attention. In that sense, he often led from behind. In his last years, he led from ahead—too far ahead, in fact, for liberal leaders of the time. In that sense, the maturation of King's vision turned him into a prophetic leader who suffered the fate of prophetic leaders: misunderstanding, anger at their message, and finally death.

The civil rights movement changed America more fundamentally than any other social movement save for abolition. Not all the way; that is too much to hope for any such movement. But further in a short time than anyone could have dreamed. It did not happen because of Martin Luther King Jr., and yet it is difficult to see how it could have happened, at least

in the same way, without him. He provided the moral force, the motivat-
ing words, the captivating oratory, and the religiously inspired visions.
All of those together were not sufficient, but they were necessary. For a
time, the arc of America's universe moved toward justice, as King had
hoped.

Whether it continues to do so, or moves in other, darker, more reactionary directions, remains difficult to see. "History does not repeat," the
historian Timothy Snyder has written in his book *On Tyranny*. It does not
offer lessons. But—"it does instruct." Martin Luther King Jr. would have
understood that, both because he grew up and lived in a particular kind
of tyranny—the tyranny of American racism—and because he so often
wove historical lessons into his addresses and sermons. He offered them
not as models to repeat or avoid but as moral lessons to learn. In that
way, he was a moral philosopher who speaks to any age and whose ideas
have empowered international movements for freedom, from Soweto to
Eastern Europe to Tiananmen Square. King's legacy, distorted as it has
become since his canonization to sainthood in the American civil religion,
continues to instruct. The moral force of his ideas moves us still.

And so, I offer this work in the hope that an examination of Martin
Luther King Jr.'s religious lives and legacies may continue to instruct a
new generation of students and readers. Many will have encountered
King in the limited and straitjacketed ways he often is presented to us
now. A quick internet search will turn up a million misuses of King and
his legacy; they grow in number and in their baleful distortion seemingly
every year. The epilogue to this book, "Afterlives," portrays some ways
King has been used, and more often misused, since his death.

I hope this book leads readers who haven't been there before back to
the original King, a man of many coats but ultimately with a powerfully
prophetic message. King's commitment, writes the religious studies
scholar Douglas Sturm, was "sustained by the black religious tradition,
informed by the Social Gospel, and expressed in diverse ways during his
tragically brief career. If we would honor the man, we must acknowledge
his dream—An America that never has been, but yet must be."

A talented and visionary minister; a conflicted and morally compro-
mised man; a radical and far-seeing social philosopher; a prophetic critic
of white supremacy and social inequalities of all forms: his vision still
resounds with a call for justice. Therein lies his redemptive power.

1

✝

Growing Up King

All is grist that comes to his mill. . . . He will probably become a big strong man among his people.

—Confidential evaluation of King by professor Morton Scott Enslin
Crozer Theological Seminary, early 1950s

I came to see that God had placed a responsibility upon my shoulders and the more I tried to escape it the more frustrated I would become.

—Martin Luther King Jr., 1949

Martin Luther King Jr. was a preacher *par excellence.* "I am funda-mentally a clergyman, a Baptist preacher. This is my being and my heritage," he said in 1965. The lineage of Baptist churches and ministers ran deep in the family into which he was born, as Michael King (his father's name, and his name, until 1934, when a trip to Germany inspired his father to change their names to Martin, after Martin Luther), on January 15, 1929. He was called Mike, and he remained Mike even after his father renamed him Martin. Born on the cusp of the Great Depression, he saw terrible suffering around him as a young boy. Yet he was a prized and precocious child, surrounded by love. He knew the reality of evil and the power of love: both were in abundant evidence in his boyhood, the first outside his home and church, the second inside them.

Later, he was a student of philosophy and theology, a social activist, a husband and father, a perpetual motion machine, an orator. But before any of those, he was a preacher. Once, when his advisors urged him to reduce his speaking events and focus on publicity and fundraising for the

Southern Christian Leadership Conference, he replied, in a rare moment of ill temper mixed with some self regard, that speaking was his art, and the artist should not "be denied his means of expression. That he liked to preach and felt that he should do it." And so he did.

He also knew church life in his bones, both literally and metaphorically. His great-grandfather Willis Williams had joined the Shiloh Baptist Church in Greene County, Georgia (an hour south of Atlanta), in the antebellum era. It was then a church of slaveowners and slaves, a fairly typical biracial church of that era. After the Civil War, the 144 black members of the church left to form their own congregation in Penfield. Later in the nineteenth century, Williams's son, Adam Daniel (who normally went by A. D.), followed his father into Baptist church membership, activism, and ministry. Seeking better economic opportunities, he eventually ended up in Atlanta in 1893 and pastored various congregations before deciding to devote his energy to Ebenezer Baptist. He also enrolled in a ministerial training program in Atlanta Baptist College (later to become Morehouse) and married Jennie Celeste Parks, then a student at the fledgling Spelman Seminary (now Spelman College for African American women). The two together raised Alberta Christine Williams, the woman who grew up to marry Martin Luther King's father.

Mike King's maternal grandparents, A. D. and Jennie Celeste Williams, not only pastored and raised up Ebenezer as a prominent congregation from the 1890s forward but also took part actively in the social movements of the progressive era. Together with illustrious figures of African American history in Georgia—including William Jefferson White (an important figure in the founding of Morehouse College), Henry McNeal Turner (one of the fathers of "black theology"), and W. E. B. Du Bois (the most important black intellectual of the twentieth century)—Williams protested African American segregation, disfranchisement, and white supremacist politics through the Georgia Equal Rights League. In the same year of its formation, however, the Atlanta Race Riot of 1906 clarified in a brutal way that mob rule would enforce violently the dictates of white supremacy. Professors from Atlanta Baptist (later Morehouse) College, doctors, ministers—the educated elite stood in the same vulnerable position, literally fighting for their lives, as all other African Americans; they all lived in a city too busy with the politics of white supremacy to control the hate that produced it.

A. D. Williams's church, ironically, benefited from a riot that, by enforcing strict segregation through violent means, encouraged the growth of black businesses for customers who could not use white-owned businesses. It grew to upward of a thousand members as Williams assumed important roles in national black Baptist politics. This was no small thing, given that the black Baptist church was the largest black institution in the country. Its National Baptist Publishing Board, led by Richard H. Boyd of Nashville, was the largest black-owned publishing enterprise in the country (and the first to produce black dolls for children, something later taken up by Marcus Garvey's Universal Negro Improvement Association).

Williams also twice served as president of the Atlanta NAACP chapter. The chapter had some brief successes and many struggles, but during his term an increase of black voter registration and pressure exerted by the black community resulted in the building of new black elementary schools and Atlanta's first public high school for black students. Named for Booker T. Washington, the favorite African American of local whites for his call for Negroes to focus on business and upward mobility rather than politics and protests, MLK would attend this high school some years later.

MLK's father, Michael King, was an undereducated but fiercely ambitious man when he came to Atlanta from rural Georgia at the end of World War I. He was the same sort of man as A. D., his future father-in-law. When he met his future wife Alberta Williams, A. D.'s daughter, he was an adult assiduously studying elementary school subjects while Alberta, a teenager, was attending Spelman Seminary. Michael King came up the hard way in a large family in rural Georgia. "My mother had babies, worked the fields, and often went during the winter to wash and iron in the homes of whites around town," he later remembered. Michael's father, James, experienced conflicts with landlords and abuse at every turn; his bitterness, worsened by his heavy drinking, made Michael's boyhood years traumatic. Whites frequently attacked African Americans who experienced any degree of economic prosperity or independence. That happened to MLK's paternal grandfather. Whites once surrounded his home and forced James King to flee and hide out in the woods for a period of some months. Michael King felt driven to escape this world, as well as his abusive father. He moved to Atlanta with that intention. He was, then, just another uneducated country preacher. Not fully literate, he supported himself with a variety of working-class jobs as he sought to better himself and his prospects. He initiated a very extended courtship in 1919 with Alberta Williams, continuing it even while she moved to attend Hampton Institute in Virginia for two years. And he struggled upward on the educational ladder, eventually managing (with some help from his father-in-law, an alumnus) to enter Morehouse College in the mid-1920s, where he studied for a ministerial degree. He failed introductory English courses twice, finally squeaking by on his third try in summer school. But he was not to be stopped; if it took him seven years of courtship to win the hand of Alberta Williams— the two married in 1926—he would press forward with his educational pursuits until he was successful there as well.

Michael King entered Morehouse shortly after the black theologian, mystic, and educator Howard Thurman had graduated. Both had come up the hard way, Thurman was born to a poor family in Daytona, Florida, where he virtually supported himself as he made his way through a private black Baptist high school in Jacksonville. During Thurman's years at Morehouse as a student (1919–1923), he developed a reputation as a young man of immense, if somewhat mysterious, intellect. Thurman's future wife, Sue Bailey, grew up in a family of black Baptist leaders in Arkansas, and Sue for some time roomed with Alberta Williams, MLK's mother, when the two attended Spelman Seminary.

The connections between the Thurmans and the Kings were deep and immensely influential on the young MLK in the 1950s. Thurman, the cultivated intellectual mystic, and Michael King, the hugely talented but rough-hewn preacher of limited academic training, both exercised a major influence on King. Martin Luther King Jr. transformed familiar sermonic material into majestic works of oral art. That skill came in part through a fusion of his father's traditional sermonic stylings and fervor together with the cultivated intellectual style of Benjamin Mays and Howard Thurman, especially his poetic way of introducing complex ideas to broad audiences. In that way, MLK represented the synthesis of the varied strands of his black Baptist ancestry. He wove those threads together as an intellectual scholar, a social gospeler, and an oral artist in the black preaching tradition.

Martin Luther King Jr. later spoke of escaping the fundamentalism of his father's generation, even as he accepted some of the deeper spiritual truths behind biblical stories. For him, the theatrical sermonizing of his father's generation—the very style captured on LP records of the mid-century from legends such as the Reverend C. L. Franklin—was embarrassing. He sought to cultivate a quieter, thoughtful style. He wanted to preach philosophical and advanced theological ideas to the masses.

But MLK's self-created narrative about escaping from a fundamentalist straitjacket is complicated by the fact that he heard all manner of sermons from his father's pulpit. Indeed, his father preached much of the same social gospel that King later extended to an international reach. Just as important, many of the best black intellects passing through town appeared at Ebenezer Baptist while MLK was a boy. Moreover, King's father urged congregants to get educated, join the NAACP, fight for the right to register to vote, and to resist the internal degradation of the caste system of Atlanta. King's father could "whoop" in the folk preacher style, but he was far from *just* a whooper.

Two years after MLK's birth, his grandfather A. D. Williams died; he was eulogized as a man of "limited literary preparation" but great natural talent and work ethic, a "preacher of unusual power, an appealing experimentalist, a persuasive evangelist, and a convincing doctrinarian." Much the same might be said of his son-in-law, MLK's father, and the generations of star ministers of that era. They represented the archetype sketched by W. E. B. Du Bois in his memorable chapter on "The Preacher" in *The Souls of Black Folk*, a poetic tribute to the native powers of ministers who emerged from rustic backgrounds and developed skills of oratorical powerful sermonizing, political intriguing, and idealistic philosophizing.

MLK's father never forgot his own limitations, least of all when raising the future civil rights leader as a boy. For black parents of that generation, strict discipline was simply a reasonable introduction to a world "where death and violence are always near you." The young King received many a "whupping," even to his teenage years; King later revolted by deliberately violating some strict norms that governed his boyhood (such as avoiding pool halls). But for Daddy King, parental training involved balancing the cultivation of self-respect together with "getting along with the enemy all around you," and his son instinctively understood that.

MLK always was a churchman; it's just what he grew up with, what he was constantly immersed in. "The church has always been a second home for me," he later reflected. "My best friends were in Sunday School, and it was the Sunday School that helped me to build the capacity for getting along with people." King's earliest correspondence as a boy, in fact, tells of his close acquaintance with the details of Baptist church life: the committees and subcommittees, the habits and customs of the people, the hymns, the exhortations at offering time to give until it hurt, the call-and-response rhythm of the sermons.

The young King enjoyed being in the choir. In December 1939, he appeared with the Ebenezer Baptist Church's boys' choir, dressed up in the costumes of slaves, as the movie *Gone with the Wind* premiered at Loew's Grand Theater in Atlanta. The producer of the film, David Selznick, was incensed that Hattie McDaniel, the African American actress who soon won an Oscar for her portrayal of a white household's slave, had not been invited. But legions of Hollywood stars were. The organizers certainly had to ensure that this was a whites-only event, but the moonlight-and-magnolias entertainment served as an appropriate role for the black choir with the young King singing. There for the day, the Atlanta of Margaret Mitchell and of Martin Luther King intersected, both playing their roles (King inadvertently, Mitchell purposefully) in perpetuating romanticized stories of the Old South that formed the falsely powerful memory of the Civil War for generations of white southerners.

King's father pressed the legacy of activism that came from his own family. The story of Ebenezer's choir at the premiere of *Gone with the Wind* is well known; it stands for the role that black Atlantans had to play in this ritualized rehearsal of the southern Lost Cause tradition. Less understood is that, in the same year, King Sr. organized a massive voter registration drive and a march to Atlanta's city hall. "I ain't gonna plow no more mules," he shouted to a crowd of one thousand. "I'll never step off the road again to let white folks pass. I am going to move forward towards freedom, and I'm hoping everybody here today is going right along with me." The next year, King Sr. campaigned to equalize salaries between white and black teachers.

King learned the racial lessons of growing up in the Jim Crow South from smaller incidents and everyday interactions. One time, as he later recalled, his father took him to a shoe shop. The proprietor demanded that they not to sit in the seats for white customers. "This was the first time I had seen Dad so furious," King recollected. "That experience revealed to me at a very early age that my father had not adjusted to the system, and he played a great part in shaping my conscience. I still remember walking down the street beside him as he muttered, 'I don't care how long I have to live with this system, I will never accept it.'" Another lesson came at the hands of the police, the primal moment of racial education for generations of black Americans, dating from the slave patrols to the present. And this was in the context of a relatively minor brush-up. The officer who stopped MLK's father addressed him as "boy." King responded angrily by pointing at his son and saying, "This is a boy, I'm a man; until you call me one, I will not listen to you."

King learned a social gospel at church. He saw in his father an angry resistance to the ritual humiliations of southern segregation. Only when ministers set the standard of political participation would their parishioners stand up for full citizenship, he insisted. And in the early 1940s, King Sr. told a group of black Baptist ministers, "God hasten the time when every minister will become a registered voter and a part of every movement for the betterment of our people. Again and again has it been said we cannot lead where we do not go, and we cannot teach what we do not know. As ministers great responsibility rests upon us as leaders."

And the young King was not afraid to call out the hypocrisy of religious white southerners whom he grew up around but not among. He got an early start on that. In April 1944, the fifteen-year-old student at Booker T. Washington High School entered himself at a speech contest in Dublin, Georgia. His topic: "The Negro and the Constitution." The young King delivered an address that was, in fact, far in advance of most mainstream historical thinking of the time; his history came more from W. E. B. Du Bois and a generation of black historians before him than from the woefully biased textbooks of the day. Most of them were too hopelessly ahistorical myths about the relatively benign nature of American slavery and the supposed awful consequences of Reconstruction after the Civil

War. King grew up with a history that placed slavery as a central part of American history.

As the teenage King orated at the contest, "Black America still wears chains. The finest Negro is at the mercy of the meanest white man. Even winners of our highest honors face the class color bar." He gave the example of Marian Anderson, the African American opera singer first denied her opportunity to perform at Constitution Hall in Washington, DC, by the Daughters of the American Revolution before the intervention of Eleanor Roosevelt led to her famous and stirring performance at the Lincoln Memorial. He referenced the "Double V" campaign—victory over fascism abroad and racism at home—noting that "as we gird ourselves to defend democracy from foreign attack, let us see to it that increasingly at home we give fair play and free opportunity for all people." King ended his address hopefully: "My heart throbs anew in the hope that, inspired by the example of Lincoln, imbued with the spirit of Christ, they will cast down the last barrier to perfect freedom," and then the "Negro could stand, as a man, alongside the Anglo-Saxon, a symphony of American brotherhood." The young King, a smart but not especially accomplished student, doubtless had considerable help in drafting his speech, but the sentiments expressed were common themes in African American history classes of the era. Unfortunately, hardly any white students outside of a few college classrooms or taken to left-wing political meetings of the time had much exposure to that history.

King's teenage dream met the reality of the American racial nightmare on the way home from a contest he did not win. As he rode the bus home to Atlanta, when a crowd of whites boarded the bus in Macon, the bus driver bellowed at King and his classmate, then sitting toward the front. He told the "niggers" and "black sons of bitches" to move to the back. King wanted to refuse but followed the counsel of his high school teacher to swallow his pride and follow the law. In fact, there were no seats available for him to sit in, and he stood up for the rest of the journey. He was tired, he remembered, but that wasn't the point; the driver had achieved his object: enforce "humiliation." He never forgot the experience: "It was the angriest I have ever been in my life," he later recounted. As King remembered, "Suddenly I realized you don't count, you're nobody." Even the scion of "Sweet Auburn," a boy raised in a loving home and experiencing about as good an education as could be expected for black students of that era, counted for nobody.

Following the year of King's speech contest in Dublin, an opportunity opened up for him to attend Morehouse College as a high school junior. It was 1944, the height of American involvement in World War II. Colleges needed paying customers to stay alive, and King had the promise and a community backing him to enter early. Before he did so, he spent the summer in Simsbury, Connecticut (near Hartford), picking tobacco alongside other boys, white and black. It was his first time away from his family for any extended time, and his first period observing life outside the segregated South. On the way, the train stopped in Hartford, where, to his amazement, he shared a meal with his companions. "After we passed Washington the[re] was no discrimination at all the white people here are very nice. We go to any place we want to and sit any where we want to," he wrote to his father in June 1944.

Patrick Parr's *The Seminarian*, an illuminating book on King's younger years as a student, memorably portrays King's time in the (relatively speaking) integrated North. King enjoyed preaching sermons to his peers, and on Sundays he attended churches mixing white and black congregants. At work, he and his black male workmates mixed with white women who worked on farms in the same era. As a peer later remembered, "they were workers, just like we were, and we could talk to them, briefly, during lunch time, and not get taken to jail for it." This was not heaven, but it also was not Atlanta.

But the trip home on the train quickly reminded King of his place. When he had to change to the Jim Crow car in Washington, DC, a waiter on the car pulled a curtain down to separate the black passengers. A few years later, then a Morehouse student, King returned for one more summer of work. In the years between those two ventures, he experienced further education from bosses on the Atlanta Railway Express Company who called him a "nigger" and in daily incidents in and out of workplaces and social settings where the veil of segregation was brutally enforced. At one point, King's anger bubbled over into a letter published in the *Atlanta Constitution*, a missive inspired by the confluence of a number of hate crimes directed against blacks in the area (including a black veteran from World War II, murdered for attempting to vote in a Georgia primary).

At Morehouse, King made up his mind to follow in his father's footsteps as a minister. His sister Christine later said, half-seriously and half-humorously, that "It was not the Lord but the hot sun of the tobacco fields that 'called him' to the ministry," replaying a bit of folk humor that long had been passed down, in one form or another, about what really explained "calls" to the ministry. But in truth, the young King already was speaking to his workmates, and to his classmates at Morehouse, about what he wanted to do with himself. They remembered that he had a vision of helping others, uplifting the race, and challenging injustice. "I could envision myself playing a part in breaking down the legal barriers to colored people's rights," he later said.

His chosen major at Morehouse, sociology, furthered that perspective. So did his relationship with the well-known Atlanta minister William Holmes Borders, a rival to his father but a representative of a well-educated race man whose Wheat Street Baptist Church was at the center of southern black social gospelism. Daddy King advised his son not to visit Borders's church—the two were rivals for congregants and money, for one thing—but the young King sought to further his education wherever he could find it. The impressively erudite Borders was a kind of de facto professor in modeling what King himself wanted to be as an adult.

King had spent some time at a short-lived Atlanta University laboratory school, designed for parents seeking a better education than could be found in the underfunded black public school system. He had also attended Booker T. Washington High School, the institution created only after his father and others had demanded a public high school that would at least approximate the education available to white children. But King's true high school and college experience came at Morehouse College.

He entered as a fifteen-year-old student. King was popular among his fellows and engaged in the usual teenage pranks and pastimes. But he was not an academic star. He generally earned Bs and Cs (his only A came from professor George Kelsey, someone whose sociological approach to religion attracted the young King greatly). Later, when applying to attend Crozer, King's recommendation letters were lukewarm, essentially saying he had not done too badly for his age. His record was "short of what may be called 'good,'" as George Kelsey put it. But then, only in his last year had King come to a full recognition of the "value of scholarship." Benjamin Mays added that King was far from "brilliant" but had a good mind and would grow intellectually as he grew in years. He might have added that King's participation with whites on the local Intercollegiate Council, as well as his work under a professor (Samuel Williams, who had been a student of Howard Thurman's) who was committed to the campaign of Progressive Party candidate Henry A. Wallace, had given the young aspiring minister a broader vision of the possibilities of what could be achieved through his pastorate. It also helped him grapple with the hatred for whites that he had developed watching the brutalities of everyday life in Jim Crow Georgia.

More important for him personally, King Jr. used his years at Morehouse to work out his personal balance of the biblical fundamentalism in which he had been raised and the modernism that he was exposed to in his college classes. "The shackles of fundamentalism were removed from my body," he later remembered of those years. And he was gradually coming to a decision to enter the ministry, something he initially resisted.

King's early self-reflections suggest a young man committed to the ministerial profession and to being an advocate for the social gospel. In one of his earliest lessons from Crozer Theological Seminary in Chester, Pennsylvania, where he began attending school in the fall of 1948, he reflected on what was required for a successful preaching ministry: "On the one hand," he scrawled out, with plenty of self-corrections and added-in thoughts along the way, "I must attempt to change the soul of individuals so that their societies may be changed. On the other I must attempt to change their societies so that the individual soul will have a change. Therefore, I must be concerned about unemployment, slums, and economic insecurity. I am a profound advocator of the social gospel." He was also convinced that the minister "must somehow take profound theological and philosophical views and place them in a concrete framework. I must forever make the complex, the simple."

In his "Autobiography of Religious Development," written for Professor Davis at Crozer and a decade later sent to a northern Baptist publication interested in King's origins, King remembered his call to the ministry as being "neither dramatic nor spectacular." It was something that came "neither by some miraculous vision nor by some blinding light experience on the road of life. . . . Rather, it was an inner urge that came upon me." It came gradually, expressed as a "desire to serve God and humanity, and the feeling that my talent and my commitment could best be expressed through the ministry. . . . I came to see that God had placed a responsibility upon my shoulders and the more I tried to escape it the more frustrated I would become."

He began with a dress rehearsal at Ebenezer in 1947 and received his ordination in 1948, just before he graduated from Morehouse and moved on to Crozer Theological Seminary in Pennsylvania. And this was not just a latter-day reflection. He wrote the same in his application to attend Crozer in February 1948: "I felt a responsibility which I could not escape." Later, he explained that "Not until I entered Crozer Theological Seminary did I begin a serious intellectual quest for a method to eliminate social evil." That was being a bit modest, as reflections of his teenage friends suggest. The ideas were clearly formulating in his head earlier. But Crozer certainly helped to cement them.

King decided to pursue ministerial study at Crozer Theological Seminary in Chester, Pennsylvania (near Philadelphia). He arrived there in the fall of 1948 and would study there three years for his bachelor of divinity degree. He followed in a long line of educated African Americans who attended black colleges but went on to other northern universities or professional schools to "validate" their degrees (a way of suggesting that their education could be recognized by whites). He followed in the footsteps of some of his Morehouse mentors, notably the University of Chicago–trained educator Benjamin Mays and George Kelsey, a professor who deeply influenced the young King as a Morehouse College student.

Most important for King, he was preceded by the Reverend J. Pius Barbour, a 1917 Morehouse graduate who attended Crozer starting in 1936 and then became a pastor in the town of Chester. Barbour was close to the King family and took the young King in as a sort of adopted son during those years. Barbour's acerbic wit attracted a seminary student who needed an outlet to balance his own propensity to overseriousness. King appreciated his elder mentor; he was, King said, "full of fun and he has one of the best minds of anybody I have ever met." Barbour enjoyed challenging the young King, pricking his pretensions and probing his mind, and the young MLK took avidly to shooting the theological dozens with the impressively well-read older minister.

In Barbour's home, black students heatedly debated issues of the day. Barbour loved to play the role of devil's advocate. King's early ideas of nonviolence got a thorough working over in Barbour's intellectual boxing ring; what good could nonviolence do in a culture so steeped in the violence of racial hate as was the United States, he challenged Martin. The preacher-in-training replied with instrumental more than philosophical arguments. It was just a question of simple arithmetic, he said: such a highly outnumbered minority as were African Americans really did not have some kind of violent revolution as an option in their arsenal; they had to seek other means. Once during this time, as a friend later remembered, King engaged in a heated argument with the noted American pacifist and advocate of nonviolence, A. J. Muste, the "American Gandhi" (as his biographer has called him). "King sure as hell wasn't any pacifist then," he remembered. King had despaired of the power of love and thought more in terms of the necessity of fighting fascism.

Barbour linked their theological training to the realities of the lives they would spend preaching specifically to black congregations. Barbour's daughter, who loved to sit and listen to the debates her father and the young King would engage in, later remembered that the ministerial courses at Crozer "had no emotion of tension." They did not "speak to the conditions of black people, because how you see Christianity depends upon what your reality is." Her father served as a translator. Barbour invited the twenty-year-old King to preach in his church in Chester first in the early months of 1949, and more frequently thereafter; partly through this experience, the young man gradually developed his own preaching style, one employing but not limited to the conventional sermonic techniques that he learned in his classes at Crozer.

King entered Crozer together with other black men (including his close friend Walter McCall, who joined him in the spring term) along with international students and older men who were war veterans. Although he had black companions, King felt self-conscious; he was the black "representative individual," and his missteps would not be his alone but emblematic of the Negro as a race. For that reason, as he later reflected, "If I were a minute late to class, I was almost morbidly aware of it and sure that everyone noticed it." He dressed the part, too, keeping a set of "perfectly shined" shoes and "immaculately pressed" clothes. Samuel Proctor, former Crozer and Boston University graduate, remembered meeting King for the first time: "Martin talked slowly, delivering every sentence with Delphian assurance and oracular finality." King always wore a formal suit and tie, and he "walked and talked slowly with a kind of Napoleonic assurance. He looked like a major event about to happen."

King did better in Barbour's pulpit than he did in some of Professor Keighton's professional preaching classes; he earned an A− in one but subsequently slipped down to a C+. That might be (so speculates the biographer of his early years, Patrick Parr) because King worked in black preacher styles alongside the carefully coiffed sermonic form he was given in class. Professor Keighton evidently was not entirely pleased with the southern intonations in King's personal repertoire. King also took classes in Old Testament. In one, he wrote about the Book of Jeremiah, noting that the Old Testament prophet was a "shining example of the truth that religion should never sanction the status quo. This more than anything else should be inculcated in the minds of modern religionists, for the worst disservice that we as individuals or churches can do to Christianity is to become sponsors and supporters of the status quo. How often has religion gone down, chained to a status quo it allied itself with." That was to be a constant theme of King's over the coming years: the capitulation of the church to the demands of the status quo instead of to the commands of God.

Ironically, Barbour later pushed King to pursue a post in education, or a pulpit in the North, rather than be trapped in a southern pulpit caught between white racism and black color and class dynamics in congregations. By then, King was coming into his own and chose otherwise. But for years afterward, Barbour maintained a fatherly and, increasingly, affectionately admiring interest as King assumed a role as one of the best-known African American ministers in the country.

King's other major professorial influence was George Washington Davis. A lifelong friend and influence on King, Davis came from a family of steel mill union activists, received theological training in Rochester and at Yale University, and had pastored Baptist churches before coming to Crozer as a professor in the late 1930s. He introduced King to Walter Rauschenbusch and other social gospelers, and King remembered him generally as someone who brought a "warm evangelical liberalism" into the classroom. Unfortunately, he also brought an inability to spot academic plagiarism, which King practiced, perhaps without fully realizing it, in his papers for Davis's classes. In spite of that, and more important in the long run, King worked out in his own mind his synthesis of evangelical liberalism and prophetic criticism.

In one essay prepared for Davis, the young MLK explained that while the Bible should be subjected to historical analysis, "this advance has revealed to us that God reveals himself progressively through human history, and that the final significance of the Scripture lies in the outcome of the progress." King also wrote on "The Humanity and Divinity of Jesus," arguing that the "orthodox view of the divinity of Christ is in my mind quite readily denied." Instead, his true significance "lies in the fact that his achievement is prophetic and promissory for every other true son of man who is willing to submit his will to the will and spirit of God. Christ was to be only the prototype of one among many brothers." Jesus's unity with God was "not something thrust upon Jesus from above, but it was a definite achievement through the process of moral struggle and self-abnegation." Professor Davis gave the young student a B+, saying that the paper proposed "a solution which would appeal to the liberal mind."

In the fall of 1950, King began some of his first autobiographical reflections in a course from George Washington Davis on "Religious Development of Personality," later given also to Charles Batten, the dean at Crozer. It was a straightforward self-evaluation. King gave his own sense of himself as called for something special. King wrote that he was a physically blessed child, "somewhat precocious, both physically and mentally," with an IQ "somewhat above average." His education at Morehouse had awakened "many doubts" within him and set him apart from his father's theological beliefs, although he retained his admiration for his father as a person. "Religion has just been something I grew up in. Conversion for me has been the gradual intaking of the noble [ideals] set forth in my family and my environment, and I must admit that this intaking has been largely unconscious." He still felt the "noble moral and ethical ideas that I grew up under. They have been real and precious to me, and even in moments of theological doubt I could never turn away from them. Even though I have never had an abrupt conversion experience, religion has been real to me and closely knitted to life. In fact the two cannot be separated; religion for me is life." As he matured, he questioned the literal truth of the Bible and disdained what he saw as his father's rigid fundamentalism. In college, however, he learned that "behind the legends and myths of the Book were many profound truths which one could not escape."

King remembered growing up in a "very congenial home environment," which he portrayed without acknowledging some of the complaints and doubts that he later expressed. No one had great wealth, but his father knew how to save money and be thrifty, and the community where he grew up, though modest, was comfortable and safe. The comfort of his upbringing gave him the ability to ponder a God of love and the universe as accommodating to men. "It is quite easy," he reflected, "for me to lean more toward optimism than pessimism about human nature mainly because of my childhood experiences." King also grew up with the reality of segregation, once having a young white playmate from whom he was forced to separate when his father informed him they could not play together anymore. His parents introduced him to the race problem, and King wrote that he grew determined to "hate every white person." How could he love those who hated him, he wondered. Only in college did he overcome this, partly through his work in interracial organizations. College further lifted the shackles of fundamentalism and made it easy to accept the liberal Protestantism he encountered at Crozer.

King was undergoing an intellectual struggle internally between what he saw as competing traditions of neoorthodoxy and theological liberalism (more recently, scholars have portrayed Niebuhrian neoorthodoxy as a form of religious liberalism). In what is his most interesting writing from his Crozer years, he pondered how to balance his developing liberal theology with the brute realities he knew from growing up. Here, using his own personal reflections and without the need to rely on scholarly authorities, his prose, uncharacteristically, shines. "The former leaning may root back to certain experiences that I had in the south with a vicious race problem," he explained. It was awfully difficult to believe in the basic goodness of man after growing up in the Jim Crow South. However, in "noticing the gradual improvements of this same race problem I came to see some noble possibilities in human nature. Also, my liberal leaning may root back to the great imprint that many liberal theologians have left upon me and to my ever present desire to be optimistic about human nature."

During his second year at Crozer, in 1950, King met Mordecai Wyatt Johnson, the legendary longtime president of Howard University. Freshly arrived back home from India, Johnson was giving a talk in Philadelphia about his thoughts on Gandhi and the possibility of a campaign of mass nonviolent civil disobedience in the United States akin to Gandhi's campaign in India. Gandhi, Johnson said, was "probably the first person in history to lift the love ethic of Jesus above mere interaction between individual to a powerful and effective social force on a large scale. Love for Gandhi was a potent instrument for social and collective transformation." When King went to hear Johnson at the Fellowship House in Philadelphia, he later said, he felt that he had heard a message "so profound and electrifying" that his vision of nonviolence shifted. He read everything he could about Gandhi and learned to speak this internationalist language of active nonviolent resistance.

Some of this story later got conveniently repackaged in *Stride Toward Freedom*, an autobiographical work that deliberately (as per the advice of the ghostwriter, Lawrence Reddick) Christianized and tamed Gandhi.

And black church folk had long heard some version or other of this message, so King's conversion experience in 1950 was probably less dramatic than the version he later told. Moreover, King already had read Howard Thurman's *Jesus and the Disinherited* and was quoting it (without attribution) in his sermons and academic work.

Clearly Johnson had a major impact on King, just as he had had on King's intellectual inspiration, Howard Thurman, when Thurman was a young student in 1918. Later, Johnson recruited Thurman to be the dean of Rankin Memorial Chapel at Howard University, where he had an illustrious career from 1932 to 1944. Much the same could have happened with King; Johnson tried hard to recruit King to the Howard University faculty in 1957, to be dean of Howard's School of Religion (where Thurman had taught). King turned down the offer, telling Johnson that for the moment his calling was to stay in the South and lead the movement that had sprung up around him; Johnson understood and wrote back admiringly of King's work.

King's social life at Crozer included plenty of clowning around with his friends, playing pool, visiting Philadelphia and nearby cities, dating, and visiting restaurants and clubs in Philadelphia and New Jersey. At times this was without incident, but the counterexamples were impossible to ignore. Once, at a restaurant in Philadelphia with a white friend, the wait staff ignored their table, until finally, upon receiving their food, King's plate had sand mixed in with the vegetables.

In another, more menacing case, King was involved with a group that had a confrontation at a bar in New Jersey. His boyhood wonder at the lack of racism in the North faded once he spent enough time there during his postgraduate training. Once, King and some companions attended a church service and decided to go to a café together in Maple Shade, New Jersey, near to Crozer. The group asked for glasses of beer, which was refused to them by the German American bartender, who later shot a gun out the back door as the group was leaving, shouting, "I'll kill for less!" King and the group sought to press charges against the establishment, which had violated New Jersey's antidiscrimination law. King offered testimony on the case, but at the same time he was rushing home to attend his brother's wedding, earning himself a speeding ticket in the process. Meanwhile, back in New Jersey, their case against Mary's Café started to come apart when whites from the University of Pennsylvania were going to testify that they had been served glasses of beer on a Sunday—the alleged reason why King and his fellows could not be served—but some of those potential witnesses were reneging, as their parents pressured them that it could hurt their law careers. It didn't help that King did not arrive back in time to testify in court, leaving only his friend Walter McCall among the original four complainants. The case was dismissed, but King never forgot it. Later, he aimed some piercing barbs at milque-toast northern liberalism, the kind that could see the splinter in some other eye but not the mote in its own. MLK portrayed segregation and racism as a national, not simply a southern, disease. He had experienced that personally.

It was in those latter experiences that King learned about how informal norms and private agreements were enforced in the urban North. In Chicago, the Congress of Racial Equality (CORE) formed in 1942 precisely to test the boundaries of racial integration in a northern city bitterly divided along racial lines. King's turn to campaign in Chicago in 1966 came about for many of the same reasons that the CORE first addressed in the 1940s. Housing segregation governed American neighborhoods nearly every-where and was enforced with federal codes of real estate and redlining, ensuring that mortgage loan money would flow into neighborhoods typically restricted to white residents, while black residents were ineligible for such loans in their own residential sectors. In his encounters with racist treatment in northern establishments during his years at Crozer, King in effect saw just the barest outline of the full scope of how institutionally racist practices governed northern cities.

"No theology is needed to tell us that love is the law of life and to disobey it means to suffer the consequences; we see it every day in human experience," King said in 1949. Perhaps he was thinking of his intense but short-lived relationship with Betty Moitz, a young white woman who was the daughter of a housekeeper at a Crozer dormitory. She later said that "one thing ML knew at age nineteen was that he could change the world." One friend warned the smitten young King, "it was a dangerous situation that could get out of hand, and if it did get out of hand it would smear [him]." For a future pastor of a black church to have a white wife was just out of bounds. The relationship ended, but by some accounts, King carried bitterness about this with him through the coming years. He still lived within the veil.

Early in his career at Crozer, King got a heavy dose of the antifunda-mentalist style of the biblical scholars there. Some of them considered it a sort of special mission to introduce undereducated students into the tradition of the higher criticism of the Bible. His professors at Crozer came to admire the young aspiring minister, and King was a popular figure on campus. In the spring of 1950, as his relation with Betty Moitz deepened, he was voted the first black student body president in the history of Crozer; at that time, half of the students in King's class were African American. One student remembered him being picked because he was "head and shoulders above anybody else. . . . He was a good speaker, a good scholar; he was . . . well liked." One professor predicted that King would "probably become a big strong man among his people," and another captured something fundamental to King's style: "All is grist that comes to his mill." Few ever better described King's ability to copy, absorb, and digest sermonic material and then repeat it but vary it in ways that made it his own. The preacher King was the riffing King, taking up and reconstructing bars and melodies until the melody sounded and felt like something different than the original. This, more than King's original thought or his often dutifully produced academic papers, captures King's quality as a preacher and religious communicator.

At the end of his first year at Crozer, King preached, "The church is supposed to be the most radical opposer of the status quo in society, yet, in many instances, it is the greatest preserver of the status quo." For that reason, the church had historically sanctioned slavery, bigotry, exploitative capitalism, and racial bigotry. King was reading Marx during the Christmas holidays in 1949, trying to understand the appeal of communism for many people. He was writing papers at Crozer such as "Will Capitalism Survive?" and expressing concern that capitalism had "failed to meet the needs of the masses." His mentor and preacher-father figure J. Pius Barbour remembered that King "thought the capitalistic system was predicated on exploitation and prejudice, poverty, and that we wouldn't solve these problems until we got a new social order."

In his second year, King's schedule during the winter of 1949–1950 included "Christian Theology for Today," "Conduct of Church Services," "The Development of Christian Ideas," and a course he audited with Elizabeth Flower at the University of Pennsylvania, "Ethics and Philosophy of History." George Washington Davis's course on "Christian Theology for Today," King later remembered, was saturated with a "warm evangelical liberalism," aided by dinner at the professor's home. In it, he considered liberal and neoorthodox perspectives and wrote that his experiences in the South "made it very difficult to believe in the essential goodness of man." In the same course, King showed how much he immediately absorbed the ideas of Howard Thurman, recounting in one passage a story that Thurman had told about his grandmother's minister telling slaves, "You—you are not slaves. You are God's children," something, King said, that established for them a "true ground of personal dignity."

King served in the summers as an associate pastor at his father's church, Ebenezer Baptist in Atlanta. And for all of King's references to breaking with his father's "fundamentalism," with what he came to see as narrow-minded literalist views of scriptural authority, in fact, as he developed his preacher chops, preaching at only twenty years of age in his father's pulpit, he carried on many of his father's emphases. In a sermon to his father's church from June 1949, reflecting on the nature of conflict in human life in everything from internal psychological struggles to international relations with other countries, he found the same conflict with southern racism. "The average white southerner is not bad," he noted. The average white southerner was a churchgoer who "worships the same God we worship," and gave generously to missionary causes abroad. "Yet at the same time," King pointed out, "he will spend thousands of dollars in an attempt to keep the Negro segregated and discriminated." King waxed philosophical: "Yes, we must admit that there is something contradictory and paradoxical about human nature." King concluded the sermon by pointing the way to overcome these social contradictions. God "transcends the world," he concluded, "yet at the same time he is immanent in the world. And so by identifying ourselves with this knowable God our wills somehow become his will. We will no longer think of our selfish desires. We will somehow rise above evil thoughts. We will no longer possess two personalities, but only one." He implied the same could happen in the social world. God's intervention could heal the wounds of broken human relationships. And in a sermon just a month later, focusing on stories of our own blindnesses, he concluded that "While we see the splinters in Russia's eye we fail to see the great plank of racial segregation and discrimination which is blocking the progress of America."

Many observers of King's life have detected his move to an increasing economic radicalism in the last few years of his life, coinciding with his attacks on the Vietnam War and the inadequacy of the "War on Poverty." On the latter, as he put it, the United States had barely conducted a skirmish, much less declared a war. But while King was certainly more open in public about these views, he long held ideas suspicious at best of capitalism and favorable to democratic socialism. These were not just the musings of a seminary student, to be left behind later as he "matured," but instead represented ideas that he carried with him over the course of the next two decades. This was King working out his ideas about social problems in his own authentic voice. He decried Marxist atheism but found much truth in a Marxist analysis of the workings of capitalism. "It is a well known fact that no social institution can survive after it has outlived its usefulness. This capitalism has failed to do" (here, the professor corrected "failed to do" with his word "done," but in fact King's original captures the idea much better).

For a course on "Christianity and Society," we have some remaining notes from King's thoughts on "War and Pacifism," in which he wrote:

> It seems to me that we must recognize the presence of sin in man and that it can be done without seeing that there is also good. Since man is so often sinful there must be some coercion to keep one man from injuring his fellows. This is just as true between nations as it is between individuals. If one nation oppresses another a Christian nation must, in order to express love of neighbor, help protect the oppressed. This does not relieve us of our obliga-

tion to the enemy nation. We are obligated to treat them in such a way as to reclaim them to a useful place in the world community after they have been prevented from oppressing another. We must not seek revenge.

About the same time, in some notes scribbled for himself about capitalism, he compared it to a "losing football team in the last quarter trying all types of tactics to survive." Capitalism was showing itself to be done, because it had "failed to meet the needs of the masses." This was a theme he returned to repeatedly through his career; in the 1960s, it got more substantive, thanks to his interactions with intellectuals who moved him to endorse specific policy proposals toward controlling unfettered capitalism, equalizing incomes, and eliminating poverty.

While romancing Coretta Scott, the two carried on their own dialogue on these issues in 1952. While spending some time apart in the summer, King wrote Scott a love letter, one of the most personal and playful writings that may be found in all of the King papers. But after noting how much he pined for her, he then sent in a lengthy reply to Coretta's query about the book by Edward Bellamy, *Looking Backward*, a nineteenth-century utopian socialist fiction. "I should be interested to know your reactions to Bellamy's predictions about our society," she handwrote on the cover of the copy she sent him. King replied at length, noting some flaws in Bellamy's utopianism (his "idealism is not tempered with realism," King said) but also acknowledging again that, whatever the initial merits of capitalism in a Europe dominated by nobles, "like most human systems it [fell] victim to the very thing it was revolting against. . . . So I think Bellamy is right in seeing the gradual decline of capitalism." King extended his critique to the church, which easily fell prey to being a "tool of the middle class to keep the proletariat oppressed." King noted that he hoped, as a minister, to "avoid making religion what Marx calls the opiate of the people.'" He concluded by stating his hopes for his ministry: "Let us continue to hope, work, and pray that in the future we will live to see a warless world, a better distribution of wealth, and a brotherhood that transcends race or color. This is the gospel I will preach to the world." Or, as he put it in his later work *Strength to Love*, his mission was to bring "the Christian message to bear on the social evils that cloud our day."

King also preached as a fledgling minister about the "False god of nationalism"—the god of nationalism could be perverted to evil ends when it became an excuse for the exercise of power over others. Such was the nationalism of Nazism and fascism, and in the United States, King added, its exponents included racists and McCarthy and his imitators, as well as "the advocators of white supremacy, and the America First movements." King was attuned to how fascism could (and sometimes did) arise in America, and he knew where the phrase "America First" came from to begin with; it was not much more than a decade old then.

And for that reason, King developed an attraction also to the pessimistic neoorthodox theology of Reinhold Niebuhr. In the social world in which King grew up, rank with the stink of segregation, perhaps it was inevitable that King would be drawn to theologies that acknowledged human evil. King could hardly help questioning whether there was goodness in humanity, given what he saw and experienced, even with the comforts and love that surrounded him in his home. As he expressed it in 1958, he "had grown up abhorring not only segregation but also the oppressive and barbarous acts that grew out of it." He saw police brutality and injustice meted out in courtrooms, and all of it imprinted him deeply. He was to explore his ideas about Niebuhr much more in depth during his years at Boston University.

During this time the young King, coming into his own both intellectually and socially, began to consider his options for further education. As far as Daddy King was concerned, King had done enough, and further education could render him practically unemployable in the southern black Baptist church. But the young King sought to combine the preaching power of the previous generation with his education. He wouldn't return to the South, as the scholar of his young life Patrick Parr puts it, until "he was able to show his father (and himself) how a preacher could sound with power *and* intellect."

William E. Gardner pastored a church in East Elmhurst, Queens, very near to King's sister Christine; King served a sort of internship there. Gardner was direct with his criticisms of a young man that he perceived as having a impressive intelligence and personality but some obstacles to being a successful minister: "An attitude of aloofness, disdain and possible snobbishness which prevent his coming to close grips with the rank and file of ordinary people. Also, a smugness that refuses to adapt itself to the demands of ministering effectively to the average Negro congregation." King liked to show off a bit, others commented, and would experiment with different dialects and styles to impress a congregation with his range. In the long run, this trait would prove central to his genius, but, as a young man, it was sometimes a little off-putting.

As his time at Crozer came to an end, King applied for further doctoral training at several institutions at home and abroad. While he was not an academic superstar, he was highly regarded, with enough intellectual smarts to hold his own and the gregarious personality that would serve him well as a minister. By January 1951, he knew that he had been accepted at Boston, and he decided to give up an idea he had entertained to go to Edinburgh.

King spent a successful last semester at Crozer, working still with George Washington Davis, absorbing the ideas of personalist theologian and philosopher Edgar S. Brightman and grappling still with the neoorthodox realism of Reinhold Niebuhr. In one of his final papers for Davis, he wrote, "I do remember moments that I have been awe awakened; there have been times that I have been carried out of myself by something greater . . . and to that something I gave myself. Has this great something been God? Maybe after all I have been religious for a number of years, and am now only becoming aware of it." As before, his personal reflections shed far more light on King's deepest thinking than do his pedestrian essays. Six of the ten graduates that year at Crozer were African American men, and after graduation, King helped his father again with his duties at Ebenezer, preparing soon to focus his PhD studies at Boston University.

His professors at Crozer sent him along with much warmer recommendations than he had received at Morehouse, and some of his Crozer teachers remained good friends with King in the years to come. George Washington Davis said that King would "make an excellent minister or teacher. He has the mind for the latter." Another professor noted that he was "very able." Dean Charles Bratten described him as "one of the best men in our entire student body," someone with a "keen mind which is both analytical and constructively creative."

Much later, at the time of the coronation of the King national holiday, King's close friend and former professor Kenneth "Snuffy" Smith could see immediately that the person he had known so well at Crozer was going to disappear into the myths of iconization: "Will the holiday be viewed as symbolic of the fact that King represented the brightest and the best of the American tradition of dissent in his struggle for social justice and peace . . . ?" Or, he asked by way of forecasting, "will it assume simply a symbolic significance transcending its actual effect, thus turning King into just another irrelevant plastic hero, like Superman, perhaps to be sold at Christmas time, along with Rambo and Rocky . . . I hope not, but I fear it will." By that time, the nation, indeed, already had "frozen Martin's feet to the steps of the Lincoln Memorial in 1963," where he had given the "I Have a Dream" speech. The person Smith knew would not be the person introduced every year on the King holiday, the icon commemorated but smelted down into an image palatable to everyone and challenging to virtually no one. Yet, as King prepared to enter Boston University as a candidate for a doctorate in theology, it would have been hard to have forecast such an outcome. The *zeitgeist* (spirit of the times) of history, as King later put it, had not yet caught up with him. Soon enough, it would.

2

+

The Young Preacher in Boston and Montgomery

Behind the legends and myths of the Book were many profound truths which one could not escape.

—Martin Luther King Jr., "Autobiography of Religious Development," 1950

This personal idealism remains today my basic philosophical position. Personalism's insistence that only personality—finite and infinite—is ultimately real strengthened me in two convictions: it gave me metaphysical and philosophical grounding for the idea of a personal God, and it gave me a metaphysical basis for the dignity and worth of all human personality.

—Martin Luther King Jr. in *Stride Toward Freedom*, 1958

Daddy King frequently expressed concern about "communist" ideas his son might pick up in the northern theological institutions. But he was also proud of his son. He could see him growing into his role during his summers at Ebenezer Baptist. His sermons, the father later wrote, showed the "probing quality of his mind, the urgency, the fire that makes for brilliance in every theological setting." Earlier, the father had insisted that the role of the church was to touch all parts of community life, to minister to the "broken-hearted, poor, unemployed, the captive, the blind, and the bruised." Doing so involved spiritual ministering but also political activism. He saw that his son combined the same sentiments, only with the addition of deeper theological training that confirmed what the son grew up instinctively knowing.

MLK learned about personalism at Crozer, and he instinctively took to it; it showed him, as the introduction to volume II of *The Papers of Martin Luther King, Jr.* puts it, that "experience as well as intellectual reflection could be the basis of religious belief." He knew from his youngest years that God was present in the soul of every person, and this gave each person an infinite worth. Personalism gave him the language to express what already was in his most basic sentiment. And King himself was personable, as well liked and sociable at Boston as he had been at Crozer. In dormitory rooms King and his fellows held bull sessions which gradually grew into a formally organized "Dialectical Society," often held in King's apartment. He was an informal leader of a group, and his student colleagues joined in with presentations on theological ideas.

The young doctoral candidate and minister-in-training also was intent on finding a wife, a requirement for any respectable man of the southern pulpit. During his first year in Boston, thanks to a mutual acquaintance, he met Coretta Scott, then a music student. She had grown up in a tough area of rural Alabama, where she later remembered, "It is a wonder that my own father did not end up in the swamp." That didn't happen, but their home and her father's sawmill was destroyed when he refused to sell out to white competitors. Scott later attended Antioch College as a music student. The experiences she had there in Yellow Springs, Ohio (later home to the family of the comedian David Chappelle), persuaded her to join the NAACP. It was not love at first sight with Martin and Coretta, but over time she warmed up to him. He made his intentions clear from the outset: "You have everything I have ever wanted in a wife . . . Character, intelligence, personality, and beauty." The two also discussed serious topics of economics, theology, and philosophy. The young King was effectively a democratic socialist in his sentiments, but it would be some years before he felt free to express those sentiments in person.

Coretta was very political from her teenage years. In 1948, she was a young supporter of the insurgent presidential primary campaign of Henry Wallace and the Progressive Party, a left-wing challenge to the mainstream (and Jim Crow–ed) Democratic Party of the era (although Truman himself endorsed a relatively strong civil rights platform). Despite her public image (partly cultivated later by Martin, who had very traditional, indeed patriarchal, ideas about family life) as a mother and helpmeet to her famous husband, she was in fact a committed political activist. As such, she came away from an early meeting with Martin impressed by his political commitments. In one of their first meetings King had "talked about working within the framework of democracy to move us toward a kind of socialism." That word "inevitably" would be misunderstood and was best avoided in public conversation, but Martin felt deeply, Coretta King remembered, that the system was "unjust" and needed a transformation. Arguably, her political views, if anything, were to the left of those of her husband; the fact that she sent him Edward Bellamy's *Looking Backward* (a story told in the previous chapter of this book) as a kind of reading assignment when they were dating suggests something of her long-held democratic socialist sentiments.

Later, Coretta urged MLK to come out against the Vietnam War, earlier than he was comfortable doing so, and after his assassination, she carried on his Poor People's Campaign and involved herself in international movements for pacifism and peace. She was on the left her whole life and at times pushed Martin in that direction, especially during his later years. But the role as wife of the famous minister and mother to their four children subsumed her image. Like Rosa Parks, Coretta Scott King has been mythologized into a kindly woman accidentally thrust into history by the force of events. This fits the narratives that Americans have demanded of women attached to great men, but it ignores their lives and fiercely held views.

King had come to Boston to study with his intellectual hero Edgar S. Brightman, the philosopher of personalism. But Brightman was in ill health and passed away during King's time there. King instead became a student of L. Harold DeWolf in courses such as Systematic Theology, Religious Teachings of the New Testament, and Seminar in Philosophy. King's academic performance dipped during a period when he had some conflicts with his father, especially regarding his desire to marry Coretta (Daddy King had some other local prospects in mind for his son), but he recovered and became a favorite student of DeWolf's. In the years afterward they maintained a warm relationship. DeWolf admired King and proudly followed his accomplishments as King rose to public prominence.

But in DeWolf's classes, King continued his practice (carried over from Crozer) of including sizable portions of unattributed quotations in his academic work. Some scholars attribute it simply to sloppiness. King took extensive notes on notecards, which he then transmitted onto the written page, often without bothering to note what were the words of others versus his own paraphrases. His sources were simple enough to track down, as he included them in his extensive bibliographies. His professors (save for one case where a paper was sent back for citation corrections) failed to note the unacknowledged quotations from secondary sources. Perhaps more important, King was reproducing pretty much exactly the theological thought that his professors wanted him to assimilate, and they praised him for it. And most of these quotations came from background material, including long historical sections that are more or less a recitation of data on this or that topic. To some degree, King continued this practice because no one caught and stopped him, and it was just easier.

Another explanation, from his biographer David Garrow, is that King was "first and foremost a young dandy whose efforts to play the role of a worldly sophisticated young philosopher were in good part a way of coping with an intellectual setting that was radically different from his own heritage." Then in his early twenties, King liked to show off. This was evident in the pleasure he took in driving the new Chevrolet his father had bought for him. It was manifest also in his desire to please his professors in a predominantly white theological institution.

Was that overcompensation? Perhaps. But the problem is that King was in fact quite self-assured in many ways, and he assimilated academic material without evidencing much fear of failure or of what we now might call "stereotype threat." He knew he was a black "representative individual," a walking emblem of the race; such was the fate of virtually all black scholars of that generation in predominantly white institutions. Still, he had warm personal relations with some of his professors, and they remained friends and mutual admirers long after he graduated. Furthermore, any number of other black scholars of that generation attended white northern schools without falling into this form of academic malpractice.

King had come from a folk tradition of the black pulpit. There, an accepted sharing of style, presentation, and material were both common and expected. Sermonizers drew from familiar wells of such sermons in the past. They copied large portions into their own sermons but then used those familiar and beloved starting points. King certainly did this throughout his career. Nearly all ministers who preach regularly do it in one form or another. He had learned that from his years growing up in the church. Preachers riffed on a sort of greatest hits catalog of familiar themes, tropes, ideas, and imagery. Preachers were like cover bands doing new versions of familiar tunes. The key was to take the familiar tune and transform it into one's own song. And King transferred that technique into his academic work, whether consciously or unconsciously.

Yet this view does not give King's engagement with his academic work enough credence. King also invested himself emotionally and intellectually in certain of the topics he was studying. He genuinely grappled with the warm social gospel, the evangelical liberalism, that came naturally to him and the darker warnings of Reinhold Niebuhr and others about the human potentiality for evil. And when he cared about the subjects he wrote about, it shows in the higher degree of originality in the work.

Perhaps the most persuasive explanation for King's plagiarizing practices is that he was interested in using scholarship for his own preacher ends, rather than creating academic tomes. As the editors of the King Papers put it in volume II, "King's actions during his early adulthood indicate that he increasingly saw himself as a preacher appropriating theological scholarship rather than as an academic producing such scholarship." Added to that, he was in a hurry; he already had accepted his position at Dexter Avenue Baptist Church in Montgomery before finishing his dissertation. As a preacher, he followed the norms that he knew and grew up with, to take tunes written by others and convey them with his own style, grace notes, and adaptations. He continued to do that throughout his preaching career. He planned to be a preacher, not an academic scholar, and he did what preachers-in-training did then and do now: take familiar material and craft it in a way that makes sense to them.

King filtered, adapted, and transformed familiar material over and over again throughout his career. One consistent pattern emerges: relatively dull background material, the kind of sentences and paragraphs that could easily be paraphrased, tended to be repeated verbatim. When King wanted to express his own ideas, he came alive. In his academic work, it happened when he took to an idea and worked through its implications for his own use as a preacher.

King sometimes longed for an academic career, especially later in his life when he sought refuge from the barrage of demands that confronted him every day. Absent the historical accident of his being in Montgomery and thrust into a role as a symbol for the movement, perhaps he would have jumped from early congregational preaching posts to a more cushy academic position. But his genius lay not in creating new ideas or conducting original research. Rather, it remained in adapting ideas for congregations and preaching them powerfully in idioms they could understand. He did this for black congregations through his career. He was equally skilled in orating for white churches, labor union meetings, social justice organizations, school assemblies, and of course the national audience as his star rose to fame.

King's dissertation, titled "A Comparison of the Conceptions of God in the Thinking of Paul Tillich and Henry Nelson Wieman," is not scintillating reading, to put it charitably. A good deal of the background material presented early in the work consists of passages taken from others but not attributed properly. He mixes paraphrasing and direct quotation without differentiating between the two. From a scholarly perspective, his practices, although unnoticed by his professors, are unacceptable. From the perspective of the student of King's life, what is interesting is not the plagiarized passages—dull recitations of factual material and summaries of various theologies—but the way King worked through the material to reach conclusions that would influence his thinking in the years to come. This is illustrated best in his sermons. There, he serves as a kind of translator of higher-order theological ideas to ordinary audiences, more so than in his academic scholarship. In short: his dissertation is pedestrian; the use of the ideas he explored in his dissertation is powerful.

Moreover, King's most avid personal study was less in the high theology assigned to him than in popular preachers of the past. He was drawn to Phillips Brooks, a nineteenth-century New England minister who provided to King the basic structure for a staple of King's sermonic oratory, "The Three Dimensions of a Complete Life," and to Harry Emerson Fosdick, the most important liberal Protestant preacher of the first half of the twentieth century, now best known for his essay "Shall the Fundamentalists Win?" King once corresponded with an elderly Fosdick, expressing his admiration and appreciation for Fosdick's body of work; Fosdick returned the favor, as he had followed King's career. King extensively annotated and copied Fosdick's collected sermons and borrowed from them extensively in a venue where academic citation practices didn't matter: his sermons.

More important than anything, King was a man in a hurry. He married Coretta Scott on June 18, 1953, in Alabama; the couple spent their honeymoon in a black funeral home, as the white-owned hotels in Perry County, Alabama, would not have given the black couple a room. Opportunities were opening up for King in pulpits and in black educational institutions around the country.

At one point, an administrator at the historically black Dillard University in New Orleans contacted Howard Thurman, dean of the chapel at Boston University (BU), asking for a recommendation for a man to serve as dean of the chapel at Dillard. They had heard that King might be their man. Thurman knew King only slightly, arriving late in King's term there. Of more consequence, Thurman and King shared an outlook deeply informed by, but also somewhat suspicious of, the rigidities of their own black Baptist tradition. It's little wonder that King responded with such enthusiasm to Thurman's *Jesus and the Disinherited*. It expressed King's vision of a liberatory gospel as much as it did Thurman's.

But King had not yet impressed everyone with his true potential. He was popular in Boston and well liked by students and professors. But he was a young man, in his early to mid-twenties in graduate school. He dressed the part, making sure to be immaculately coiffed. He enjoyed sporting an academic language that veered toward the pretentious. Once or twice, his professors warned him not to sail too high above his audiences (advice that he quickly took to heart). Thurman responded somewhat hesitantly, as he did not know King well, that "I understand that he is a good preacher," perhaps with little experience directly with students, but "a man has to start some time." Thurman later reflected, with ironic humor, on his relationship with King during that short time when their paths intersected in Boston: "I suppose I am one of the few members of the faculty of the Graduate School of Theology at Boston University that while he was there had no influence on his life." That was a self-deprecating exaggeration. Thurman had a long relationship with King's family. And his master work *Jesus and the Disinherited* was a key milestone in developing King's social consciousness as a theology student. King later used it in his sermons as a kind of urtext.

King was also busy making a name for himself nationally. An Atlanta radio station broadcast King's sermons at Ebenezer, including those in which he urged parishioners to not only seek salvation in their souls but also struggle for justice in this world, to be what he often referred to as "transformed nonconformists." He preached at the annual meeting of the National Baptist Convention and there joined with younger progressives in seeking to overturn an increasingly sclerotic leadership in the nation's largest African American religious body. That proved to be a failure, and in later years King would join with others in forming a splinter body, the Progressive National Baptist Convention, precisely to have a group of black Baptists aligned with civil rights activism in a way that the historic church body (formed originally in 1895 and through the twentieth century a power base for a succession of presidents who clung to their powerful positions in the black world) simply would never be.

Writing to George W. Davis in 1953, his old mentor from Crozer days, he said that he still held to a "liberal position," and there were "certain enduring qualities in liberalism which all of the vociferous noises of fundamentalism and neoorthodoxy can never destroy.'" King was still attracted to the "primacy of experience over any external authority," which he told his professor he had encountered in Schleiermacher but which he had imbibed from all his years in African American churches. As King continued, he found more sympathy now for neoorthodoxy; he could see its theological points as a "necessary corrective for a liberalism that became all too shallow" and one that "has the merit of calling us back to the Christian faith." But while it served as a corrective, it was never definitive, because it lacked the sense of hope that he always sought. King further commented on this in his qualifying doctoral exam in December of 1953 (he received a B), in which he noted that the question was "not revelation *or* reason, but revelation *and* reason. The one must supplement the other."

King presented his paper on Niebuhr's theology to the Dialectical Society, expressing his appreciation for but also criticisms of Niebuhr. "Within such a view is there no hope for man?" he asked of Niebuhr's skepticism. As King saw it, original sin for Niebuhr and the fall are not literal events in history; they are rather "symbolic or mythological categories to explain the universality of sin." King appreciated that Niebuhr's piercing skepticism showed that the "particular sort of optimism" characteristic of much twentieth-century theology "has been discredited by the brutal logic of events. Instead of assured progress in wisdom and decency, man faces the ever present possibility of swift relapse not merely to animalism but into such calculated cruelty as no other animal can practice. Niebuhr reminds us of this on every hand." But King doubted whether Niebuhr's views were "as orthodox and Biblical as he assumed them to be." Christ was so symbolic as practically to be "shorn of flesh and human meaning." In this section, King borrows liberally and without attribution from BU dean Walter Muelder's work "Reinhold Niebuhr's Conception of Man," particularly in pointing out that "Niebuhr's extreme agnosticism as to the God concept is far from biblical religion."

At Boston University, Harold DeWolf was his primary mentor in the philosophy of personalism. He also had a full-fledged socialist-personalist-pacifist model in his dean at BU, Walter Muelder. King was in the process of blending black church religion, modern intellectualism, anticolonial internationalism, and social justice politics.

Scholars make mistakes in minimizing his theological commitment to liberal theology and personalism, and caricaturing personalism and liberalism as weak on sin. They were not. "The theologians King studied practically battered their readers with descriptions of sin as badness, depravity, selfishness, and collective evil," writes theological historian Gary Dorrien. King's teachers, especially DeWolf, reinforced this emphasis. Muelder exemplified the fusion of vibrant personal faith and social justice passion that King admired and emulated. King buttressed his black church faith with a personalist theological variant of the modern West's richest intellectual tradition, post-Kantian idealism. He fused black church faith and liberal personalist theology. He gave his highest place to his belief in a personal God and the infinite value of human personality. If the worth of personality was the ultimate value in life, racism was distinctly evil. Evil is precisely that which degrades and annihilates personality.

King cared about the theology he was learning. He recognized that the social gospelers, contrary to reputation and misrepresentation, knew about evil. He struck everyone in Boston as an engaged scholar. King did not have to be convinced by Niebuhr that idealistic versions of liberalism underestimated the ravages of human evil. Later, he wrote, "My study of Gandhi convinced me that pacifism is not nonresistance to evil, but nonviolent resistance to evil. Between these two positions, there is a world of difference. Gandhi resisted evil with as much vigor and power as the violent resister, but he resisted with love instead of hate. True pacifism is not unrealistic submission to evil power, as Niebuhr contends. It is rather a courageous confrontation of evil by the power of love." He added that his "personal idealism" remained his most fundamental philosophical commitment: "Personalism's insistence that only personality—finite and infinite—is ultimately real strengthened me in two convictions: it gave me metaphysical and philosophical grounding for the idea of a personal

God, and it gave me a metaphysical basis for the dignity and worth of all human personality."

Thanks to the work of the Martin Luther King, Jr. Papers Project, which uncovered (with the cooperation of Coretta Scott King) boxes of hand-written or mimeographed original sermon material from King's earliest years, we have a much more profound sense now of how deeply rooted King was in the traditions of the social gospel and more broadly of the black left. Later, King wrote with some understanding of the attractions of certain features of communism (even while denying that one could be a communist and a Christian at the same time), about the contributions of black intellectual figures such as W. E. B. Du Bois (a professed atheist later in his life), and of the relationship of white supremacy at home and colonialism abroad, two halves of the same coin, as King saw it. "It should challenge us first to be more concerned about social justice," he said of communism.

And he placed this centrally in his sermons that he gave even while in graduate school and in his earliest years as a pastor. In an early sermon from 1953 titled "First Things First," King riffed on a familiar sermon from one of his favorites, Harry Emerson Fosdick, the source of much of his early sermonic material. Much of the sermon deals with famil-iar advice: put righteousness first in one's personal and home life, for example, in order to achieve the biblical promise that all things would be added unto you. But King usually added his own spin on this material that he copied from others; the melodies of these older sermons were in effect raw material for his own improvisations. In this particular sermon, he added a sociopolitical component to the term righteousness: "So long as the nations of the world are contesting to see which can be the most imperialistic, we will never have peace. So long as America places 'white supremacy' first we will never have peace. Indeed, the deep rumbling of discontent in our world today on the part of the masses is actually a revolt against the imperialism, economic exploitation, and colonialism that has been perpetuated by western civilization for all these many years." Military buildup, threats to use the atomic bomb, aggressive action abroad—none could bring peace, for "only through placing love, mercy, and justice first can we have peace." King concluded the sermon condemning America's boasts about the atomic bomb: "if we do not place something deeper than this first we too will be plunged across the abyss of destruction."

King carefully considered "Communism's Challenge to Christianity" in a 1953 sermon given in Atlanta, concluding that communism "should challenge us first to be more concerned about social justice." The sermon enumerated the incompatibility of communism and Christianity, but discovered that Marxism emphasizes many essential truths that must forever challenge us as Christians. "Indeed, it may be that Communism is a necessary corrective for a Christianity that has been all too passive and a democracy that has been all too inert." The proper response was a reawakened Christianity: "a passionate concern for social justice must be a concern of the Christian religion."

King's friend Walter R. McCall had interviewed for the preaching post at Dexter, then recruiting for a replacement for its cantankerous legendary leader Vernon Johns. McCall's outing at Dexter failed to impress the (reputedly) haughty parishioners, but McCall was excited about King's prospects there. "Take it from me, that is a Great Church, Mike," he told the young King. "Much honor will go to the man who gets it. Frankly, I have fallen in love with those people. Don't let anybody tell you that that church is such a hell raiser! It has some laymen, men who are concerned about the future of our preaching ministry among young men. That is a healthy sign." King's old mentor from Crozer days, J. Pius Barbour, had a different view of King's future as a black southern pastor: "You will dry rot there. I feel sorry for you with all that learning." His intellect would die in a conventional black southern pastorate. Barbour turned out to be wrong, of course, but his advice made perfect sense in the context in which it was given.

As King concluded his studies in Boston, his princely background in the black Baptist world, his service with his father as associate pastor at Ebenezer, and his training in the highest reaches of the American academic worlds, both black and white, made him an attractive candidate for a number of pulpits. The world of academia was open to him, and a number of black institutions contacted his professors at Boston University for recommendations.

In February 1954, King came to Detroit's Second Baptist Church, part of his beginnings in the nonstop travel that would occupy most of the rest of his life. There, he addressed a theme he returned to repeatedly in the coming year: how only in the process of "rediscovering lost values" could American culture truly move forward constructively, because scientific progress had outpaced moral advance. "The real problem is that through our scientific genius we've made of the world a neighborhood, but through our moral and spiritual genius we've failed to make of it a brotherhood." A few weeks later, on March 7, 1954, he received by telegram his "call" to the Dexter Avenue Baptist Church. In mid-April, King accepted the call, stating as his condition that he would take a salary of $4,200 and be granted a furnished parsonage, but that he would also be given time to complete his doctoral work, meaning he would not be a full-time pastor until September.

For years, King scholars have fulminated against the oversimplification and deification of King as a civil saint. In the process, they have (correctly) argued, the most challenging and radical parts of his message, particularly the messages he delivered in the last three or four years of his life, have been lost. What has been less well understood is how much this later radicalism reflected not so much a new departure but a further development and application of arguments he had made as a young man and minister. This misunderstanding arose from a reliance on his published work without an investigation of the material in his papers. King often spoke of wanting to find a quiet pastorate where he could preach. But in fact, he had a social justice ministry in mind from the beginning, emphasizing racial justice. King came to Montgomery determined to be a civil rights activist and was ahead of other local ministers when he arrived. He had long been a profound advocator of the social gospel; his first set of congregants in Montgomery were soon to learn that.

In his "trial" sermon for the Dexter Avenue Baptist congregation in Montgomery in January 1954, King drew on one of his standbys, the nineteenth-century pastor Phillips Brooks, whose "The Symmetry of Life" provided King with his fundamental structure and outline. King preached the sermon to white and black audiences, and "Paul's Letter to American Christians" was modeled on Presbyterian minister Frederick Meek's "A Letter to American Christians." But King spoke to huge black Baptist meetings using language he deployed in all kinds of settings. As the scholar Jonathan Rieder puts it, "King's personal copies of the books of these ministers indicate his heartfelt grappling with this liberal Protestant material. The underlining and the scribbling of inspired sermon ideas suggest the primal acts of incorporation through which he took them in and chewed them over."

King was borrowing from himself as much as from outside sources. He also took black mentors who had shown him how to merge white sources into black sermons. And the basic theme—that God expects us to care for others, and that it is a part of a fully three-dimensional life— remains the same. But King took Brooks's point into directions beyond the nineteenth-century context, into the world of the social gospel and of international relations. Preaching on the Good Samaritan story, for example, he concluded that "there is another aspect of Christian social responsibility which is just as compelling. It seeks to tear down unjust conditions and build anew instead of patching things up. It seeks to clear the Jericho road of its robbers as well as caring for the victims of robbery."

Here, King preached on a theme close to his heart, one he repeated many times over the years: "our material and intellectual advances have outrun our moral progress," he told the congregation. Certainly that was a common theme of much sermonizing from the era, to be expected in a time when Christians grappled with the immense moral implications of nuclear weaponry, for example. In future years, King elaborated further on this sermon. In the process, he developed his thoughts on the content of character and other phrases that would come down as sacred scripture in American history. In the 1960s, continuing with this same theme, he noted that "it is one of the ironies of history, that in a nation founded upon the principle that all men are created equal, men are still arguing over whether the color of a man's skin determines the content of his character."

King accepted the pastorate of Dexter Avenue in May 1954 and continued traveling back and forth between Boston and Montgomery before settling in Montgomery (still in the process of writing his PhD dissertation) in September 1954. He was determined to change the image of Dexter; he did not want a dead middle-class social club "with a thin veneer of religiosity." He considered his work with the NAACP, civic groups, and the Alabama Council on Human Relations part of the church's mission: "Our church is becoming militant, stressing a social gospel as well as a gospel of personal salvation." Another sermon from around the same time, delivered to the women's Auxiliary of the National Baptist Convention (led by the long-time religious activist Nannie Burroughs), demonstrates King's early global consciousness. In it, he spoke explicitly to colonialism and imperialism leading to domination and exploitation. The old order of ungodly exploitation and crushing domination was passing away. There would be a daybreak of freedom, not just in Montgomery or Alabama but throughout the United States and the world.

In May, as he began his ministry in the fabled "cradle of the Confederacy," he compared white people to Pilate. They knew what was right and what was unjust, but they sought to wash their hands of the situation. "Many white people are against many of the practices of their group, but they are afraid to take a stand," he concluded. But as a result, they were still "caught in the clutches of slavery," beholden like slaves to a system they could not summon the fortitude to resist. They were like Pilate, who knew Jesus was innocent but also knew that "to free him would jeopardize his position. And so he crucified upon the cross of his self-interest." In many cases, it was worse, because whites were not like Pilate but instead like the crowd chanting for the crucifixion of Christ. In a sermon from December 1955, just at the beginning of the bus boycott, King commented on the jury in Mississippi that had freed the murderers of Emmett Till, a fourteen-year-old African American boy whose brutal killing had received international attention. That jury, King said, which had "freed two white men from what might be considered one of the most brutal and inhuman crimes of the twentieth century," consisted of white churchgoers. The perpetrators of many of the greatest evils in our society worship Christ: "These . . . people, like the Pharisee, go to church regularly . . . pay their tithes and offerings, and observe religiously the various ceremonial requirements," only to actively perpetrate evil.

King's self-description as a "profound advocator of the social gospel" fits his Dexter Avenue sermons well. In July 1954, for example, he told the congregants, "Christ is more concerned about our attitude towards racial prejudice and war than he is about our long processionals. He is more concerned with how we treat our neighbors than how loud we sing his praises." Countless "Christians" were "worshipping Christ emotionally but not morally," including white lynchers of Negroes and white southerners who advocated segregation.

King came with some decided ideas about authority structures in the church. "Implied in the call," he told the church in his recommendations for their first fiscal year, "is the unconditional willingness of the people to accept the pastor's leadership. This means that the leadership never ascends from the pew to the pulpit, but it invariably descends from the pulpit to the pew." Congregants obviously were not to submit "blindly and ignorantly," as if the pastor were some superhuman figure, but likewise the pastor "must never be considered a mere puppet for the whimsical and capricious mistreatment of those who wish to show their independence."

King had learned from his father's reorganization of Ebenezer Baptist on taking the pulpit in the early 1930s, and he proposed plans similar to those his father had used, including implementing a unified budget to replace separate rallies for individual causes. Congregants were assigned to birth month clubs; committees for raising building funds, recruiting new members, and organizing cultural events were formed. Most important for our purposes here, King recommended the creation of a "Social and Political Action Committee," in order to keep the "congregation intelligently informed concerning the social, political and economic situation." Its job was to raise awareness of the local NAACP and to encourage voting. King thought that a church following this plan would inevitably achieve success and that the success of his leadership depended on the quality of their followership. "Dexter will rise to such heights as will stagger the imagination of generations yet unborn," he concluded. Surely the older members saw this as the enthusiastic prognostications of a very young pastor. A year later, King reported back overjoyed at the progress made in the first year in all of the areas he had outlined, a success he attributed to the "greatness of your followership." He hoped the church would continue "to inject a new spiritual blood into the veins of this community, transforming its jangling discords into meaningful symphonies of spiritual harmony"; the latter phrase would become a staple of King's oratory, often deployed at the end of sermons and public addresses to register his hope for a better future to come.

By the end of 1954, King was still occupied with completing his dissertation and beginning his new work with his church. He had thoughts of staying there perhaps some years, and later coming back to academia, or being a dean of a college chapel. At the same time, he continued making a name for himself regionally and nationally through his sermonizing. After one successful venture, his father wrote to him that King Jr. had "swept" (as in carried away, inspired) the audience, and King's father frequently received correspondence about how his son was becoming the greater preacher of the two despite his young age. The father warned his son, "You see young man you are becoming very popular. As I told you you must be much in prayer. Persons like yourself are the ones the devil turns all of his forces aloose to destroy." It's hard to know exactly what King Jr. made of that, whether he took in that fatherly advice or brushed it aside as he sometimes did with some of his father's fundamentalisms. But his father was right; forces were about to engulf King that he could scarcely have imagined by the end of 1954. And there were plenty of forces loose in the world that would seek to destroy him.

Early in 1955, King addressed the NAACP in Birmingham; his speech there forecast the themes he would pursue in the pulpit and in his public addresses to come. "A voteless people is a powerless people," he said (repeating a catchphrase initiated by a black college fraternity in the 1930s, in a protest against black disfranchisement); the ballot provided the power to change the conditions of segregation, which was simply a "form of slavery." Depending on some divine force to sweep away injustice would not suffice; action was required. For example, in his own church he had created the Social and Political Action Committee to register and motivate voters and to join the NAACP.

King kept in contact with his informal mentor from Crozer days, the irascibly funny minister J. Pius Barbour, who had made sure to give King and his student colleagues lessons in staying tuned to learning to minister and preach specifically in black churches. Barbour was not overly impressed by some of the contemporary high theologians of that era, including Paul Tillich, about whom King had written part of his PhD dissertation. "Tillich is all wet. There is no 'being-itself' . . . Being-itself is a meaningless abstraction," he scribbled in a letter to King, poo-pooing Tillich's best-known contribution to twentieth-century theological vocabulary. Barbour urged King to cut his losses as soon as he could and move on to "a big metropolitan center in THE NORTH, or some town as ATLANTA," for fear he would "dry rot" in the cradle of the Confederacy in Montgomery. "I feel sorry for you with all that learning," he gently scolded King, given the lack of opportunities in the South for black preachers of intellectual interests.

But here Barbour turned out to be the one all wet, because the spirit of the times was moving in Montgomery.

3

The Montgomery Uprising

Agitation Among Negroes

—Handwritten note on FBI memo from Mobile office, January 4, 1956

If we are wrong, Jesus of Nazareth was merely a utopian dreamer that never came down to earth. If we are wrong, justice is a lie, love has no meaning.

—Martin Luther King Jr., Holt Street Baptist Church, December 4, 1955

A little less than midway into his second year at Dexter Avenue Baptist Church, his PhD now in hand and a successful fiscal year in church celebrated, an NAACP activist in Montgomery named Rosa Parks refused to give up her seat to a white man on a city bus line. Legend later created a quiet "Rosa Parks" who just happened to be tired one day. But the real story is completely different from the myth.

Parks had a long history of working against the system. As the secretary to E. D. Nixon, a local labor and NAACP leader, she had investigated unprosecuted rapes of black women by white men, including the horrendous gang rape of a young black woman named Recy Taylor by six young white men. Risking her life, she pursued her investigations throughout Alabama to collect testimony and information. And for years she had fumed, as had local African Americans in general, about the abuse they had to take at the hands of bus drivers whose talent for torturing black riders with everyday indignities seemed boundless. In a previous episode, a bus driver named J. P. Blake, a particularly noxious enforcer of bus seating segregation, had forced Parks off the bus when she objected to (as was the common practice) paying her fare at the front but then exiting to enter the bus in the back. She had been trained in activism through her work with the NAACP and workshops at Highlander Folk School in Tennessee.

Parks was a determined foe of segregation ready to move—or, in this case, not to move. That day, that same driver, J. P. Blake, demanded that she move from her place in the "neutral" section while four white men were standing nearby, so that the white men could sit. Three other black passengers moved and stood in the back; she did not. Parks had decided to see, finally, "what rights I had as a human being and a citizen, even in Montgomery, Alabama." That famous day, December 1, 1955, history moved rapidly in her wake.

By that time, King had preached for the local NAACP, developed relationships with the professional people in his congregation who would go on to lead the bus boycott, and had led his church on the path toward social activism. He also had connected with the white activists Clifford and Virginia Durr, who would (along with the local Lutheran pastor Robert Graetz) became key white allies of the movement; so had Rosa Parks, who had attended a workshop about school desegregation at the Highlander Folk School.

Just a few days later, what was supposed to be a one-day bus boycott to make a symbolic point was quickly morphing into something much greater. And King's symbolic place as a newcomer to town, not having the grip of the white establishment squeezing him, propelled him to the leadership of the Montgomery Improvement Association (MIA). It also helped that he was not yet allied with any particular faction within what had been a fractious black community and that he had a distinctively smooth voice attractive to national media. It had "happened so quickly that I did not even have time to think it through," King recalled; if he had, he might have turned it down. The black Alabamians initially sought not an end to segregation on public transportation but simply more equitable treatment for blacks riding segregated bus lines. The city resisted.

On December 2, 1955, Montgomery ministers met at an AME Zion congregation to discuss a possible boycott of the city buses. "When the Women's Political Council officers learned that the ministers were assembled in that meeting," key organizer and Dexter Avenue church member Jo Anne Gibson Robinson later recounted, "we felt that God was on our side. It was easy for my two students and me to leave a handful of our circulars at the church, and those disciples of God could not truthfully have told where the notices came from if their very lives had depended on it. Many of the ministers received their notices of the boycott at the same time, in the same place. They all felt equal, included, appreciated, needed. It seemed predestined that this should be so." Local clerics quickly discovered that the congregants were "quite intelligent on the matter and were planning to support the one-day boycott with or without their ministers' leadership. It was then that the ministers decided that it was time for them, the leaders to catch up with the masses."

Congregations that had been relatively quiescent served during the boycott as organizing centers as well as spiritual refreshment stations. After the initial one-day trial, attendees at a mass meeting demanded that the action be extended. As congregants offered up prayers for "misguided whites," the people "felt the spirit. Their enthusiasm inundated them, and they overflowed with emotion." Some months later, when Jo Ann Gibson Robinson, Mary Fair Burks, and other women took their turns being arrested, supporters came to the Dexter Avenue church for a mass meeting. In her memoir of the boycott, Robinson recounted how she felt that "certainly the Spirit from above must have been among the crowd, for people were mentally, spiritually, psychologically serene inside. . . . A quiet calm seemed to invade and relax me." Later, Robinson, Nixon, and others grew angry that the national media fixated on King, ignoring those who had done the actual initial organizing.

Local white reaction to the boycott made the job of organizing easier. On one day of arrests, the Reverend M. C. Cleveland, an older pastor of the Day Street Baptist Church and a man "so upright and so cautious" that he never attended a single mass meeting, sat "forlornly in the jailhouse, signing a piece of paper." When authorities harassed a man well known for being the "epitome of prudence and conformity," the old strategies of accommodation appeared more bankrupt than ever. At the same time, veteran southern liberals such as Clifford and Virginia Durr expressed their support, sometimes publicly but more often privately. A "white friend" wrote to Martin Luther King Jr. early in 1956, telling him that although the White Citizens' Council would meet that night, "they can't make you ride and you are not breaking any law, so continue in the spirit of Christ. He is your real leader. Don't forget him!" Mass meetings kept the spirit up in Montgomery. Ninety days into the boycott, one minister exulted that "it was in Montgomery that God chose us to play this all-important role. We must accomplish the will of God." Because the white church would not practice what it preached, he urged one crowd, "we must grab whites with a spiritual hand, and tell them we love you as though you were our very own."

That did not mean they did not recognize the evil at the core of segregation and within the hearts of those whites. Evil was present, but, as scholar Jonathan Rieder has put it, so was God and the possibility of realizing his Kingdom on earth. This was a political culture fashioned by the "churched part of the movement," a "far cry from liberal perfectionism and sunny rationalism." King exhorted the people, bringing to bear the entire history of African American preaching, connecting them to their own long social gospel tradition, but also pointing them toward universal themes of American civil religion and Christian humanism.

Although new to town, King committed himself to being the profound advocator of the social gospel that had been his self-description some years earlier. He saw the possibility that the church would at last awake and take center stage in the movement. Knowing little substantively about the philosophy of nonviolence, the young King applied for a firearms permit and purchased a gun to keep at home. As the bus boycott episode gained national attention, he consulted with veterans of nonviolent civil disobedience. King had yet to form fully his ideas of nonviolence. Soon he had help at the hands of white Methodist and Fellowship of Reconciliation national field secretary Glenn Smiley and black organizer extraordinaire Bayard Rustin. Both had logged long years in movements for peace and justice. Both recognized in King a vehicle to carry forward their hopes for a mass movement.

Bayard Rustin, brilliant political strategist and committed advocate of nonviolent resistance, became another influential theorist and advisor to King. Rustin came to Montgomery partially at the behest of white southern liberal writer Lillian Smith. They had worked together during the 1940s, he as race relations director and she as a board member of the Fellowship of Reconciliation (FOR). Rustin's homosexuality and political radicalism forced him to keep his distance from civil rights organizations. Rustin's role was to advise and ghostwrite generally from a distance, in such a way that his influence (generally very much welcomed by King) would not be publicly evident. Rustin wrote some of the first articles advertising the bus boycott for a larger audience, published under King's name. He persuaded King to accept nonviolence as a fundamental philosophical principle. As a short-term stratagem, Rustin insisted, it would be seen as a political ploy, not as the *satyagraha* ("soul force") that empowered the Indian independence movement. King was deeply influenced by Rustin's philosophical nonviolence. But King had not yet learned fully the lessons of how to develop organizations that themselves worked democratically. King developed the SCLC more as a small and hierarchically controlled organization dependent on the charismatic authority of leading ministers.

The Fellowship of Reconciliation sent Glenn Smiley, its national field secretary, from Texas. The white pacifist clergyman, who had worked with FOR and had been imprisoned during World War II as a draft resister, advised King in all he knew about nonviolence. At the same time, Smiley in particular saw that King was well intentioned but young and surrounded by friends who would too easily resort to violence should the situation arise. Smiley's impressions of King were mixed: "so young, so inexperienced, so good," perhaps a "Negro Gandhi," or possibly "an unfortunate demagogue destined to swing from a lynch mob's tree." King talked a good game about nonviolence, Smiley thought, but not really: "The whole movement is armed in a sense, and this is what I must convince him to see as the greatest evil. . . . If he can *really* be won to a faith in nonviolence there is no end to what he can do."

Smiley set up meetings with white churches and encouraged interracial ministers' associations and prayer groups. He pushed King into developing a small grassroots interracial organization that could organize spontaneous protests and avoid dependence on charismatic leaders—something like what the SNCC (Student Nonviolent Coordinating Committee) eventually became. Smiley said that King "had Gandhi in mind when this thing started ," but he was "too young and some of his close help is violent. King accepts . . . a body guard, and asked for a permit for them to carry guns . . . the place is an arsenal. King sees the inconsistency, but not enough. He believes, yet he doesn't believe." He pondered what the FOR could teach King and vice versa. Certainly the broader movements for nonviolence and pacifism could learn from "their plain earthy devices for building morale, and they can learn from us, King runs out of ideas quickly and does the old things again and again. He wants help, and we can give it to him without attempting to run the movement or pretend we know it all." American Gandhism was already a highly mediated tradition. For many (although not for Howard Thurman), it was basically pared back to nonviolence, and Smiley helped transmit that to King. And yet, as King saw it, "there is something about the protest that is suprarational; it cannot be explained without a divine dimension."

Martin Luther King Jr. once said that while Christ gave the civil rights movements its goals, Gandhi taught it what tactics to use to achieve those goals. More than just tactics, though, Gandhi and the Indian independence movement supplied a stirring example of the power of mass nonviolent resistance to oppression. It provided a model for any number of movements worldwide. Gandhi drew from many sources for those ideas, from Tolstoy to theosophy to vegetarianism to Indian philosophy. His ideas traveled abroad and adapted themselves to new situations and conflicts, including in the land where Gandhi practiced his barrister trade as a young man (South Africa) and in the American South (although, ironically, as a young lawyer Gandhi had nothing to do with Africans in South Africa, considering them too spiritually unformed to understand nonviolence). It was in those two places where civil rights struggles carried on by people of color historically oppressed and legally ostracized would be felt at their most dramatic. Religious ideas and institutions were key in making both happen.

That adaptation of Gandhi's ideas to the black freedom struggle had a long history; King learned from a previous generation who had met Gandhi and/or imbibed his ideas. Beginning in the 1930s, young American

idealists who were to become central to the American civil rights movement visited India to learn Gandhi's ideas. They realized how much
his methods could be applied to the situation of black Americans, who
were also a colonized and oppressed class. Key in taking ideas from
the radical and pacifist left and translating them into wisdom directly
applicable to the freedom struggle were Unitarian and humanist theologian Howard Thurman, King's longtime Atlanta friend and Morehouse
president Benjamin Mays, and Howard University president Mordecai
Wyatt Johnson, whose speech on Gandhi in Philadelphia in 1949 had lit
a fire in the young seminary student King. Later, the Methodist divine
and activist James Lawson, and a white Texas veteran of the Fellowship
of Reconciliation and the Congress of Racial Equality, Glenn Smiley,
also educated King in applying Gandhian ideas to the American context. All emerged from southern Protestant backgrounds and developed
ideas of pacifism and nonviolent civil disobedience through the 1940s
and 1950s. They drew heavily from the philosophy of Richard Gregg, a
former Quaker and pacifist. Gregg's 1934 work *The Power of Nonviolence*
taught a generation about the "moral jiu-jitsu" of nonviolence. It was,
he said, a force powerful enough to defeat the oppressor without needing to land a physical blow. Thurman and Lawson learned those lessons
during their sojourns in India, in 1935–1936 and 1953–1956, respectively.
At the end of Thurman's visit, according to one account, Gandhi had
told Thurman, "it may be through the Negroes that the unadulterated
message of nonviolence will be delivered to the world." Leaders of the
founding meeting of King's Southern Christian Leadership Conference
two decades later remembered it; they understood themselves to be
carrying out Gandhian principles of social struggle. For Thurman, this
would be through small groups of dedicated activists, what he called
"apostles of sensitiveness," rather than through a major mass national
movement. But later, when the latter actually arose, he threw his spiritual resources behind it.

Initially, Martin Luther King Jr. was reluctant to do adopt the philosophy. It seemed suicidal, and King earlier had resisted pacifism as a viable
option. For the same reason, numerous everyday folk in the movement
were unconvinced, particularly those who lived in dangerous rural areas.
As one put it, "This nonviolent stuff'll get you killed." King noted that
every man in town owned a gun, so how could he leave his own family
unprotected? Given how many bombings of homes and churches were
about to happen, that was a good question. Gradually, and through the
tutelage of a generation of pacifists, labor organizers, and religious idealists, the ideas that would form the southern freedom movement found
their way to southern communities. Martin Luther King Jr. then articulated them to a national audience.

On December 5, King began to make his legend with a speech at the Holt Street Baptist Church, a church squarely situated in an ordinary black neighborhood of Montgomery. With little time to prepare (especially in comparison with the meticulous notes that he took and wrote out for his normal weekly sermons), King fell back on his old sermonic standbys but reframed them in a way that moved his audience. In a sense, that was the night he became the public icon *Martin Luther King Jr.* From that time on, King understood his role to be one of "racial diplomat," as the biographer Peter Ling has expressed it. Later, he said that his job was to thread the needle between a "speech that would be militant enough to keep my people aroused to positive action and yet moderate enough to keep this fervor within controllable and Christian bounds." King understood the depth of anger in black communities, that "many of the Negro people were victims of bitterness that could easily rise to flood proportions. What could I say to keep them courageous and prepared for positive action and yet devoid of hate and resentment?" Or, as he later explained it, "You just can't communicate with the ghetto dweller and at the same time not frighten many whites to death. I don't know what the answer to that is. My role perhaps is to interpret to the white world. There must be somebody to communicate to two worlds."

King threaded that needle perfectly, giving vent to the anger and frustration but letting the audience know that "the only weapon that we have in our hands this evening is the weapon of protest." It was the "glory of America, with all of its faults," that provided the space for protests. Indeed, "if we are wrong, the Constitution of the United States is wrong," and "if we are wrong, Jesus of Nazareth was merely a utopian dreamer that never came down to earth." King made reference to the connection of white supremacy and capitalism: "When labor all over this nation came to see that it would be trampled over by capitalistic power, it was nothing wrong with labor getting together and organizing and protesting for its rights."

King reminded his audience that it was not enough to pray without acting, and it would not suffice to call for love when the demand was for justice: "And justice is really love in calculation. Just as love correcting that which revolts against love." He concluded the speech by exhorting people that in the future someone could say, "there lived a race of people, a *black* people . . . a people who had the moral courage to stand up for their rights. And thereby they injected a new meaning into the veins of history and of civilization." By that time, he held the crowd in his hand. This was a generation ready to move, and they had found someone who could articulate their grievances, hopes, and aspirations in a language that spoke to their everyday experiences but at the same time pointed to universal aspirations for freedom and liberty that could not be denied.

The actual demands of the MIA were almost absurdly minimal. The group sent its requests to the National City Lines, the parent company that ran the city bus company in Montgomery, simply asking for "courteous treatment by bus drivers" and a system of seating with blacks sitting from the rear to the front, whites from the front to the rear, but with no specifically racially assigned seating. "Since 44% of the city's population is Negro, and since 75% of the bus riders are Negro, we urge you to send a representative to Montgomery to arbitrate," they advised the company, which subsequently sent a company official to investigate. In short, the MIA asked not for an end to segregation but a more flexible interpretation of the law which could accommodate the needs of bus riders in the city. The city government of Montgomery, however, would not budge an inch. "We are going to carry out the law as we see it, and state law and city law call for segregation on buses," the mayor said after several meetings with black leaders and city attorneys in the first two months of the boycott. The absurd lengths to which whites went to defend indefensible and now illegal customs in Montgomery were the best ally of a movement that depended on dramatizing and publicizing such injustices. Their white opponents at nearly every turn made that strategy look like genius.

As the Montgomery story hit the national press, King's name soon ascended. A former friend and fraternity brother, writing to King a few weeks after the start of the boycott, grew excited in contemplating the possibilities of "large scale, well disciplined, nonviolent civil disobedience to segregation laws." Such a movement gave people a sense of personal participation, and because the movement came out of "good Christian doctrine, it makes it all the more difficult for the conscience of the white South to rationalize its opposition to it." Thus, the movement could be just as potent a political weapon in the hands of southern blacks as it had been in the hands of Gandhi.

As the press caught hold of the developing King story, so did the FBI. Two days after the Holt Street Baptist church meeting, agents from the Mobile, Alabama, office of J. Edgar Hoover's agency started to send reports to their boss. Headlined "Racial Situation," with the handwritten addition of "Agitation Among Negroes," the memo informed their superiors in Washington that someone had been charged with the task of digging up dirt on King and the movement. It likely was someone in the Montgomery police department, as policemen there guarding such events often double-timed as spies who transmitted information about movement plans to police departments, and sometimes to the FBI as well. Local authorities also recruited local prisoners to attend mass meetings to report on what happened, as well as one woman who served as a cook for the mayor and gave him information on what she had heard.

This kind of infiltration would be common through King's career. It started small in Montgomery. Later, it included his accountant, a photographer (who took a number of famous photographs from that era), and others from King's circle who worked in the movement but also were moles for the FBI and other federal agencies. The government surveillance of King started early and escalated over time, including cops on the beat in Montgomery, authorities in the various southern states, and then attorney general Robert Kennedy and, most notoriously, FBI director J. Edgar Hoover. At first it was more casual than systematic. Later, in the last six years of his life, it was relentless, intended to destroy King's career, and conducted with the voyeur's vengeance that was J. Edgar Hoover's stock-in-trade.

The local authorities harassed King as well. In January 1956, while driving home from his church and taking along some passengers in the car pool system, policemen stopped King and cited him for speeding—he was five miles over the twenty-five-miles-per-hour speed limit. For this violation, the police threw King in jail. Obviously they wanted him to know that they knew who he was and what he was doing and that they could have control over his life when they wanted, simply through the exercise of the "law." King's later reflections on distinguishing between just laws and unjust laws, memorably placed with the text of "Letter from a Birmingham Jail," arose from such constant petty harassment. He knew ordinary black citizens faced such brutality at a much more elemental level nearly every day of their lives. King's success in the bus boycott only fueled the desire of state authorities to surveil and harass him. Any minor offense would work, even traffic offenses. Driving five miles over the speed limit could be cause for jail time, after all, if one followed the full letter of the law.

The local harassment continued with a court case filed against the leaders of the boycott, a case that became *State of Alabama v. M. L. King, Jr.* in March 1956. The trial attracted national attention and a crowd too large to fit into the courthouse. Prosecutors charged King with leading an illegal conspiracy against an institution of the state government. The prosecuting attorneys brought in bus drivers to recount supposed incidents of violence directed against them and the buses, as well as a few black witnesses to suggest they had been coerced physically into staying off the buses. The defense separated King himself from the boycott and asked for testimony from numerous witnesses to recount the abuse they suffered daily at the hands of bus operators. Black passengers who tried to enter through the front, for example, were verbally abused and, after exiting to enter in the back, were stranded when the bus sped away.

Eventually the judge found King guilty and fined him. The sentence was suspended while appeals were heard. A crowd gathered to hear King after the hearing concluded; King repeated that the glory of America was the right to protest for rights and reminded all that "we still advocate nonviolence and passive resistance and still determine to use the weapon of love." Later that day, he returned to Holt Street Baptist Church, where he was greeted as a figure akin to Christ. "You don't get to the promised land without going through the wilderness," he told the congregants, after another speaker had proclaimed that King was "nailed to the cross for us." King expressed again his faith in democracy, the basis of the right to protest, and again eschewed violence. "This is a spiritual movement," he said, "and we are depending on moral and spiritual forces. That is the only weapon we have."

Admirers from around the country sent him fan mail to encourage him, as did many of his former colleagues and professors. Samuel DuBois Cook, King's classmate at Morehouse, wrote him, "You have achieved that rare combination of social action and love. When one acts on the presupposition of love, who can condemn, who can fail to admire? History knows of many who have traveled your present journey," including Socrates, Christians in Rome, Gandhi, and Thoreau.

Still in Montgomery, King was arrested in September 1958 and found guilty of loitering. The court fined him and sentenced him to fourteen days in the jail in Montgomery—this was at the very time that *Stride Toward Freedom* was being published. Later the Montgomery police commissioner, realizing the hopeless strategic stupidity of the local police action, paid the fine. He recognized King's tactics as "just another publicity stunt intended to further his self-assumed role as a martyr." Before then, King issued a statement denying he was interested in any "histrionic gesture" or "publicity stunt." Instead, he felt compelled to register his protest because of his love of country, of the principles of liberty and equality: "I have come to see that America is in danger of losing her soul and can so easily drift into tragic Anarchy and crippling Fascism. Something must happen to awaken the dozing conscience of America before it is too late. The time has come when perhaps only the willing and nonviolent acts of suffering by the innocent can arouse this nation to wipe out the scourge of brutality and violence inflicted upon Negroes who seek only to walk with dignity before God and man."

Earlier, King had described his "conversion" as one that diverged from the standard evangelical narrative; it involved the "gradual making of the noble ideas set forth in my family and my environment, and I must admit that this intaking has been largely unconscious." While he may not have been saved in the traditional ecstatic catharsis, he experienced his own crisis moment on January 27, 1956. Sitting in his kitchen after receiving a threatening phone call—one of many during those early days of the Montgomery bus boycott—he realized "religion had become real to me and I had to know God for myself. And I bowed down over that cup of coffee, I never will forget it." He heard the voice of Jesus urging him to "fight on" and that "He promised never to leave me, never to leave me alone." At that moment King "experienced the presence of the Divine as I had never experienced Him before. . . . My uncertainty disappeared. I was ready to face anything." His vision that troubled evening steeled his resolve. Three nights later, following the bombing of his home, an angry crowd gathered outside. King calmed them, possibly preventing an ugly confrontation. In doing so, he sealed his growing reputation as an orator with near magical powers of persuasion.

King's own theology emerged from the Old Testament teachings of the moral absolute of justice, a historic black Christian emphasis. To that, King added in diverse and to some extent contradictory influences, ranging from liberal Protestantism, his own reading of Niebuhrian neoorthodoxy, and Gandhian maxims. Together, the mixture inspired active nonviolent resistance to injustice, and a faith and hope that conquered despair. Local whites admonished the young preacher to stick to the gospel and let other things alone. King would have none of it. There remained, he believed, a "material connection between man and his environment and this connection means a material well being of the body as well as the spiritual well being of the soul is to be sought."

More than any theology or philosophy, King's oratorical artistry moved people in ways that were difficult to articulate but powerfully present. Andrew Young remembered King's "strong biblical metaphors, drawing upon his scholarship and sophisticated knowledge. Martin had the ability to make us feel as if we were more than our daily selves, more than we had been—a part of a beautiful and glorious vision that was enabling us to transcend ourselves. It was a marvelous quality he had, not ever fully captured on the printed page or in recordings, to lift the people to another place so that they could almost feel themselves moving." At that point, parsing King's theological influences mattered less than understanding his ability to move the spirit of people.

In the coming months he increasingly adopted a spiritually profound and committed rhetoric of Gandhian nonviolence. One black newspaper called him "Alabama's Gandhi." To a congregation in Brooklyn, he said, "Christ showed us the way, and Gandhi in India showed it could work." Increasingly, King attached the movement about practices on the city buses of Montgomery to larger struggles for justice and freedom everywhere. As well, he saw the connection to anticolonial movements and international revolutions. "The great struggle of the Twentieth Century," he told one congregation, "has been between these exploited masses questing for freedom and in the colonial powers seeking to maintain their domination." At the same time, King avoided any association with communism. He criticized the Soviet system as a denial of freedom with no hope (as in the United States) of winning changes from within that system and tiptoed around a public association with Bayard Rustin, a gay man arrested for homosexual conduct in the past, who had long identified as a man of the Left.

King understood what could be discussed privately versus what should be open publicly. He had cultivated an oratorical manner readily adaptable to different audiences. He knew that the success of a nonviolent movement in Montgomery and elsewhere lay in keeping its image squarely within the American civic tradition of protest against injustice. His brilliance in oratorical adaptability had won him admirers, including his old mentor and theological sparring partner, J. Pius Barbour. The young theology student still in formation just a few years ago had taken command of the stage in ways that Barbour could scarcely believe. And King was, he said, "the first PhD I have heard that can make uneducated people throw their hats in the air over philosophy."

A perfect example of this comes from a sermon King delivered to MIA boycotters in January 1956. The full address King gave is not available, but we have notes taken by some Fisk University researchers at the time. King told of conversations with "good white citizens" (the kind of "moderates" he would later deride), who worried that the "good relations" that had existed between whites and Negroes could be destroyed by outsiders who disturbed a properly functioning southern social order. They told him he should spend his time preaching the gospel and "leave other things alone." King responded that it little suffices to preach about honesty to people who experience economic conditions that effectively compel dishonesty as a survival strategy, nor could he preach about truth in a social order that depended on fictions such as "warm relations" and "southern way of life." As King put it, "You see God didn't make us with just soul alone so we could float about in space without care or worry. He made a body to put around a soul. When the body was made in flesh, there became a material connection between man and his environment and this connection means a material well being of the body as well as the spiritual well being of the soul is to be sought. And it is my job as a minister to aid in both of these."

King's gift for digesting theology for his audiences was fully in evidence even as a young minister in Montgomery. And the contrast between his trenchant observations here and the stilted academic prose of his productions just a few years earlier clarify what his deep dive into the realities of his parishioners' everyday lives had given him. Whatever Paul Tillich or Edgar Brightman said or didn't say paled in comparison to what King now had to say to Montgomery citizens whose backs had been against the wall for so long. They now responded with astounding unity of purpose and spirit to King's call to move toward the daybreak of freedom.

King soon had reason to put into practice his theology of nonviolence, when, on January 30, 1956, dynamite landed on his front porch. Coretta and a church member from Dexter were home, and King's first daughter slept in the back room. The bomb blast damaged a part of the house. King raced home; outside stood a crowd ready to move at a moment's notice and unwilling to listen to police orders to disperse. King told the crowd to avoid panic, eschew violence, and continue loving their enemies. Even if someone got to him personally in an act of violence, the movement had not started with him, and it would not stop with him, for "if anything happens to me, there will be others to take my place." The crowd sang "My Country 'Tis of Thee" and left at 10:45 p.m., about an hour and a quarter after the bomb had arrived. This would be the first of a campaign of harassment, bombings, arrest, and threats that King and others endured during the 381-day boycott, continuing on afterward. It was severe enough, in fact, to compel Rosa Parks eventually to leave town.

In a sermon soon afterward, King noted that too often "Christianity has been relegated to a bundle of sentimental teachings." He was referring in part to the prosperity gospel stylings of people like Norman Vincent Peale. At that very time, Donald Trump's father was listening to Peale and introducing his son and family to the gospel of prosperity. Later, that prosperity in real estate in New York involved a deliberate program of discrimination against blacks seeking housing. Already, by the 1950s, what Niebuhr, Howard Thurman, and Gandhi were for King, Norman Vincent Peale was for the Trumps and a generation who enjoyed the fruits of American postwar success and prosperity and saw it as evidence of their righteousness. To King, this showed how Marx was right in pointing out how religion could become an opiate of the people. "We have a high blood pressure of creeds and an anemia of deeds," King said of that prosperity gospel.

King received much correspondence after this first bombing. One came from Pinkie Franklin, a member of the Sixteenth Street Baptist Church in Birmingham, Alabama; Franklin was still in that church when it was bombed in 1963, and spent two days in jail during the Birmingham campaign of that year. "For years, we Negro Mothers of the Southland have prayed that God would send us a leader such as you are. Now that the Almighty has regarded our lowly estate and has raised up among us, I am indeed grateful," she wrote to him. "The Arm of God is everlastingly strong and Sufficient to keep you and yours." King treasured these kinds of letters and conversations with ordinary parishioners. Frequently, he sprinkled memorable quotes and phrases from them into his own sermons to humanize broader philosophical points he wanted to make.

Cultural and intellectual figures across the country joined in the praise. Renowned sociologist St. Clair Drake, wrote that King would find his "place among that small group of prophetic figures who have tried to teach the world how to fight for justice with weapons of the spirit. . . . Destiny has called you to participate in that process." He remembered discussions at the Quaker school, Pendle Hill, in Pennsylvania from the 1930s, when people dreamed of a mass movement to confront injustice; Reinhold Niebuhr had come and talked to them about "the possibilities of non-violent direct action among Negro Americans" (although Niebuhr himself had little use for Gandhi). That was not the time, but now St. Clair Drake saw King putting into action all they had been talking about and was busy wiring everyone he knew to send funds and support.

Another letter came from a fellow black fraternity member from Boston University who highlighted the precise problem of structurally racist institutions that King faced: "We realize the trying hours you are experiencing as the object of a white council-controlled police department, and bomb wielding segregationists." Similarly, Ralph Bunche, well-known diplomat and recipient of a Nobel Prize (and former activist and socialist), knew that King would "stand firm and united in the face of threats and resorts to police state methods of intimidation." Another minister from Baltimore, who had attended Crozer Seminary with King, wrote to urge him, "Fight on and if necessary ask God to stop the sun or close up the heavens and let no rain or dew fall on the soil of Alabama until judgment shall come to town with righteousness in his suitcase." And his closest mentor from Crozer, George W. Davis, sent him a note of encouragement, that "the strain of these days will soon be but an unhappy memory and that the day of our equality before men as before God may not be far away." A letter from J. Martin England, a fellow graduate of Crozer and former founder of the Koinonia Farm in Americus, Georgia, advised King on the meaning of *satyagraha*, noting that the point was to redeem rather than conquer the enemy. "Non-violence is such a powerful tool that when its advocates discover its strength they may be tempted to use it for the same ends for which others use violence: to conquer the opponent, rather than redeem him." He would not want King to use Gandhi's name "glibly."

Through the spring of 1956, the same time that the University of Alabama prevented a young black woman named Autherine Lucy from attending, King spoke to his congregation on what "peace" meant. In particular, he explored how a false "peace" was an enemy of justice. Peace had been restored to Tuscaloosa, he said, via the exclusion of this young black woman, but "it was peace that had been purchased at the price of capitulating to the force of darkness"; it was the kind of peace that "stinks in the nostrils of the Almighty God." Peace without justice is not peace; it's a peace purchased "at the price of allowing mobocracy to reign supreme over democracy. It was peace that had been purchased at the price of . . . capitulating to the forces of darkness. This is the type of peace that all men of goodwill hate." Jesus was a "fighting pacifist." Peace is not the absence of tension but the "presence of justice." Christians should not accept a false peace in place of the positive affirmation of "justice, goodwill, [and] the power of the kingdom of God. . . . If peace means a willingness to be exploited economically, dominated politically, humiliated and segregated, we must revolt against this peace," he concluded. A few weeks later, King emphasized again how constructive tension would disturb the peace in the short run but lead to justice over the longer run. The tension in Montgomery, he said, was "due to the revolutionary reevaluation of the Negro by himself"; as a result, the cradle of the Confederacy was "rocking."

King took the opportunity to say the same to James P. Coleman, the governor of Mississippi. King had been invited to speak in Mississippi in April 1956, and the governor wrote to ask him to cancel his visit, given the "tranquil" conditions existing in the state; his appearance would be a "great disservice to our Negro people." King responded the next day that actually he was not coming because he already had a prior commitment, but if he had planned to come, he would be even more determined to do so now. "Certainly I think the state of Mississippi could well profit from a gospel of love," which was the "pivotal point around which my whole philosophy revolved."

White southern liberals also were inspired by King. The white southern author of the novel *Strange Fruit*, Lillian Smith, wrote to King. She had been a longtime "inside agitator" in the South and warned King about the influence of "outsiders"; the movement would work best if it came across as southern-born and southern-led. The deep-rooted racist resistance in the South was vulnerable, she thought, precisely because of the common regional heritage of Protestantism; whites shared, she thought, "the profoundly religious symbols you are using and respond to them on a deep level of their hearts and minds. Their imaginations are stirred; the waters are troubled." As a long-time follower of the Gandhian movement and method, but as a Deep South white Methodist, she understood the "deep ties of common songs, common prayer, common symbols that bind our two races together on a religio-mystical level, even as another brutally mythic idea, the concept of White Supremacy, tears our two people apart." She also sent him her advice as a fellow southern activist: "don't let outsiders come in and ruin your movement. This kind of thing has to be indigenous." Better to keep the northern "do-gooders" out, as it would "break my heart were so-called 'outsiders' to ruin it all."

In one year he had come a long way. King quickly had absorbed these lessons on nonviolence, as is evident from an article in *Liberation* in April of 1956. Ghostwritten by Bayard Rustin, it provided one of the first full-length published explanations for a national audience of the philosophy underlying the Montgomery movement. Key points included an emphasis on how "economics is part of our struggle," that nonviolent resistance was a "new and powerful weapon," that the "church is becoming militant," and that black southerners had learned to come together. King's article concluded with some sharp words for southern gradualists and moderates, who had now come to see that "even the slow approach finally has revolutionary implications." One was William Faulkner, Nobel Prize–winning novelist, who had implored southern blacks to "stop now for a moment"—more or less the same advice that evangelist Billy Graham gave just a few years later during the Birmingham campaign ("put the brakes on a little bit," as he put it). The brilliant novelist Faulkner, whose literary works probed with unmatched power the deeply rooted maladies of white southern psychology, could not see what was right in front of his face outside of his incomparable fiction (Faulkner later, weakly, protested that his statement had been made while drunk and should be ignored). "It is hardly a moral act to encourage others patiently to accept injustice which he himself does not endure," King furiously responded. The real issue was not buses but injustice. By attacking the basis of injustice—"man's inhumanity to man"—there could emerge "an interracial society based on freedom for all."

King delivered a similar message at the Cathedral of St. John the Divine in New York that spring. "We have seen evil in all of its tragic dimensions," he told several thousand gathered to hear the new national star minister. The struggle of good and evil, a constant of human history, had been played out in the contemporary world in the struggle for freedom and justice against oppression and colonialism: "The Red Sea has opened, and today most of these exploited masses have won their freedom from the Egypt of colonialism and are now free to move toward the promised land of economic security and cultural development." God sought at every moment to lead men out of Egypt, bring them through the "wilderness of discipline," and finally arrive at the "promised land of personal and social integration."

King took these points even further in an address to the NAACP Legal Defense and Educational Fund in June 1956. There as well, he developed the critique (repeated numerous times in the coming years and in some of his best-known writings and addresses) that while laws cannot change people's souls, they can "control the external effects of those internal feelings." The law could not make a white man love a black man, but it could keep the white mob from lynching the black victim. The law could prevent employment discrimination, no matter how much white businesses would want to practice it. King concluded with a broad survey of injustices to which he would remain "maladjusted." This theme of King's drew from the popular psychology of the era and from a particular sermonic favorite of King's, Harry Emerson Fosdick:

> I never intend to adjust myself to the viciousness of lynch mobs. I never intend to become adjusted to the evils of segregation and discrimination. I never intend to adjust myself to the tragic inequalities of an economic system which takes necessities from the masses to give luxuries to the classes. I never intend to become adjusted to the madness of militarism and the self-defeating method of physical violence.

He would remain maladjusted because the "salvation of the world lies in the hands of the maladjusted."

King developed similar themes at even greater length in addressing the NAACP convention in San Francisco that summer. Here, too, as in the previous address, he gave a sweeping overview of African American history dating from 1619, going through slavery, and arriving at the present day as the "Negro masses all over began to reevaluate themselves." King's brief history was far superior to whatever one would find in a standard textbook of the era, beholden as most of them were to Lost Cause myths of slavery and the South. This fundamental change in psychology, a new sense of dignity and self-respect, produced a new generation determined to resist injustice. That was the only way to understand Montgomery—it required a shift in collective psychology. King's address provided a brilliant historical and psychological exploration of how this new collective consciousness had arisen. It was a *tour de force* of American history, civil religion, early liberation theology, and internationalist anti-colonialism.

Only a short time ago, King pointed out, bus drivers routinely harassed and grotesquely insulted black passengers. Empty seats in the front remained vacant as blacks stood in the back. Then came Rosa Parks, the incident that compelled the new spirit into action. "There comes a time," King said, "when people get tired of being plunged across the abyss of exploitation where they experience the bleakness of nagging despair." King recounted the multiple ways that white reactionaries had tried to kill the movement, through "legal" means as well as through the bombings of his home and others, all to no avail. The key was the philosophy guiding the movement, its faith in a future, and the fact that it was a "spiritual movement" guided by a "cosmic companionship. We feel that the universe is on the side of right and righteousness." Again, as he did frequently through this era, here King was channeling Howard Thurman's most fundamental ideas (and sometimes his exact language).

The movement in Montgomery had likewise become part of the rising of all peoples living under the yoke of colonialism and imperialism. The black revolution in America would stanch the tide of communism, by showing that democracy could work, but the motive was not just one of expedience but also one of right: "it must be done because it is right to do it." American segregation was the "cancer in the body politic which must be removed before our democratic health can be realized." In another version of the address, he added that the cries of the contemporary southern politicians, attempts to outlaw the NAACP, and other repressive measures were but the "death groans from a dying system. The old order is passing away, and the new order is coming into being. We are witnessing in our day the birth of a new age, with a new structure of freedom and justice."

King already had established the whirlwind pattern of travel that would characterize the rest of his life. He crisscrossed the country addressing churches, synagogues, labor unions, NAACP conventions, Baptist assemblies, and numerous other groups, explaining again and again his message of nonviolent civil disobedience. He brilliantly adapted his addresses (generally ghostwritten originally but modified and changed over time according to audience) to the needs of the moment. As he saw it, in the struggle against injustice, retaliatory violence remained an option, but "history is replete with the bleached bones of nations who refused to listen to the words of Jesus at this point." Aside from being immoral, it was not practical for black Americans, as they would simply be outmatched and outgunned by the white majority. Thus the method of nonviolent resistance stood out.

King insisted that nonviolence was not about submission but, instead, was a way of activating mind and body in resisting evil and emotionally affecting the evil-doer: "This method is nonaggressive physically, but it is aggressive spiritually. It is passive physically, but it is active mentally and spiritually . . . it is not a method of surrender, or a weapon or a method of submission, but it is a method that is *very* active in seeking to change conditions, and even though it is passive it is still resisting." And those schooled in nonviolence sought to redeem rather than humiliate the opponent, for ultimately "the end is reconciliation." The contest of the day was not between different people in Montgomery, or between white and black, but ultimately about good and evil, justice and injustice; therefore victory in the struggle would be a victory for democracy and justice. The nonviolent method, besides resisting violence, "seeks to avoid internal violence of the spirit. And at the center of the method of nonviolence stands the principle of love. Love is always the regulating ideal in the technique." Soul force offered a way to defeat socially structured evils without resorting to weapons. Violence could coerce, but it could never convince.

King's idealism came together with his political realism. As he spread his philosophical messages, he also interacted with friends and foes alike in the political arena and behind the scenes plotted strategy with his advisors. He testified before the platform committee of the Democratic National Committee in 1956, urging them to acknowledge that the federal government should "guarantee to all of its citizens the rights and privileges of full citizenship. The state of affairs in the South has come to such a point that the only agency to which we can turn for protection is the Federal Government. Without this protection we will be plunged across the abyss of mob rule and tragic anarchy." Democrats should understand that segregation and democracy were incompatible, and the conjunction of them in the United States simply fed communist propaganda. King understood that the rhetoric of the Cold War could be a powerful ally of the movement, given foreign propaganda about America's most brutally undemocratic practices. King kept his own economic views, which were far to the left of those considered acceptable in the mainstream, under wraps in his most public addresses. Later, he understood more clearly that Cold War rhetoric would only serve as an ally so far and that it had to be overcome in order to address deeper issues of economic inequality and structural racism.

During these years, King and civil rights groups frequently petitioned to meet with President Eisenhower and to compel the Republicans to take similar stands. In August, for example, following the bombing of the home of the white Lutheran minister and King ally Robert Graetz, King and the MIA wrote to Eisenhower, urging him to use federal power to investigate acts of violence committed against African Americans. With blacks being randomly arrested and handed crippling fines for alleged offenses, the revival of the Klan, and the denial of voting rights, only federal power could address local tyrannies that reigned throughout the South. While African Americans had started moving their votes en masse to the Democratic Party during the New Deal of the 1930s, there still remained a strong residue of historic support (dating back to Reconstruction) among many blacks for the Republicans. This included, for example, Martin Luther King Jr.'s father and Jackie Robinson.

Martin Luther King Jr. was skeptical of both political parties. He saw, correctly, that both historically had deep investments in white supremacy. Neither party had civil rights as a central part of its platform. In the 1960s, King tied his hopes onto the Democratic presidencies. In Congress, though, in order to pass the Civil Rights Act of 1964, northern Republican votes were key; southern Democratic congressmen threw up every legislative barrier they could manage. Yet in 1964 the Republicans were captured by the forces of Barry Goldwater, also a staunch opponent of federal civil rights measures. As King put it to a fellow Morehouse graduate and Eisenhower supporter in Michigan, "The Negro has been betrayed by both the Democratic and Republican Party. The Democrats have betrayed us by capitulating to the whims and caprices of the southern dixiecrats. The Republicans have betrayed us by capitulating to the [blatant] hypocrisy of conservative right wing northerners. This coalition of southern dixiecrats and right wing northern Republicans defeats every move toward liberal legislation in Congress." King felt it better to remain independent of either party. That remained King's view for years, expressed repeatedly in speeches and addresses on blacks and partisan politics. Later the "white backlash" of the 1960s hardly came as a surprise to him; it was more of the same thing he had experienced his whole life.

King's *realpolitik* likewise comes across in his correspondence with his staff and advisors. In October 1956, traveling to Hampton Institute (a historically black college, which Booker T. Washington once had attended), a lengthy plane delay resulted in the passengers deplaning and being given vouchers for a meal. King was the only black passenger. He entered with the other passengers into a restaurant in the Atlanta airport but was forced to sit separately, in a "dingy" area in the back. King pointed out to the manager that he was an interstate passenger and that he would "rather go a week without eating before eating under such conditions." King described the situation to an Atlanta NAACP attorney, who responded that they would pursue his case. King responded enthusiastically, hoping that his experience would serve as an excellent test case for the courts. Ironically, three years later King had the same experience and again sought to provide an affidavit and testify. But just a few months later, in *Coke v. City of Atlanta*, involving the same restaurant in the Atlanta airport, the judge ruled against the restaurant, and the Atlanta airport was at least partly desegregated.

All the while he remained pastor of the Dexter Avenue Baptist Church. There, he produced annual reports urging the church to mount evangelism campaigns and seek higher levels of spirituality. Yet he felt guilty of neglecting his pastoral duties. In his fall 1956 fiscal year summary, he explained his deeply felt sentiment that he was torn too many different ways, unable to attend to any of his duties and responsibilities (whether just a part of his normal work or imposed on him by force of circumstance). Demands on his time had mounted exponentially. The international attention focused on Montgomery required King to travel, raise funds, publicize the movement, and act as its spokesperson. He expressed appreciation to the church for its "deep sympathetic understanding," for providing encouragement when his life was in jeopardy. King still saw himself as a pastor. He sometimes dreamed of simply returning to pastoral anonymity. That never happened. When he left the pulpit of Dexter in 1959, it was in part because he simply could not serve as a pastor. The movement threatened to swallow him.

At the one-year anniversary mark of the formation of the Montgomery Improvement Association, King and other leaders looked to create an organization that could carry on the struggle elsewhere. At an Institute on Nonviolence and Social Change, held in December 1956, King and others brought together activists, ministers, and organizers who looked to put into practice some more permanent organization. They sought to "rededicate the community and the nation to the principle of nonviolence in the struggle for freedom and justice." King sensed that African Americans had joined a struggle that had international implications and that they would be the "proving ground for the struggle and triumph of freedom and justice in America." Meanwhile, protests spread to other cities, including Tallahassee and Birmingham. In the latter, the courageous Baptist minister Fred Shuttlesworth faced arrests and savage beatings for attempting to enroll his daughter in a whites-only school. The spirit of Montgomery seemed to be catching.

Capitalizing on that spirit, King and his associates began to organize what became the Southern Christian Leadership Conference (SCLC). It rose in part from a plan developed by Bayard Rustin, always King's adviser in things practical and political. Rustin described how they could capitalize on their accomplishments: "The achievement of unity, the intelligence in planning, the creation of a competent, complex system of transportation, the high level of moral and ethical motivation, all combined to give the closed mind of the white southern an airing it has never before had."

At the same time, King already faced dilemmas that would remain difficult for him throughout his career. He knew full well that without the movement, there would be no Martin Luther King; he would be just another black pastor of a mid-sized church in the South. He sensed that the "zeitgeist" of the times carried him along. Future scholars of the movement would emphasize how the activism of everyday folk—in the case of Montgomery, through phone trees, a taxi system, insurance pools, and restoring themselves through singing at mass meetings—made the movement possible. King became its voice, the most articulate orator of its aspirations, but he had created neither the conditions that led to its rise nor the intricate networks that predated him that sprang into action when the movement arose. At the same time, people did look to him. King's pulpit hero, William Holmes Borders of Atlanta, told him, "There is no position in any church, religious body, University and etc., which you could not fill."

And King knew the price many people had paid for their heroism. His own home had been bombed, and there would be further attempted

bombings. But King was a celebrity; many others who suffered might-
ily were not. Later, Lawrence Reddick, Jo Ann Gibson Robinson, Mary
Fair Burks, and other stalwarts of the Montgomery movement lost their
jobs at Alabama State college, victims of a purge by the president who,
under pressure from officials of the state of Alabama, determined to
rid the black college of "disloyal faculty members." Rosa Parks eventually moved away, her husband having been driven nearly mad by the
harassment, and her own health and finances in bad shape. Movement
leaders had to be shamed into taking up collections to keep her (barely)
afloat financially. Numerous others lost jobs and livelihoods. Moreover,
desegregating the bus lines did little to improve economic conditions for
most blacks in Montgomery, something King understood all too well. The
bus boycott strategy employed in Montgomery proved difficult to scale
up; when tried in another city, for example, the bus company declared
bankruptcy and went out of business. While the national press celebrated
the boycott as a kind of victory, an accomplishment of the goals of the
movement, King knew it was only the beginning. New tactics would be
required in other cities.

With the Supreme Court decision in November mandating the desegregation of buses in Montgomery, King and the movement held a meeting to celebrate the coming victory. The white Lutheran minister Robert
Graetz read the Scripture: "Soon there was shouting, cheering, and wav-
ing of handkerchiefs," which King saw as "an exciting, spontaneous
expression by the Negro congregation of what had happened to it these
months. The people knew that they had come of age, that they had won
new dignity. They would never again be the old subservient, fearful
appeasers. But neither would they be resentful fighters for justice who
could overlook the rights and feelings of their opponents." For King, this
signaled the moment when "nonviolence, for all its difficulties, had won
its way into our hearts." Black churches had learned the lessons that an
otherworldly gospel ignoring daily life was inadequate; instead, the true
gospel concerned itself, "as Jesus did, with the economic and social problems of this world, as well as with its otherworldly gospel. As our church
has played a leading role in the present social struggle, it has won new
respect within the Negro population." Later, in his address at the end of
the boycott to the annual meeting of the Institute on Nonviolence and
Social Change, he ended with a stirring affirmation about letting freedom
ring, one that forecast the celebrated conclusion to his 1963 address at the
March on Washington: "Freedom must ring from every mountainside."

King announced the end of the bus boycott on December 20, 1956,
repeating many of the lessons he had been proclaiming for the year. But
he introduced a new phrase, another that would become a trademark. He
told a crowd of about 2,500, "But amid all of this we have kept going with

the faith that as we struggle, God struggles with us, and that the arc of the moral universe, although long, is bending toward justice." He continued, "We have seen truth crucified and goodness buried, but we have kept going with the conviction that truth crushed to earth will rise again." That phrase may have originated in another article published in *Liberation* that year by John Haynes Holmes. He had quoted the nineteenth-century abolitionist minister Theodore Parker, who had said, "The arc of the moral universe is long, but it bends toward justice."

Meanwhile, King himself felt both called to his position and thrust into it in a way that exceeded his capacities. He felt compelled to capitalize on his celebrity, and he felt guilty for the fame that had come to him so early. And as he told a group of boycotters at one MIA meeting, "I want you to know that if M. L. King had never been born this movement would have taken place. I just happened to be there." There were times that were pregnant with possibilities for social change, and "That time has come in Montgomery, and I had nothing to do with it." He meant that; he felt it. And he didn't totally mean it, because he also felt called by God to be a leader, to articulate the grievances of the people and empower them to act against their own oppression.

He also was worried, as he told J. Pius Barbour, that a man who peaks in his mid-twenties "has a tough job ahead." It already was tough in Montgomery; after the boycott, the MIA more or less collapsed, and E. D. Nixon, who had been key in selecting King originally to head it, was furious that King's celebrity had overshadowed local Montgomerians (such as himself) who had been doing the work for years. King reflected to Barbour that "people will be expecting me to pull rabbits out of the hat for the rest of my life." That rabbit had practically jumped out of the hat on its own in Montgomery. Whether it could happen again, or how to reproduce the magic, was difficult to see. In the last years of the 1950s, it would not get much clearer.

4

Montgomery and the SCLC

Love has within it a redemptive power. And there is a power there that eventually transforms individuals . . . if you hate your enemies, you have no way to redeem and to transform your enemies. But if you love your enemies, you will discover that at the very root of love is the power of redemption.

—Sermon "Loving Your Enemies," Dexter Avenue Baptist Church, 1957

Martin Luther King Jr.'s mastery of the language of reconciliation and redemption made the seemingly impossible, possible. Indeed, it is difficult to conceive of what else could have moved masses of black people to confront a system whose violent backing had been evident to all for decades. But even the smallest of accomplishments, such as desegregating the bus lines in Montgomery, required Herculean feats of faith and organizing. King and the movement sought to capitalize on the boycott. Successes in doing so proved elusive over the next few years.

King championed the cause of nonviolent civil disobedience and spoke to local people's grievances as well as national political issues. He translated movements' aims and objectives carried forward by others for a broader audience. He did so by combining prophetic black church Christianity, social gospel liberal Christianity, Gandhian nonviolence, and the best of American civil religion. By doing so, he realized the dream of generations before: to create a protest movement coming out of churches imbued with a religious vitality that propelled social reforms. He called on America to honor its ideals and on local people to organize against the betrayal of those ideals they had experienced their whole lives. In doing so, he reenergized the frequently untapped potential of the black church as a social institution.

King assimilated and synthesized the ideas of his childhood in the church, his training with theological scholars in the North, and his experiences on the ground in the South as a pastor. His ideas shaped that reality on the ground. Meanwhile, the experiences he saw in the lives of his parishioners also significantly shaped his ideas. Likewise, while "the movement made King" (as legendary black organizer Ella Baker put it), the movement could not have been what it was without him.

King identified the purposes of social reform with those of Christianity. White Christians *would* listen to King because he was speaking their language. He routinely cast the struggle for civil rights in terms of light and darkness, good and evil, and the two kingdoms. "In the act of interpreting the black experience for his crossover audience," writes scholar Jonathan Rieder, "King was simultaneously interpreting for whites the true meaning of *their* professed creeds." He knew how to play the racial diplomat, with enough prophecy and anger to empower black organizing and enough American civil religion to translate his message for wider audiences. It was a perspective that "blended black church religion, liberal theology, Christian philosophy, and racial justice and social justice militancy like nothing else."

King had absorbed the lessons of nonviolent civil disobedience from his tutors during the boycott. He also got it from the experiences of seeing it happen in front of him. King took his Niebuhr seriously and preached on themes of human evil frequently. He also was by the later 1950s a full-fledged Gandhian who embraced nonviolence as a way of life. Later, he wrote, "My study of Gandhi convinced me that pacifism is not nonresistance to evil, but nonviolent resistance to evil. Between these two positions, there is a world of difference. Gandhi resisted evil with as much vigor and power as the violent resister, but he resisted with love instead of hate. True pacifism is not unrealistic submission to evil power, as Niebuhr contends. It is rather a courageous confrontation of evil by the power of love." Thus, King straddled Gandhian idealism and Niebuhrian neoorthodoxy; his training in the black church gave him the capacity to understand both and to envision a beloved community beyond Gandhi's purified visions of a spiritual elite and Niebuhr's cold analysis of human evil.

King's advisors, meanwhile, were determined to capitalize on the Montgomery breakthrough. The CORE had already demonstrated the limitations of interracial Gandhian organizing; it simply could not pull together a mass movement. But the churches could. Indeed, the existence of a mass movement that came out of churches was something like the fulfillment of the dream of the black social gospel, a realization of the power always potentially there, but often unrealized, of the most basic institution of the black community.

In an Easter sermon from April 1957, a few months after the end of the boycott, King reflected on what had transpired during those epic months. As usual, he put it in larger, biblical contexts, wondering specifically what the meaning of Easter was for those suffering under southern oppression. People naturally "wonder why it is that the forces of evil seem to reign supreme and the forces of goodness seem to be trampled over." King asked God why injustice so often beat Negroes down, why slavery and exploitation had been allowed to continue. "*Why* is it, God? *Why* is it simply because some of your homes are bombed, their *children* are pushed from the classrooms?" It seems that the "forces of injustice reign supreme." But he could hear someone saying, "*Easter* is coming! One day truth will rise up and reign supreme!"

King and his colleagues hoped to capitalize on the apparent triumph in Montgomery and attack segregation throughout the South. They formed the Southern Christian Leadership Conference (SCLC). They faced huge challenges in scaling up a movement based in the very particular community of Montgomery and frequently floundered. As biographer Peter Ling puts it, "caught in a double bind, the SCLC could only launch programs if it had sufficient funds and would only receive ample funds if it were seen to have effective programs." King's constant time out on the road mostly involved fundraising, but that same time away made it difficult to organize the programs for which the funds were raised. Master organizer Ella Baker, sent in to bring order to the SCLC's chaos, found herself in a sexist and patriarchal world of black ministers who knew oration better than organizing. She eventually gave up but found a more congenial world in young students who would carry out the SCLC's philosophy of nonviolent civil disobedience with a verve and bravery that eventually shamed the SCLC into doing the same.

King was coming to know the perils of celebrityhood as well. He complained, "I can hardly go into any city or any town in this nation where I'm not lavished with hospitality by peoples of all races and of all creeds. I can hardly go anywhere to speak in this nation where hundreds and thousands of people are not turned away because of lack of space. And then after speaking I often have to be rushed out to get away from the crowd rushing for autographs." He felt it in trying to be a pastor of a local church while also being thrust into the limelight. As he told his church, in one of his annual year-end report letters, "Through the force of circumstance I was catapulted into the leadership of a movement which has succeeded in capturing the imagination of people all over this nation and the world," but he admitted that "in the midst of so many things to do I am not doing anything well." Tugged in every direction all the time, he felt summoned by God to answer nearly every call, frequently without much of a plan ahead of time. He knew how to improvise brilliantly, but he worked best when his colleagues and coworkers in the SCLC did the everyday work that King never had the time, or inclination, to handle.

His message remained the same, and his message extended to larger worlds of black internationalism and anti-colonialism. After the first meeting of the SCLC, as reported in the *Christian Century* in 1957, King wrote, "The determination of Negro Americans to win freedom from every form of oppression springs from the same profound longing for freedom that motivates oppressed peoples all over the world. The dynamic beat of deep discontent in Africa and Asia is at bottom a quest for freedom and human dignity on the part of people who have long been victims of colonialism. . . . When oppressed people rise up against oppression there is no stopping point short of full freedom. Realism compels us to admit that the struggle will continue until freedom is a reality for all the oppressed peoples of the world." He understood the southern freedom struggle as part of a much broader movement. No one needed to instruct him on that. Later depictions of King that stress his emphasis on brotherhood without understanding his devastating critique of colonialism fail in grappling with his whole philosophy. King also developed close relationships with peace activists, democratic socialists, and anti-colonial leaders and anti-apartheid activists abroad.

King outlined the principles of nonviolence that had been learned in the movement. It was not a method for cowards, for it involved resistance. It was just that the "nonviolent resister is just as strongly opposed to the evil against which he protests as is the person who uses violence." The point was not to defeat the opponent but to "win his friendship and understanding." The methods of boycotts and means of economic pressure were not ends in themselves but a "means to awaken a sense of moral shame in the opponent." The attack was to be "directed against forces of evil rather than against persons who are caught up in those forces. It is evil we are seeking to defeat, not the persons victimized by evil." It was key to avoid not only physical violence but also an "internal violence of spirit. . . . Along the way of life, someone must have sense enough and morality enough to cut off the chain of hate. This can be done only by projecting the ethics of love to the center of our lives." The struggler would keep the faith that the "universe is on the side of justice . . . in his struggle for justice he has cosmic companionship. This belief that God is on the side of truth and justice comes down to us from the long tradition of our Christian faith."

King himself was a relative newcomer to nonviolence, but he quickly mastered the art of explaining it to those who knew nothing of it. That included both black church congregants and broad national audiences.

In 1957, King explained the power of nonviolence before the YMCA in Berkeley, California. He noted that movement leaders used mass meetings to "explain nonviolence to a community of people who had never heard of the philosophy and in many instances were not sympathetic to it." Through weekly meetings, institutes on nonviolence and social change, and constant reiteration of the principles of nonviolence, King preached that nonviolence was "merely a means to awaken a sense of shame within the oppressor, but the end is reconciliation, the end is redemption." The personality of whites had been "greatly distorted by segregation," and as a result their souls were "scarred," in need of love. Therefore, "the Negro must love the white man, because the white man needs his love to remove his tensions, insecurities, and fears." The language of Christian redemption, Gandhian nonviolent resistance, and midcentury popular psychology mixed together freely here. King readily drew from all three throughout this period.

King pointed out that nonviolence was nothing more than "Christianity in action. It seems to me to be the Christian way of life in solving problems in human relations." Gandhi had made the technique famous, but its principles derived from Christianity. King often spoke of how he intended to be "maladjusted," drawing from the psychological lingo of the era and from a sermonic chestnut that he used for his text of departure.

He got this idea from Harry Emerson Fosdick, the early and midcentury liberal Protestant preacher who provided him with a wealth of source material to use. Fosdick wrote about prisoners of conscience, those in the past who could not be "adjusted" to a society that denied religious liberty: "To war, to the evils of predatory economics, to racial prejudice, totalitarian dictatorship, or whatever other social ill confronts them, they refuse comfortably to adjust themselves." King relied heavily on his well-marked-up version of Fosdick's *On Being a Real Person*; Fosdick's deployment of psychological theories particularly appealed to King, who drew on them extensively and wove them into his own sermons for both white and black audiences. His sermon "Conquering Self-Centeredness," for his congregants in Montgomery in April 1957, reflected on his own experience of being captured by the *zeitgeist* and thrust into celebrityhood, and the role of religion in providing a proper sense of equilibrium.

King was fond of analogies drawn from popular (if sometimes outdated) psychology, none more so than the metaphor of personal maladjustment writ large to the social order. In this sense, King took in the lessons he learned from Harry Emerson Fosdick, Howard Thurman, and an entire generation of mainstream Protestant ministers who thoroughly incorporated the language of psychology into their sermons. Thurman, for example, often spoke of the "psychic wounds" of racism, and Fosdick's sermon on being maladjusted to the evils of life became one of

King's primary themes for much of his preaching career. For a number of white Protestant mainstream ministers, the language of therapy and healing nearly supplanted the historic themes of sin and redemption. That was not the case for King. He retained his attraction to preaching against evil while also embracing the "warm evangelical liberalism" that had attracted him at Crozer. But he found the language of psychology useful particularly in dissecting the deeper and more obscure sources of white racism and hatred, and the psychologically freeing aspects of liberating one's self from the sin of racism. It was a burden experienced by blacks but carried by whites as well. King preached through the 1950s that the freedom struggle could be as liberating for whites psychologically as it would be for blacks socially and economically.

In another sermon from the era, King analogized African Americans to the prodigal son, kicked around and pushed down to an "inferior economic and political position. And now you have made them almost depersonalized and inhuman." King considered what Freudian psychology had to offer, its analysis of the id and superego, but found that after all the psychologizing, it still stood true that man was a sinner before God. Therefore, "at bottom, the conflict is not between the id and the superego but the conflict is between God and man. And the universe stands with that glaring picture of the reality of life—that man is a sinner; man is a sinner in need of God's redemptive power. We can never escape this fact." King paraphrased the famous dissection of human psychology from the apostle Paul in the New Testament, how humans do what they most want not to do, and fail to do exactly what they know they must do. King came to know this all too painfully in his own personal hypocrisies, his morally conflicted personal life: "We know how to be just and moral, to live and to be faithful; yet we are unjust and immoral, unloving and unfaithful." On the broader stage, as King put it, "We know how to achieve peace and yet seek war. And thus we must all see ourselves as sinners." For King, this meant that "there is something about it that causes us to know that as we look down into the deepest resources of our souls that we are in eternal revolt against God."

The hope of liberation from that sin and revolt, both in the individual person and in the struggle against social evil, pushed him forward. The vision was one of freedom for all, a liberation from the shackles of hatred and segregation that held whites as well as blacks in bondage. In a piece for *Liberation* in 1958, King portrayed how freedom for black Americans would result in freedom for all. Calling for free elections abroad meant nothing when there were of course no free elections at home. Social change always took place through struggle, and the beneficiaries would be whites as well as blacks. Poor whites, after all, "bore the scars of ignorance, deprivation, and poverty." Because of the historically inequitable voting system in the south, reactionary men gained and controlled power, keeping everyone else in servitude.

King looked to a growing tide of African American activists and white allies, people such as white southern writer Lillian Smith, liberal southern newspaper editor Harry Ashmore, and a growing list of ministers whose "voices represent the true and basic sentiments of millions of southerners, whose voices are yet unheard, whose course is yet unclear and whose courageous acts are unseen." King frequently pointed to them as emblems of hope, and he encountered or knew many of them personally and corresponded with them frequently. The problem was that they were few and far between and not usually blessed with positions of much power. Even worse was the ordinary southern moderate, who mouthed sympathetic words of reconciliation but never turned out to be an ally in the practice of seeking justice.

King held hopes for the role sympathetic white southerners could play. He held many treasured friendships among them. At a conference on Christian Faith and Human Relations in the spring of 1957, he announced that the nation looked to southern white ministers for such leadership: "Every minister of the gospel has a mandate to stand up courageously for righteousness . . . to lead men from the desolate midnight of falsehood to the bright daybreak of truth." King continued with some of familiar lines about remaining "maladjusted" to segregation and discrimination, to economic injustice and the "madness of militarism." At an SCLC Crusade for Citizenship in Miami in February 1958, King extended his view that good-hearted (white) southerners could no longer permit their heritage to be dishonored and smeared by the worst elements of the region. Black voting crusades were not just about rights guaranteed by the Constitution but also a "moral obligation," a "duty to remove from political domination a small minority that cripples the economic and social institutions of our nation and thereby degrades and impoverishes everyone." More important was the broader vision of the struggle: "we are opposed to all injustice, wherever it exists."

In 1959, for example, a white Tennessean had written to King that "the South has been waiting a long time for a leader such as you!" He had been on the mailing list of the MIA and wanted to know how to be involved in the movement. King wrote back appreciatively and advised him to find an organization "working in the area of human rights" and throw his energies there; an "individual witness" was important, but real change came only through organized efforts. He added, "I have always longed for a white southerner to come into some predominantly Negro organization and work side by side with Negro leaders. This would lift it above a mere racial struggle, and people would come to see that the tension is at bottom between justice and injustice rather than between Negro people and white people," something that inspired King about the Indian struggle.

Most southern moderates, however, never failed to miss an opportunity to miss an opportunity. Their consistent prevarications, inaction, and pleas for patience and against pressure and protests wore King down. In April 1958, for example, more than a year after the settlement of the bus boycott, three hundred white religious leaders from Montgomery condemned mass protests, with their "exaggerated emphasis on wrongs and grievances," and called for "conversations among responsible leaders" of both races. Of course, they were lying. Montgomery SCLC leaders reached out, inviting dialogue and asking for a good date and time to meet. They got no response. That was how most whites defined "dialogue"—vapid pronouncements followed by no response.

This was the common experience of civil rights leaders and southern moderates; the calls for dialogue in place of protests invariably went nowhere. Much the same could be said for King's relationship with Billy Graham. In 1957, King appeared at a rally for the massively popular evangelist at Madison Square Garden. King learned from Graham important lessons in how to attract people, draw crowds, and move people to action. And King admired preachers who were good at their craft, as Graham certainly was.

Initially, King praised Graham's willingness to hold desegregated evangelical meetings. At the same time, Graham invited segregationist southern politicians to appear with him, including Texas senator and then governor Price Daniel, one of the signatories of the "Southern Manifesto" of 1956, a group of white southern politicians inveighing against *Brown v. Board*. King wired Graham that appearances by people such as Daniel, so openly associated with the growing "massive resistance" to desegregation, would impact the black struggle for "human dignity" and would "greatly reduce the importance of your message to them as a Christian Minister who believes in the fatherhood of God and the brotherhood of man." King received a snippy letter back from Graham's close associate and assistant Grady Wilson, informing him that local ministers in San Antonio had selected Price to appear. Wilson lectured King on how he should treat a fellow brother in Christ and "Governor of the Sovereign State of Texas." King's participation was welcome—exactly on the same level as those of the most racist and segregationist politicians of the region. That was the meaning of fellowship, for white moderates. They failed to understand King's most fundamental message about a social order defined by justice.

In a Prayer Pilgrimage for Freedom in May 1957, commemorating the third anniversary of the *Brown v. Board* decision, King pivoted again toward the coming voting rights campaign. He spoke on the theme "Give

us the Ballot, We Will Transform the South." His talk generated some controversy among his colleagues, who were undecided on what course the
SCLC should set. King knew that political power equaled social power.
King's close advisor Bayard Rustin didn't like the speech to be given,
considering it impolitic, perhaps too aggressive. But King told him, "I'm
better at words than you are." Take care of the organizing, he implied,
and leave the preaching to me.

King had the better of the argument here. (Years later, ironically, it was
Rustin making this exact argument, in his famous essay "From Protest to
Politics"; by that time, King had grown more wary of political solutions.)
His address is a masterpiece of clarifying the moral point of a complex
issue. Give us the ballot, King preached, and "we will fill our legislative
halls with men of good will." Influence at the ballot box would end the
need to depend on the federal government for civil rights, or to plead for
an anti-lynching law. Men who would sign the Southern Manifesto (a
pro-segregation document from that era, signed even by the future hero
of foreign relations, J. William Fulbright) could be replaced by those who
might insist on the implementation of *Brown v. Board*. Instead, because
of the disastrous voting system, reactionary politicians from both parties
maintained control. Moderate and liberal white southerners were desperately needed in the political arena. "There are in the white South more
open-minded moderates than appear on the surface," King said. "These
persons are silent today because of fear of social, political, and economic
reprisals." A change of political winds would augur more in their favor.

So would a stronger stance on the part of the Eisenhower administration. King had some hopes of effecting that through his correspondence
with Richard Nixon, Eisenhower's vice president. Nixon seemed the
kind of moderate in national politics who could be swayed. King had an
ongoing correspondence with the political figure who had risen through
the ranks, thanks to his anti-communist fervor. They kept up a dialogue
through the late 1950s. King frequently sent him telegrams urging him
to adopt the same rhetoric that he used in reference to people suffering
under the Soviet regime to the conditions faced by black southerners. He
urged Nixon to make a fact-finding mission to the American South and
investigate the "reprisals, the bombings and violence directed against the
persons and homes of Negroes who attempt to assert their rights under
the United States Constitution." Nixon carried on a cordial correspondence with King, who found himself interested in the ambitious politician, despite Nixon's association with certain far-right groups from the
McCarthy era. Nixon could be a progressive force, he surmised. He was
not yet sold all the way. As he told a biographer of Nixon who wrote King
asking for his opinion, "I would conclude by saying that if Richard Nixon
is not sincere, he is the most dangerous man in America."

King pressured the Eisenhower administration to take a more forthright stance, never getting what he hoped for despite Nixon's inklings of support. For King, a strong word from the president, the use of executive power, and the bully pulpit could bolster the suppressed southern liberals who knew what was right but were afraid to push for it publicly. "The southern white liberal stands in a pretty difficult position because he does not have anywhere to turn for emotional security," noted King, in comparison to the multitude of hate groups offering security and group empowerment for the most vile of racists. And yet "with a word from the president of the United States, with his power and influence, it would give a little more courage and backbone to the white liberals in the south who are willing to be allies in the struggle of the Negro for first class citizenship." Eisenhower only reluctantly intervened in the Little Rock school crisis of 1957 and generally wanted to leave matters up to state authorities. King knew that these "state authorities" defended segregation and intimidated opponents of it. Thus, King remained disappointed in his forays with Eisenhower administration officials. At the same time, the southern Democratic Party was dominated by the die-hard opponents of black civil rights. Some of them spent the first years of the 1960s trying to filibuster to death civil rights legislation—and nearly succeeded in doing so. In King's (accurate) view, the political options available were bleak in the late 1950s. There were good reasons that figures such as Jackie Robinson believed that the GOP had a better chance of being the party of civil rights than the Democrats. The young John F. Kennedy had little substantive to say about civil rights; he was seen more as Cold Warrior than as a politician affiliated with the black freedom struggle.

While King remained more of a "warm evangelical liberal" than the neoorthodox Niebuhr, he had learned his lessons from Niebuhr about social evil. The evidence was obvious in the South, and King preached on it frequently. The same white southerners who would give a needy person the shirt off their backs also made it impossible for that person to have a shirt on his back in the first place. A brutal system of segregation operated with the massive complicity of churchgoers who professed the love of Christ for everybody. Good people had created and continued to maintain an evil system, the very system that King's father said he could never tolerate living with. The paradox was painful and demanded an explanation. Niebuhr provided one.

King explained to numerous congregations and audiences the thesis of Reinhold Niebuhr's book *Moral Man and Immoral Society*, adapting his language and explanation to the level of his listeners. Individuals may be good, he explained, but when man begins to interact in society, he gets caught up in all of the evils of society. And so that is why people caught in society will do things that they probably never would do as an individual. They want to be approved socially. They get courage to do things that they could never do by themselves. The crowd is doing it, and so in order to be in social line with the crowd they do it. And so man rises to the tragic level of social sin. And then the real tragedy of man's social and collective existence is the fact that sin is almost inescapable in this level.

Or, as King summed it up colloquially on another occasion, groups tended to be a little more "naughty" than individuals. (Although King also believed, it should be noted, that properly channeled collective action could lead to a more moral society; here, he was somewhat at odds with the later writings of Niebuhr.)

King remained a profound advocator of the social gospel, pointing to the social conditions which produced sinful acts. One example comes from his sermon "The Christian Doctrine of Man," delivered to an audience in Detroit. One has to believe that men and women *should* be good, he said, "but I must be concerned about the social conditions that often make them bad. . . . I must be concerned about the poverty in the world. I must be concerned about the ignorance in the world. I must be concerned about the slums of the world. . . . And any religion that professes to be concerned about the souls of men and fails to be concerned about the economic conditions that corrupt them, the social conditions that damn them, the city governments that cripple them, is a dry, dead, do-nothing religion in need of new blood." He added that "when we look at our collective life, we must cry out, 'We are sinners. . . . We need to repent.'" The emphasis here is on *collective* life.

At this time, in 1957–1958, King was busy taking ghostwritten drafts of the book that became *Stride Toward Freedom* and working them toward the final product. The first draft came from King's companion and writer Lawrence Reddick. King's old Morehouse teacher George Kelsey took a look at the first draft of *Stride* and advised King to sharpen the "fact that the movement which you so nobly led was Christian in motivation and substance. Christian love remained on the 'ground floor,' [Gandhi] furnished the techniques, including the 'operational principles', which you spell out at the end of the chapter." He advised using words such as "substance" and "philosophy" in a Christian sense, as "I am convinced that the Spirit and worldview of Christian Faith informed it," a position not inconsistent with acknowledging the "operational principles" and techniques of Gandhian thought. King needed to further Christianize Gandhi. King in short order did so, in large part because his knowledge of Gandhi came secondhand through American Christian sources. Again, King had a nearly unmatched genius for assimilating secondary material (including works *about* Gandhi or other thinkers) into words that moved masses of people.

The philosophy of the movement was noncooperation with evil, a concept he got from Gandhi but also from Thoreau's essay "Civil Disobedience," which had moved him as college student. The people of Montgomery had said to the white community that they would not cooperate anymore. Further, and less explicably, King averred, there was just something about the protest that was "suprarational." It could not be explained without a "divine dimension," without pondering the "extrahuman force [that] labors to create a harmony out of the discord of the universe. There is a creative power that works to pull down mountains of evil and level hilltops of injustice. God still works through history His wonders to perform."

A further inspiration was the Sermon on the Mount; it had inspired the blacks of Montgomery to "dignified social action. It was Jesus of Nazareth that stirred the Negroes to protest with the creative weapon of love." This was the part where Kelsey's influence showed through most clearly. King Christianized Gandhi while keeping an emphasis on the international nature of the freedom struggle. Nonviolence was presented to locals as simply an expression of Christianity in action, giving them the permission, within their own religious culture, to use the technique. But the determination to win freedom also arose from the "same deep longing that motivates oppressed peoples all over the world. The rumblings of discontent in Asia and Africa are expressions of a quest for freedom and human dignity by people who have long been the victims of colonialism and imperialism. So in a real sense the racial crisis in America is a part of the larger world crisis." And it was a crisis that should not go to waste, because it had the "potential for democracy's fulfillment or fascism's triumph; for social progress or retrogression. We can choose either to walk the high road of human brotherhood or to tread the low road of man's inhumanity to man."

Government action against evil social systems was not the whole answer, but it was an indispensable one. "Morals cannot be legislated, but behavior can be regulated": King gave that answer repeatedly to the same vapid suggestion that simply changing the hearts of men would address the problems faced by oppressed people. "The law cannot make an employer love me, but it can keep him from refusing to hire me because of the color of my skin. . . . Moreover the law itself is a form of education." Laws took on the force of morality. King warned against thinking that change would work out on the wheels of inevitability: "If we wait for it to work itself out, it will never be worked out. Freedom only comes through persistent revolt, through persistent agitation, through persistently rising up against the system of evil." King here also applied his version of social psychology, believing that forcing changes in outward behavior would eventually lead to internal conversions.

King had all the resources of the theology of evil and human suffering, Gandhian resistance, and American civil religion from within his own tradition. His Afro-Baptist faith had the stuff of American civil religion and of Gandhi. He also knew how to draw on "white" sources, especially his favorite sermonizers from the past, to frame his messages for larger audiences in a way that appealed to them. As scholar Jonathan Rieder puts it, "King was not passive in his poaching; he always wove the sources seamlessly into his own voice"; theologian Richard Lischer makes much the same point in arguing that "He was no captive of words; he owned them, made them work for him and for black people and the nation at large."

Academics have a fancy name for King, derived from the Italian social thinker Antonio Gramsci: organic intellectual. It means a thinker whose most profound work derives from a direct engagement with ordinary people. King represents such a figure well, and he was conscious of it. For all of his theological education, his immersion in the highfalutin theologies of the day, it was ultimately his experience with the Mother Pollards and Rosa Parkses of Montgomery that had clarified his thinking "more than all of the books that I had read. As the days unfolded I became more and more convinced of the power of nonviolence. Living through the actual experience of the protest, nonviolence became more than a method to which I gave intellectual assent; it became a commitment to a way of life. Many issues I had not cleared up intellectually concerning nonviolence were now solved in the sphere of practical action." In addition, it had deepened his faith. He had become more convinced of a personal God. He had seen God as some kind of "metaphysical category" but now understood Him as a "living reality that has been validated in the experiences of everyday life."

King connected the movement to the broader struggles for freedom and independence sweeping the world. In "A Tough Mind and a Tender Heart," from August of 1959, he told an audience, "Many social revolutions in the world growing out of the legitimate aspiration of man for political independence, economic security and human dignity are all too often believed to be communist inspired because a large segment of the press reports it as such. . . . The soft minded are susceptible to belief in all kinds of superstitions. Almost any irrational fear can invade the soft mind without any sign of resistance," and they feared change. Such had been the case with the resistance of religion to scientific advances.

However much King's legend grew from the triumph in Montgomery, there had in reality been no miracle. The end of the boycott saw some of the worst episodes of violence and harassment directed against King and others associated with the movement, including Rosa Parks. King's life and the safety of his family continued to be in peril. In January 1957, observers discovered a fake bomb on the sidewalk outside of church. White men attacked a young black woman waiting on a bus and shot at another who was pregnant, seriously injuring her legs; black bus riders were harassed constantly; and in Birmingham whites dynamited the home of King's colleague Fred Shuttlesworth, who had the temerity to try to enroll his child in the public school. The constancy of the violence, both real and threatened, exhausted the newly famous pastor. King confronted the evil they had all experienced with the question on the lips of all oppressed people and the disinherited: "Where is God in the midst of falling bombs?" He urged parishioners to "continue to love" but also foresaw the possibility of death: "Certainly I don't want to die. But if anyone has to die, let it be me."

King carried a guilt, as he would in the subsequent years, fearing that the worst might come, that one of the ordinary people empowering the movement might be killed, and that he was asking for too much sacrifice. Speaking one night early in 1957, at the very end of the boycott, he nearly collapsed. He concluded by noting that if it was his turn to die, "I would die happy because I've been to the mountain top and I've seen the promised land and it's going to be here in Montgomery." This was one of his earliest uses of this promised land image, implying that he would be the Moses to lead them partly there but never make it himself. Most famously, he deployed that image powerfully the night before his death, in Memphis, often seen now as a kind of divination of what was to come. It was one of his most common themes in the years leading up to Memphis. And it's understandable why. Martyrdom was an ever-present possibility. It was a reality, not just a complex.

The strength to withstand the constant assaults came from King's faith in the ultimate triumph of justice. Later, he expressed more doubts about it, but in the later 1950s he preached on it constantly. King increasingly took on the role of a spokesman for a tough-minded but warm evangelical and political liberalism. The role of the church, he told a conference in Nashville in the later 1950s, was for a "strong ethical Christian liberalism, which will take a definite stand in the name of Jesus Christ." King connected his evangelical preachings with his social democratic political leanings, understanding political means to be a way to achieve moral ends.

He also articulated hopes that, at long last, the Old South would soon be gone, never to return. "Many of the problems that we are confronting in the South today grow out of the futile attempt of the white South to perpetuate a system of human values that came into being under a feudalistic plantation system which cannot survive in a day of democratic equalitarianism. Yes, the Old South is a lost cause," he quipped, poking fun at the catchphrase of southern romanticism from the late nineteenth century. At Highlander Folk School in 1957, he returned to his favorite text of Fosdick's about remaining maladjusted to segregation, inequality, and violence. He saw industrialization as a force for change, and organized labor as an ally in the struggle for freedom. He hoped activists could be nonconformists to the tragic inequalities of the economic system as it stood. They should be "maladjusted as Jesus of Nazareth, who dared to dream a dream of the fatherhood of God and the brotherhood of man. He looked at men amid the intricate and fascinating military machinery of the Roman Empire, and could say to them, 'He who lives by the sword will perish by the sword.'"

At the conferences at Highlander during this time, organized by long-time southern radical Myles Horton (a white Tennessean who had studied with Reinhold Niebuhr in New York), an entire generation of civil rights activists plotted the future of the movement. There, too, was Ed Friend, a "reporter"/spy. He had come to the twenty-fifth anniversary of Highlander on Labor Day 1958, introducing himself as a photographer. Later he took a photo plastered on the famous billboard, "Martin Luther King at Communist Training School." King's friend Anne Braden, a white left-wing activist from Louisville and longtime sympathizer with the movement, explained to King what had happened—that the spy would fabricate damning stories based on what allegedly he had seen. Later, Friend testified that at Highlander the goal preached was that "*white people should be murdered to force the Federal Government to support integration in the South—that was Martin Luther King.*"

Challenged by Highlander lawyers, Friend later backed down from alleging King had said this at Highlander but suggested that King might have said it at Spelman College in Atlanta. Anyway, the "facts" of this professional liar didn't matter; the point was simply to propagate misinformation. And it worked. Eventually, the relentless harassment that the state of Tennessee pursued against Highlander ended up shutting it down, supposedly because it had violated state alcohol laws by serving drinks. Obviously, the real reason was its central role as a place for civil rights and labor organizing. Previously it had been able to fly under the radar, but with the presence of King and others, it attracted the scrutiny of state authorities.

Added to the constant threats, governmental surveillance and harassment, and internecine warfare between various civil rights organizations, King had a growing family, with another child born just after the end of the Montgomery boycott. Two more children would soon come as well. He repeated his apology to his own church at the end of 1958 before finally resigning that pastorate and joining his father at Ebenezer Baptist. Along the way, he received contradictory advice from friends and counselors on how to divide up his time. His old mentor from seminary days in Pennsylvania, J. Pius Barbour, advised him, "Now, buckle down and preach and let Reform alone for a while." Others suggested that by remaining in Montgomery, he was endangering his wife and children. "How much does a leader owe his people?" one friend asked him. "How much is he called on to suffer from them?" This correspondent thought King should join forces with an established group, such as the NAACP.

King straddled the divide between various civil rights organizations. But given that he later came under some criticism for being too cautious, or not willing to put his life on the line the way SNCC students were, in 1957 he seemed at the vanguard of activism. He seemed the leader best capable of combining a critique of segregation in the United States, capitalist exploitation of labor, and colonialism abroad. At the same time, he preached black self-help staples of self-improvement and Christian "uplift," sounding a theme familiar from earlier generations of Booker T. Washington–derived black oratory. At Holt Street Baptist Church in Montgomery, for example, during an institute on nonviolence, he blasted the lower standards of teachers who "can't even speak the English language," quack doctors, and preachers more interested in "whooping" than developing the moral caliber of their flock. These uplift sermons were expected of ministers (and King exemplified it through the elevated literary style of his own sermons). Their job was to urge their flock to higher moral standards. With King, however, they remained secondary or tertiary themes in comparison to his true passion for justice.

At the same time, King found it difficult to capitalize on the momentum of the Montgomery movement. The SCLC searched for its role, looking for a place to re-create the magic of Montgomery. But as King himself had pointed out, people would always be expecting him to pull a rabbit out of the hat. That was easier said than done. The later 1950s saw the beginnings of citizenship programs, small local movements, and organizational and fundraising drives, but the SCLC itself lacked focus. Its organizational structure seemed to be perpetually in chaos, despite the entrance later of veteran organizer Ella Baker, soon to become a figure revered particularly by SNCC students.

Despite the difficulties, King's star attracted younger people around the country. One of them was John Lewis, the future hero of the Selma movement. He grew up poor in rural Alabama. Having heard MLK on the radio, the young Lewis, an aspiring Baptist minister, gravitated toward him as his hero. Lewis later studied under James Lawson, a Methodist minister who had lived in India for three years and later brought back ideas of nonviolence, which he spread to younger men and women under his influence in Nashville.

James Lawson spent three years (1953–1956) teaching in India and studying Gandhian philosophy and tactics after being released from prison for refusing to register for the draft for the Korean War. He subsequently formed a chapter of the Fellowship of Reconciliation in Tennessee. Thurman and Lawson introduced the message of Gandhian nonviolence as the key to an American social revolution to nascent civil rights groups in the years after World War II, including the Congress of Racial Equality (formed partly by Howard Thurman's student James Farmer in 1942). Lawson met King when King came to speak at Oberlin College in 1957; not long after, Lawson moved to the South, studied at Vanderbilt University for his theological degree (where he was expelled for his civil rights activities), and closely advised King and the SCLC for a number of years.

Lawson served as a kind of conduit transmitting ideas of nonviolence, the official philosophy of the SCLC, to students (including Lewis) who would form the vanguard of the movement in the 1960s. Another student inspired by King was Ezell Blair. While attending an address at Bennett College in Greensboro, North Carolina, as a high school student, Blair heard King urge young black southerners to move forcefully against segregated public accommodations. "His words were such that the vibrations that come over the microphone, over the loud speaker. . . . It was so strong, I could feel my heart palpitating, it brought tears to my eyes." Blair would soon form part of a small group that sat in at segregated lunch counters in Greensboro, the event that sparked similar movements across the South and revolutionized the region in the early 1960s. Underneath the surface the currents of change grew stronger. And King's presence, his constant traveling and speaking, was indispensable to that.

Critics who saw (and some who still see) King as a kind of professional orator, lacking in the substance of organizing ordinary folk to empower themselves, miss how much King's oratory actually *did* empower ordinary folk. That's why King's student critics on the left, such as Stokely Carmichael, maintained their admiration and respect for him, even while debating and disagreeing with him. They understood he was indispensable and inspiring, even when they parted ways with him on the philosophy of nonviolence or the tactics necessary to push the movement forward. They understood that, even if the movement made the man, King defined the movement for a larger public in words that appealed to them and to ordinary black southerners at the same time. He spoke to everyone at once; no one else could do that. There would have been a movement without him; there had been one for decades. Yet he was indispensable to inspiring it, clarifying its philosophy for the masses, and pushing it forward toward larger ends over time.

Introducing King at an Emancipation Day Rally in the late 1950s, Samuel Williams, a mentor of King's at Morehouse, noted that King was indeed a student of Gandhi, but "long before he heard of Mahatma Gandhi," via the preaching of his grandfather and father and family life with his mother and grandmother, "he heard and learned of Jesus of Nazareth, whom he now follows in all that he does." King told the crowd that day that their movement was part of the same struggle against colonialism that was igniting colored peoples abroad and that colored people were in fact a majority of the world's population. All was evidence that the old order was dying, with its politicians' words of "nullification" and "interposition" serving as nothing more than the "death groans from a dying system." King cleverly employed metaphors of deathbeds and wheezing patients on their last breath and funerals in his depiction of the dying of the old order. Congregants ate up his sarcastic humor in those contexts.

But the older order would not die on its own. Students would have to "speed up the coming of the new order," with urgency, as the patient on the deathbed, segregation, always has his attendant guardians "on hand with their oxygen tents to keep the older order alive." But more important, "we know if democracy is to live, segregation must die." Ultimately, the moral cosmos of the universe would move to justice; "the universe is on the side of justice." And the Christian faith assures us that "when we would give up in despair and we would think that we're struggling alone; it says to us that God is struggling with us." The masses of people had gained a vision, "they've tasted freedom," and now they were ready to go to the promised land.

King explained it a little differently in an article that appeared in the *Hindustan Times and Peace News*: "When I was in theological school . . . I felt that the Christian ethic of love was confined to individual relationships. I could not see how it could work in social conflict. Then I read Gandhi's ethic of love as revealed in Jesus but raised to a social strategy for social transformation. This lifts love from individual relationships to the place of social transformation."

Likewise, in his most extended reflection on Gandhi given on Palm Sunday in 1959, just after King himself had returned from a visit to India, King portrayed how Gandhi had caught the spirit of Jesus. It was, King said, one of the "strange ironies of the modern world that the greatest Christian of the twentieth century was not a member of the Christian church. He had defeated the great Empire of the modern world without firing a shot, without having any weapons or army, through the force of the power of his message of loving nonviolence as the means of an active resistance to evil." Then, later, he paid the sacrifice of his life, as had Abraham Lincoln. Now, as Edwin Stanton had said of Lincoln, "he belongs to the ages." The implication for African Americans was obvious.

For his audiences, King frequently connected the struggle of African Americans in the South with the movement of the worldwide struggles of oppressed peoples. "The old order of colonialism is passing away, and the new order of freedom and equality is coming into being," he told one group in Atlanta at beginning of 1957. For King, there was "no basic difference between colonialism and racial segregation . . . at bottom both segregation in America and colonialism in Africa were based on the same thing—white supremacy and contempt for life." King knew the history of white supremacy at home and abroad.

King frequently preached on the themes of international movements for freedom to his congregants in Montgomery. In "Birth of a New Nation," a sermon at Dexter Avenue from April 1957, he portrayed what the Ghanian independence movement had to say to black Americans: "Ghana has something to say to us . . . the oppressor never voluntarily gives freedom to the oppressed. You have to work for it." The independence movement in Ghana had shown precisely that when an oppressor was in domination, it would not end without a struggle; "he never voluntarily gives it up . . . Privileged classes never give up their privileges without strong resistance."

King also involved himself in causes of peace. In a speech to the War Resisters League in 1959, he articulated his view that true pacifism "is not nonresistance to evil, but nonviolent resistance to evil. . . . I feel free to say that we who believe in nonviolence often have an unwarranted optimism concerning man and lean unconsciously toward self-righteousness." The pacifist position was not "sinless" but the "lesser evil in the circumstances. . . . We who advocate nonviolence would have a greater appeal if we did not claim to be free from the moral dilemmas that the nonpacifist confronts." King had learned his Niebuhr but moved in his own direction, one contrary to the more conservative and pessimistic track Niebuhr of later life took.

For King, history had shown the "throbbing desire" of man, something that could only be suppressed temporarily until it "breaks out. Men realize that . . . freedom is basic. To rob a man of his freedom is to take from him the essential basis of his manhood." He added his characteristic emphasis on what he later called the fierce urgency of now: "If we wait for it to work itself out, it will *never* be worked out! Freedom only comes through persistent revolt, through persistent agitation, through persistently rising up against the system of evil." The struggle would have to be waged cleanly, without "falsehood and violence and hate and malice," so that when segregation finally collapsed, there would be a chance at brotherhood. But until then, "there is no crown without a cross," and

before Canaan there was the Red Sea and a "hard-hearted Pharaoh to confront." But God was moving in history, breaking down the "bondage and
the walls of colonialism, exploitation, and imperialism. To break them
down to the point that no man will trample over another man," but all
would respect the "dignity and worth of human personality." Speaking
in St. Louis a few days later, he envisioned a world of peace—swords into
plowshares—but also one of economic justice, where "men will no longer
take necessities from the masses to give luxuries to the classes." He concluded there again with the repetition of "freedom must ring from every
mountainside. . . . Let it ring," six years before its triumphant invocation
at the March on Washington.

King's celebrityhood also extended to the role of advice columnist.
A syndicated column of his appeared in black newspapers around the
country. Advice-seekers wrote him on numerous issues, often seeking
advice on marital problems, family conflicts, and ruptures in personal
relationships. A number of people involved in interracial relationships
queried the pastor on what to do when their families would not abide
that situation.

But the most interesting exchange came when King received this
question: *Why did God make Jesus white, when the majority of peoples in the
world are non-white?* King's response remains fascinating. He begins,
predictably, by noting that the color of Jesus's skin "is of little or no
consequence," nor is the color of anyone's skin any more consequent.
Jesus's importance lay in his spirit, his being the human form of God on
earth representing an "internal spiritual commitment" to bring salvation.
But then King concludes, "He would have been no more significant if
His skin had been black. He is no less significant because His skin was
white." In denying the importance of Jesus's supposed skin color, King
unconsciously affirmed it, repeating (without intending so) the deeply
ingrained power of the perception of Jesus's whiteness as it had been
passed down in American art and imagery starting from about the 1830s,
but ascending in significance from the 1930s and 1940s through the production of Warner Sallman's classic "Head of Christ." Here, King was as
beholden, without even realizing it, to the power of whiteness to define
divinity. Late in his life, responding to movements and currents of black
theology in the 1960s, he began to better understand the power of this
kind of imagery to demonize blackness.

King also fielded questions about what young Christians should and
shouldn't do in the realm of popular culture. Here he showed his complete
absorption in the typical moral clichés of his day. Writing to one young
musician who had asked him about playing gospel or rock and roll, and
whether rock was sinful, King replies, "The two are totally incompatible,"
because the "profound sacred and spiritual meaning of the great music of

the church" should never be mixed with the transitory pop music of the day: "The former serves to lift men's souls to higher levels of reality, and therefore to God; the latter so often plunges men's minds into degrading and immoral depths." King began the first paragraph of his book *Stride Toward Freedom* by telling a story of listening to the Metropolitan Opera on the radio as he drove from Atlanta to Montgomery early in 1954. And indeed, he was a great lover of classical music, as had been Howard Thurman, W. E. B. Du Bois (a great fan of Richard Wagner), and others. Later, though, he was captured by the soul music of the 1960s, and especially by James Brown, once leaving a meeting by announcing that "I'm sorry, y'all. James Brown is on. I'm gone." His colleagues enjoyed this playful side of King, one unknown to a more general public.

King also addressed concerns about the social gospel from the pulpit. One correspondent complained about a preacher who mixed God and the NAACP in the pulpit; there were too many "worldly things in his sermon." King responded, "I know of no way to separate God from the noble work that the NAACP is doing. Religion at its best is a two-way road," seeking both to change the individual soul and to "change environmental conditions so that the soul can have a chance once it is changed. Therefore any religion that professes to be concerned about the souls of men and is not concerned about economic conditions that cripple them and the social conditions that damn them is a dry as dust religion in need of new blood."

While leading the movement in the late 1950s, King kept receiving offers of professorships, administrative posts, and other positions that would suit his periodically expressed desire to be a kind of professional thinker. He clearly was attracted to it; he enjoyed his time in the higher realms of theological discourse. But he consistently turned them down. Responding to one offer from Garrett Biblical Institute at Northwestern University, "I have a deep sense of responsibility at this point and feel, for the next few years at least, that my place is here in the deep South doing all in my power to alleviate the tensions that exist between Negro and white citizens." He had embarked on this "challenging venture of love," finding it to be sorely needed in the segregated South and hoping ultimately to be able to "carry this approach far beyond the bounds of Montgomery." He had said much the same to Mordecai Wyatt Johnson when Johnson, the president of Howard University, tried to recruit King to be dean of the chapel there. It was fortunate that he had this self-recognition; his academic record was lackluster compared to his matchless talents as the voice that moved a generation.

By this time, King's life was a whirlwind of activity that would not cease until his assassination ten years later. On September 20, 1958, a mentally disturbed African American woman named Izola Ware Curry came to a store in Harlem, in uptown New York City. Martin Luther King

Jr. was signing copies of his new book *Stride Toward Freedom: The Montgomery Story*. She took out a sharp-edged letter opener. Then she stabbed the twenty-nine-year-old minister. King barely survived. Doctors later told him that if he had sneezed, he could have died.

Resting in the hospital afterward, King received a visit from the African American minister, theologian, and mystic Howard Thurman. The two had met before. Thurman served from 1932 to 1944 as dean of the chapel at Howard University; then as minister of the Church for the Fellowship of All Peoples in San Francisco during 1944–1953; and then as dean of Marsh Chapel and professor in the School of Theology at Boston University from 1953 to 1965. King was a student there when Thurman first assumed his position in Boston, and he loved to hear the renowned minister preach.

But the two were never personally close. Thurman was the age of King's father and, indeed, was closely connected with King Sr. through his years at Morehouse College in Atlanta. But they were close intellectually and spiritually. One legend has it that King carried around his own well-thumbed version of Thurman's best-known book, *Jesus and the Disinherited*, in his pocket (or, in some accounts, in his briefcase) during the long and epic struggle of the Montgomery bus boycott. Whether true in a literal sense, it certainly was true in terms of the ideas that formed the young civil rights leader. King quoted and paraphrased Thurman extensively in his sermons during the 1950s and 1960s. Drawing from Thurman, King understood Jesus as an emblem of the dispossessed—both to a group of Jewish followers in ancient Palestine and to African Americans under slavery and segregation. That was precisely why Jesus was so central to African American religious history.

Thurman felt called to visit King in the hospital. There, he gave the same advice he gave to countless others over the decades: that King should take the unexpected, if tragic, opportunity to step out of life briefly, meditate on his life and its purposes, and only then move forward. By doing so, he could recover in both body and soul. Thurman urged him to take additional time for recuperation, beyond what the doctor had ordered. It would, Thurman thought, "give him time away from the immediate pressure of the movement to reassess himself in relation to the cause, to rest his body and mind with healing detachment, and to take a long look that only solitary brooding can provide. The movement had become more than an organization; it had become an organism with a life of its own to which he must relate in fresh and extraordinary ways or be swallowed up by it." King replied to Thurman that "I am following your advice on the question."

For a few weeks, he did. After leaving the hospital, King took an unexpected respite from his public duties, one of the few in his adult life.

Soon enough, however, King returned to his frantic schedule, his already pronounced tendency toward tardiness made worse by the nonstop demands that spontaneously fell to him nearly every day. Expressing his frustration to a former Boston University professor, he wrote that "in many instances I have felt terribly frustrated over my inability to retreat, concentrate, and reflect." He wanted more time to "meditate and think through the total struggle ahead," but it was impossible. Aside from the chaos inherent in directing a growing national movement of nonviolence, there was the constant harassment by state authorities (including a falsely trumped-up prosecution for tax evasion; this imbroglio depressed him because of public allegations against his character, and because King was always careful about living relatively frugally and turning down offers for larger paydays), the demands of celebrityhood, and the suspicion of him held by some in the NAACP as well and the ongoing internecine conflict within black Baptist organizations.

In February 1959, he had a chance to travel to India, following a course set by a number of African Americans through the past two decades, including Howard and Sue Bailey Thurman, Juliette Derricotte, Benjamin Mays, William Stuart Nelson, Mordecai Wyatt Johnson, and James Lawson.

The trip was portrayed as King's homage to Gandhi and chance to learn from the spiritual wisdom derived from the Indian independence movement. The reality was rather different. It became something like a publicity and autograph-signing tour. Lawrence Reddick, King's close advisor and ghostwriter, thought that King would have to devote himself to either "full time to Crusading" or digging into his local work as a pastor; King would thus remain a "crusader in a gray flannel suit" rather than becoming the self-sacrificing apostle of the new world to come. King's associate in India, James Ellery Bristol, a lifelong pacifist and peace activist, expressed a similar frustration about how the tour in India "clearly appeared to be to build up King as a world figure, and to have this build-up recorded in the U.S." Snapshots and photo opportunities seemed sometimes a higher priority than dialogues. All the same, Bristol found the overall experience a positive one, noting the positive reaction of Indians who came to hear him. He did worry about whether King could "stand the adulation without having it go to his head."

For generations before then, dating from the late 1920s, African Americans had been going to India to study its Gandhian legacy of nonviolent anti-colonial struggle. In 1935–1936, King's intellectual mentor and influence Howard Thurman had a crucial three-hour long dialogue with Gandhi at the end of the journey, recounted in the previous chapter. By that time, Thurman had exercised an outsized intellectual and spiritual influence on an entire generation that became the leadership of the civil rights movement. Thurman's session with Gandhi was a key moment in the translation of the Indian nonviolent struggle for independence into the African American struggle for freedom. No wonder that, at the close of the meeting, Gandhi told Thurman (according to the account of the meeting published in India) that "it may be through the Negroes that the unadulterated message of nonviolence will be delivered to the world." Gandhi and Howard Thurman thought of this in terms of a small group of spiritually prepared elites who would show the way to the new age. Later, when King transmitted that philosophy to the rank-and-file of ordinary black southerners, Thurman was thrilled. It was not what he had envisioned, precisely, and yet he knew that King and the movement represented the fulfillment of much of his life's work.

Unlike Thurman, King traveled as an internationally known figure; he could not sit for hours with audiences or other religious figures, as his trip had more the feel of an extended visit of a head of state. And in a sense, he was a head of state, as Indians perceived it, for African Americans. King sent out a statement at the end of his journey, commending the Indian government's determination to move against the problem of untouchables in Indian society, contrasting that unfavorably with the support many American politicians expressed for segregation. Untouchability was, legally speaking, dying in India (King did not grasp fully how much it continued to live on in a de facto sense), but the American problem of untouchability, represented by segregation, lived on. Reactionary forces breathed new life into the dying corpse of old racial order: the untouchability of Negroes.

King drew deeply from the works of Thurman and others when he reflected on the legacy of slavery. In "Unfulfilled Hopes," preached to his Montgomery congregation in April 1959, he took on the tragedy of slavery and the lives of slaves tracked by bloodhounds and cut off from their roots. Thurman's *Deep River* provided King's inspiration here, as he both quoted from and just slightly paraphrased Thurman's writings about the cruel injustices of the denial of freedom to slaves. Slavery, Thurman had written, had been romanticized by the moonlight-and-magnolias myth, when in fact it was a "dirty, sordid, inhuman business." And yet there remained the hope fostered by preachers who may not have known grammar or higher learning but who know how to give people the hope of survival; and of ordinary slaves who "gave to America the spiritual, which is the only original and creative music in this nation."

In his Easter sermon "A Walk through the Holy Land," he fleshed out a full analogy of the meaning of Easter specifically for African Americans: "We've been buried in numerous graves—the grave of economic insecurity, the grave of exploitation, the grave of oppression. We've watched justice trampled over and truth crucified. But . . . Easter reminds us that it won't be like that all the way. It reminds us that God has a light that can shine amid all of the darkness." King reiterated his opposition to war, his stance of pacifism, in spite of the criticism that came to him. He had stated repeatedly "my hatred for this most colossal of all evils and I have condemned any organizer of war, regardless of his rank or nationality. I have signed numerous statements with other Americans condemning nuclear testing and have authorized publication of my name in advertisements appearing in the largest circulation newspapers in the country, without concern that it was then 'unpopular' to speak out." King's vision was growing, extending outward, and taking in the broadest international meanings of the most local of racial conflicts. He was tying together the violence of southern racism with the violence that undergirded the American social and economic order more largely. These would be the themes that consumed his later life.

1959 was a key year in his leadership for another reason: the SCLC had come to loggerheads over how to proceed in its organizing mission. The indomitable Ella Baker challenged SCLC leadership: "Have we been so busy doing the things that *had* to be done that we have failed to [do] what *should* be done? Have we really come to grips with what it takes to do the job for which SCLC was organized; and are we willing to pay the price?" She pushed the SCLC to develop local leaders who would then carry out the program of "nonviolent direct mass action." She challenged King directly: "I am convinced that SCLC can and should play a unique role in the struggle for human rights; but I am equally convinced that this can not be done by following, or even approximating 'usual procedures.' SCLC must present creative leadership that will bestir dynamic mass action." The top-down authoritarian style of the SCLC, an ironic repetition of the "organization man" ethos of the 1950s, would not cut it. Baker was looking to the creative experiments that would soon come in the 1960s. As Lawrence Reddick described her, Baker "really came to lay him out and abuse him. She gave him the devil for not spending more time with the SCLC." She blasted him for "speaking everywhere on every subject," to which King responded with pain: "He said that an artist should not be denied his means of expression. That he liked to preach and felt that he should do it. It was almost touching the way he said it and at that point I became convinced that he of himself does not have the [*toughness?*] to say no when these invitations flood in on him."

As Baker saw it, it was a "handicap for oppressed people to depend so largely on a leader," because that leader, willingly or not, hogs the spotlight. This means that "the media made him, and the media may undo him," and that person can start to believe that "he *is* the movement. Such people get so involved with playing the game of being important that they exhaust themselves and their time and they don't do the work of actually organizing people."

Baker's acute analysis in fact nailed King on some of his weakest points. King's charisma naturally suggested a tendency toward a cult of personality. Moreover, as one scholar has put it, "King had a complete conviction that God had called him to his task of sacrificial leadership, which helps to explain partially his rigid, initially authoritarian leadership style. When you're being led by God, it's hard to listen to mere mortals." People reinforced this notion by calling him messiah and portraying his sacrifices as akin to those of Jesus. King both resisted it and felt compelled to live and represent it for his people.

As Ella Baker and others at the time saw it, "the movement made Martin rather than Martin making the movement." Ironically, that was akin to how King portrayed himself to the Montgomery boycotters; he repeatedly said that if there were no Martin Luther King Jr., there would still be this movement. The scholar Richard Lischer has provided an important counterargument. As he puts it, "King was summoned by events he did not initiate and exposed to conditions he did not create, but his response was so powerful an *interpretation* of events that it reshaped the conditions in which they originated." King wasn't first to struggle for rights but was "the first to name the struggle and to declare its meaning."

There is no resolution to this philosophical and historical chicken-and-egg, whether the priority should be on the person or the movement that the person comes to symbolize. King himself was torn between the two, often humbly portraying himself as swept up in the currents of history, while at other times feeling deeply responsible, in an almost single-handed way, for carrying the movement forward. His colleagues and contemporaries appreciated his role as a spokesman and fundraiser; that was simply indispensable. They also resented the media focus on the person and King's own tendency to withdraw from local social struggles that he helped to initiate. Those in the movement could both appreciate and distrust the oral artistry of the man some mockingly (in private) referred to as "De Lawd."

King's blunt-talking ministerial colleague Fred Shuttlesworth, a ferociously combative pastor in Birmingham, wrote him in April 1959, "I have often stated that when the flowery speeches have been made, we still have the hard job of getting down and helping people to work to reach the idealistic state of human affairs which we desire." He found the civil rights leadership in Alabama "less dynamic and imaginative than it ought to be," to say nothing of the upsurge of violence directed against locals active in the movement and the determination of Alabama's political leaders to defend segregation to its dying day.

King knew he had to leave his beloved congregants in Montgomery. He needed to be at a more central location, and he needed to share duties in pastoring a church, rather than doing too many things halfway at the same time. He acknowledged this at an address at the Fourth Annual Institute on Nonviolence and Social Change on December 3, 1959. In his parting address, he felt he had a "moral obligation" to "give more of my time and energy to the whole South," requiring a move to a more central location. "It was not easy for me to decide to leave a community where bravery, resourcefulness and determination had shattered the girders of the old order and weakened confidence of the rulers, despite their centuries of unchallenged rule. It was not easy to decide to leave a city whose Negroes resisted injustice magnificently and followed a method of nonviolent struggle that became one of the glowing epics of the twentieth century." Later King spoke more personally of the costs he had paid in Montgomery, faced with the task of "trying to do as one man what five or six people ought to be doing . . . what I have been doing is giving, giving, giving and not stopping to retreat and meditate like I should—to come back. If the situation is not changed, I will be a physical and psychological wreck. I have to reorganize my personality and re-orient my life."

Late in 1959, he told his congregants on leaving Dexter Avenue Baptist Church, "I can't stop now. History has thrust something upon me which I can't turn away. *I should free you now.*" But King was not freeing himself. Far from it. He wrote to another former BU professor that, while he had gone to Atlanta for that reason, "things have happened as you know which have made my schedule more crowded in Atlanta than it was in Montgomery." He had tried to set aside one day a week for prayer and meditation, but "things began to pile up so much that I found myself using that particular day as a time to catch up on so many things that had accumulated."

The movement, again, was about to swallow him. The next few years would be the King years.

5

✝

The Dream, the Letter, and the Nightmare

And so a passionate concern for social justice must be a concern of the Christian religion.

—Martin Luther King Jr., Ebenezer Baptist Church, 1962

As he left his Dexter Avenue congregation in Montgomery in late 1959, Martin Luther King Jr. envisioned bigger campaigns to come. He rejoined the congregation of his boyhood, Ebenezer Baptist in Atlanta. He would be co-pastor with his father, allowing him more time to devote to the SCLC. Yet at the time, he was something like a movement leader without much of a movement. King and the SCLC talked a big game, but Ella Baker was challenging him, and his colleagues, about doing the hard work of organizing to achieve their dreams. They had helped sprout local movements throughout the South, but the SCLC itself had not managed to mount much of a campaign since Montgomery. King's words and speechgiving across the country inspired and moved people. In that sense, he was right in his argument with Baker: he wanted to keep preaching because it was his art form, and the artist should not be denied his means of expression. And those means resulted in some remarkably far-reaching consequences.

The year 1960 was a turning point for the movement. King used his new pulpit in Atlanta and capitalized on a remarkably quickly organized national student movement to bring the civil rights cause to a new era. Stumbles, missteps, and internal conflicts inevitably appeared, unsurprisingly for a movement with such audacious plans to shake up the country. At times, movement leaders faced wily resistance from local whites.

Meanwhile, relentless scrutiny by local, state, and federal authorities sought to crack King's credibility. The day-to-day chaos of managing a movement that produced offshoots in every direction, with an assortment of idealistic but eccentric and headstrong personalities, would have been a challenge for anyone.

In retrospect, what King and the movement accomplished from 1960 to 1965 is all the more astonishing. It is all the more admirable for the obstacles, both internal and external, they confronted constantly. As always, King was carried along by the course of events that he often had little part in creating. He then spoke for or explained those events to a larger public. His role as a public moral philosopher, communicating the complex set of ideas he delivered to both white and black audiences, was indispensable.

King had come into his own as a preacher in Montgomery. He was, in the words of biographer Peter Ling, "America's preeminent racial diplomat." His role crested from 1961–1965, as the civil rights movement entered a new phase and surged to national prominence. For King, the personal peak was the March on Washington address on August 28, 1963, the moment that has since come to define as well as restrict and constrain him. That day, King took portions of sermons he had preached for years before and put them together in a brilliant pastiche. His speech became embedded in the national imagination. But the lines most quoted are those taken out of context. In that sense, his mountaintop moment has had the effect in his afterlife of ghosting him misleadingly.

For King, the boycott was the "daybreak of freedom," the small event that had cracked the stone wall of white supremacy and portended larger changes to come. He also understood it within his worldview of social democracy. In his talks with King in 1960, socialist writer and activist Michael Harrington saw that the young minister was coming to understand the need for a "thoroughgoing democratization of the economy and the political structure of society. He understood that full civil rights for an exploited and hungry mass of black Americans constituted only a first step in the transformation of the intolerable conditions under which they lived. He therefore struck me as having a socialist orientation." As Harrington later said, this "warm and luminous man of the South had, in the course of a much more profound political and intellectual journey than mine, come to a view of America and the world that I largely shared." The two worked together through the 1960s, and by the end King had moved beyond Harrington in terms of his daring radicalism; Harrington would be one of those advisors (like Rustin) who pushed King leftward earlier in his career and warned him against taking his visions too far, outside the liberal mainstream.

King's goal, writes theologian and historian Richard Lischer, was the "merger of black aspirations into the American dream. To do this he had to convince black Americans that his methods represented their best interests, and he had to convince white Americans that his vision was consistent with their heritage and in their best interests as well." He did this best and most effectively in the early 1960s. The currents of history moved in his favor, as his vision drew national sympathy from whites while continuing to attract mass black support. This was a delicate balancing act, and ultimately the center would not hold. But for a few years, it grabbed hold of the national imagination. For that reason, Taylor Branch's first volume in his epic trilogy, *Parting the Waters*, is subtitled *America in the King Years*.

King was often enraged but felt constrained to play the role of diplomat in public. He expressed black rage in sermons and black forgiveness in public addresses. He "often hid his passion behind a mask of dignity," as historian Jonathan Rieder has put it. King acknowledged with pleasure the activist white ministers who spoke out against racists, even if far too few dared to do so. Then, in the "Letter from a Birmingham Jail," he blasted southern moderates as a greater danger to justice than the KKK.

King also showed his understanding of the limitations of relations with whites. In an exchange with Elijah Muhammad, the Nation of Islam leader noted to Dr. King that "you and me both grew up in Georgia, and we know there are many different kinds of snakes. The rattlesnake was poisonous and the king snake was friendly. But they both snakes." They shared a laugh. Yet, as a child, he had sung "I Want to Be More Like Jesus." Jesus as an extremist was a common theme in his addresses, and King defiantly embraced the extremism of Jesus, even while acknowledging the truth of Muhammad's sly wit. "King did not try to suppress dislike of the white man so much as to reframe it," one historian has astutely noted. King reframed it with the message of redemptive nonviolence and agape love. His prophetic sermons portrayed both a God of love and a God of wrath, a familiar figure to generations who had grown up with black sermons. King read civil religion in light of slave experience. America, in this view, was a nation in need of redemption—not a redeemer nation.

Even as King learned the ropes of creating pressure points to move legislation along through democratic institutions, he came to understand the flawed nature of American democracy. He took aim at people who thought of themselves as decent and forward-looking; those who would condemn the most public acts of violence but ignored the daily silent brutalities spoke empty words. The "daily violence which our society inflicts upon many of its members" was just as cruel as Bull Connor's dogs; "The violence of poverty and humiliation hurts as intensely as the violence of a club."

As the decade progressed, King called for more radicalism from churches. He attacked the evils of unfettered capitalism, promoted the

redistribution of economic power, and lent support to the peace movement. He also developed his understanding of anticolonial struggles at
home and abroad: the connection between the African American freedom struggle and anti-colonial movements in Africa. He saw and com-
municated especially to black audiences the international nature of the
black freedom struggle. Meanwhile, he was careful to stay in the lanes
of American civil religion. In an interview for NBC's *Meet the Press*, he
rebutted the contention that he was soft on communism just because he
had pointed out that Marx had "challenged the social conscience of the
Christian churches." He responded that he had made it clear that "communism is based on an ethical relativism and a metaphysical materialism
that no Christian can accept." King had to tread the waters of Cold War
rhetoric carefully.

Over time, King the racial diplomat morphed into King the prophet.
Sometimes, as in Birmingham, the two were there together. King knew
the price that prophets usually paid. As King scholar and theologian
Lewis Baldwin has written, King knew that the "same religious community which produced the prophets also produced the conservative
religious forces which stoned the prophets to death."

He soon had equal renown among black congregants across the country and with white audiences including labor union halls, academic conferences, nonviolence workshops, civic organizations, and interreligious
gatherings. His message was not different, but his mode of presentation
was skillfully modulated to fit the audience. His book *Stride Toward Freedom* was carefully edited to meet the expectations of a mainstream white
audience. Publishers urged him to put out a book of sermons. Eventually
he did so, under the title *Strength to Love*; it, too, underwent considerable
redaction by editors determined to smooth it out for a mainstream audience. In the meantime, he reveled in his art form and exercised his gifts
in a nearly nonstop road show. Meanwhile, he led the SCLC, dealt with
constant and very real threats to his life, remained a target of government
surveillance, and negotiated both with national political figures and with
rival people and organizations within the black community.

A friend later commented that it would kill him to be Martin Luther
King Jr. for twenty-four hours, because the pace of activity was simply too
much. King's celebrityhood was both his opportunity and his burden; he
was equally attracted and flattered by it and frustrated by the boxes into
which he had been put. He exploited his fame for the goals of the movement, but he also sought to escape it. This was an impossibility. In 1963,
he traveled 275,000 miles and gave more than 350 speeches. "I have lost
my freshness and creativity," he complained. He had to rely on speech-
writers and ghostwriters for his material and almost never had a moment,
except when in jail, to sit and create his own ideas. And yet, in the process

of speaking, he created ideas that, if not new, were perfectly calibrated revisions of standard tropes; "I have a dream," in fact, was one of those. In the haste of having to "rehash" (as he put it) old material, his artistic means reached its peak. His genius in improvising was akin to John Coltrane's take on "My Favorite Things," the too-familiar tune transformed into something of an epic force.

King both felt and resisted the idea that his role was to be something like a suffering messiah for a people. In an Atlanta radio interview shortly before the 1960 election, he said that he had "no desire to be a martyr . . . I don't enjoy suffering, and I don't have any desire to die." His involvement, rather, came because of the reality of the problem of race in America, and he felt compelled not merely to "save the Negro" but also to "save the soul of America." He also came to see America as a "sick nation," one that would inevitably claim him as a martyr. As it did.

King bid farewell to his congregants in Montgomery in December 1959 and moved to Atlanta partly to throw himself into the movement in a more consistent way and enjoy the benefits of a centrally located southern city. He was soon in the thick of things in Atlanta and involved, partly by accident, with the presidential campaign of 1960. Young people on the move throughout the country jump-started a movement that had stalled out in the later 1950s. Many of those people (including some who later distrusted or mocked King's apparent pretensions and his tendency to stay above the fray just when the fray was at its most intense) were inspired by King's addresses.

King reintroduced himself to the Ebenezer congregation with a reprise of one of his standbys, "Three Dimensions of a Complete Life." It had been his trial sermon in Montgomery in 1954, tailored to meet the expectations of that particular audience. "Many of our white brothers are concerned only about the length of life," he said, and "their preferred economic positions, their political power, their so-called way of life. If they would ever rise up and add breadth to length, the other-regarding dimension to the self-regarding dimension, we would be able to solve all of the problems in our nation today." Later, he preached that "segregation would be dead as a doornail in the South today if the Southern white church took a stand against it." He had not given up on the southern moderates—yet. That hope would not survive the coming years; those moderates ended up being his rhetorical foils in his written masterpiece from 1963, "Letter from a Birmingham Jail."

King's homilies from this era continued in the vein he had developed in Montgomery. He took standard sermonic themes from the past, including from the reservoir of "white" sermons (from Phillips Brooks, Harry Emerson Fosdick, and others), and reworked them into black sermons on sin, struggle, judgment, and deliverance. Jesus was central, and King sounds like an evangelical. He also wove black protest into orthodox explorations of biblical texts. He spoke the language of black demands for equality into ideas comprehensible by white audiences, alternately emphasizing the demands or the possibility of brotherhood for all depending on the audience. In this way, King managed to take pleas for justice that had been on the table for blacks for decades, even centuries, and translated them into idioms available for white audiences and black audiences alike. That was central to his oratorical genius.

He also traveled the country preaching on the heresy of white supremacy. In "The Man Who Was a Fool," given at Detroit in 1961, he worked over the parable of the rich fool from the Bible and applied it to contemporary race relations. White supremacy was nothing more than the notion that "God made a mistake and stamped an eternal stigma of inferiority on a certain race of people? What is white supremacy but the foolishness of believing that one race is good enough to dominate another race." The same went for black supremacy. The freedom struggle for citizenship was not about "asserting advantage, but achieving justice." King critiqued America for using its wealth to "establish military bases around the world rather than establishing bases of genuine concern and understanding." Such a policy ignored the fundamental truth that "we are tied in a single garment of destiny, caught in an inescapable network of mutuality."

King's enemies pursued him relentlessly through his career. They included some of the greatest villains of this era. And his philosophy required him to love them, assuming his love would shame them into a look into the psychology of their own hatred. That was a tall order, and King knew it. Loving an enemy did not mean one liked him, King explained in exploring this paradox, because "it's kind of difficult to like some people. . . . And you can't like anybody who's bombing your home and threatening your children. It's hard to like a senator who's spending all of his time in Washington standing against all the legislation that will make for better relationships and that will make for brotherhood." But Jesus said to love them, and "love is understanding, redemptive, creative goodwill for all men."

King understood that he had to contain his own fury, to maintain that "mask of dignity" in the face of white supremacist murderers. The internal pressure of trying to channel such rage into a rhetoric of love was at once enormously powerful and internally explosive. Hate was destructive for both parties, King said, "but so often we overlook the fact that hate is as damaging to the subject of hate as it is to the object of hate. Hate damages a white man, in many instances, more than it damages the Negro, for it does something to the personality; it does something to the soul." Here, King drew directly from the life and work of Howard Thurman, who explored the destructive psychology of hatred with unmatched insight. And thus the struggle, as he often said, was in part to "free our white brothers from their fears, from their prejudices, from their hate, and all of those attitudes that destroy and damage the soul." Psychology said the same thing—that hate "disrupts the personality, that makes for inner conflicts and guilt feelings and, thereby, develops neurotic personalities." The question that remained was the damage inflicted in one's own soul, in doing so.

Love was more powerful, King insisted. "Send your propaganda agents around the country and make it appear that we are not fit morally, culturally, and otherwise for integration," King said, and "we will still love you. Send your hooded perpetrators of violence into our communities at the midnight hours, and drag us out on some wayside road and beat us and leave us dead, and we will still love you . . . But be assured that we will wear you down (*Yes indeed*) by our capacity to suffer. (*Yes*)." King drew the contrast with a man he had met in Albany, Georgia, who had said that he didn't love Negroes like he used to back when everyone knew their place. Of course, such a person never understood what true love was. His love was contingent "upon the Negro staying in his place." It was a "utilitarian love," the opposite of *agape*. People could find it easy to love "humanity" in general, raise money for missions abroad, but hate their neighbors. And thus, King concluded, "They love humanity in general but they don't love Africans in particular." That was the love preached by the white southern church, the kind that could not see, or denied, the strange fruit swaying on southern trees.

King's preachings on radical love already faced the beginnings of the kind of criticisms that would confront him later in the 1960s. In a special issue of *Liberation*, he and North Carolina black activist and advocate of self-defense Robert Williams debated the issues of whether nonviolence should be the philosophy of the black freedom struggle. Robert F. Williams had grown up in Monroe, North Carolina. There, Jesse Helms, father of the future senior senator from the state, ruled the city streets as chief of police. Like many other black veterans, Williams swore not to take what his father's generation had endured. North Carolinians knew that men like Williams used guns for self-defense. Later, Williams lived in exile, first in Cuba in the early 1960s, where he beamed a 50,000-watt broadcast he dubbed "Radio Free Dixie" to the United States (until the CIA managed to jam his airwaves), and later in China.

Williams had challenged the strategy of "turn-the-other-cheekism." King's method might work "when the opponent is civilized, but nonviolence is no match or repellent for a sadist." King replied that he had never condemned self-defense per se, and neither had Gandhi. Blacks engaging in self-defense would find defenders, but African Americans who initiated violence would inevitably fail and bring discredit on the freedom struggle: "There is more power in socially organized masses on the march than there is in guns in the hands of a few desperate men. Our enemies would prefer to deal with a small armed group rather than with a huge, unarmed but resolute mass of people." But following Gandhi's method, the key also was relentlessness, "never letting them rest," and facing up to "the vicious and evil enemies squarely. It requires dedicated people, because it is a backbreaking task to arouse, to organize, and to educate tens of thousands for disciplined, sustained action."

That dialogue between King and advocates of self-defense would intensify through the next years. It became a central theme of the last few years of his life. King understood their point of view, all the more so as the 1960s progressed, but repeated his arguments, both practical (black were outgunned) and philosophical (if the end was the beloved community, violence could never achieve reconciliation at the end of the struggle). Robert Williams and others, meanwhile, suggested—with good reason—that the implicit threat of violence was one of the engines that in effect made nonviolent campaigns actually work.

King also preached on the broader implications of the civil rights struggle. In a piece for *Challenge*, from the Young People's Socialist League, King presented a capacious vision of what would be required for complete equality, including many measures that would go far beyond segregation. Such a vision was dependent on a "gigantic and integrated alliance of the progressive social forces in the United States." It was no coincidence, he pointed out, that reactionary forces were allied against labor, against African Americans, and against any form of equality and progressive legislation. The broad civil rights coalition, the grouping of progressive and liberal forces, could be an effective coalition not only on civil rights but also on the entire spectrum of problems facing the nation. The progressive alliance was seeking "new ways of human beings living together, free from the spiritual deformation of race hatred—and free also from the deformations of war and economic injustice. And this vision does not belong to Negroes alone. It is the yearning of mankind." To the War Resisters League, King added that "no sane person can afford to work for social justice within the nation unless he simultaneously resists war and clearly declares himself for nonviolence in international relations." Through such sermons and addresses, King connected the dots for congregants and listeners who may have held a more limited idea of the meaning of the struggle.

King and other SCLC leaders organized a recruiting meeting at Shaw University on Easter weekend, 1960. There, famously, Ella Baker told the students that they were after more than a hamburger in the sit-in movement. Sit-ins sprang up through the South, most famously in Greensboro, North Carolina, in early February 1960, and then in Nashville. By the end of 1960, thousands of students had sat in at a lunch counter or otherwise demonstrated. At this Easter weekend meeting, originally designed to organize a youth auxiliary wing of the SCLC, Baker urged the students to follow their own path, not that of their elders. Thus was born the Student Nonviolent Coordinating Committee.

The SNCC's original statement had been drafted by James Lawson. Its idealism infused the student civil rights movement and pushed the broader movement forward. The first part of it reads, "Nonviolence, as it grows from the Judeo-Christian tradition, seeks a social order of justice permeated by love.... Through nonviolence, courage displaces fear. Love transcends hate. Acceptance dissipates prejudice; hope ends despair. Faith reconciles doubt. Peace dominates war. Mutual regards cancel enmity. Justice for all overthrows injustice. The redemptive community supersedes immoral social systems." The students enacted King's vision of nonviolent civil disobedience on a mass scale in a way that King and his organizations rarely could themselves pull off in their campaigns. Sometimes in civil rights literature, the SNCC (mostly because of later developments) is portrayed as being more politically conscious and savvy, as seeing nonviolence as a technique in contrast to King's philosophical approach. If anything, it's close to the opposite. The SNCC soon put into action exactly what King had preached about for years, while the SCLC, the organization based on the ideas of nonviolent civil disobedience, often acted in pragmatic ways, utilizing protests strategically to effect change and then withdrawing to turn over the work to locals.

Often, King is portrayed as somehow in conflict with the SNCC and the student movement. At one point, during a tense moment of the Freedom Rides campaign in 1961, violence in Birmingham and Anniston had called a halt to the journey. SNCC and CORE leaders, including Diane Nash and John Lewis, determined that it would continue. King himself demurred from joining. The reason was pragmatic and supported by SCLC leadership: somebody had to be out on the road raising funds that would finance freedom rides and other protests. They were expensive, mostly because of the necessary bail money. King's explanation, however, angered students: "I think I should choose the time and place of my Golgotha," he said, referring to the story of Jesus's crucifixion in the Bible. That was, as students saw it, a pretentiously pious response. It seemed to suggest that King actually was not willing to put his life on the line even as the students were. King's life already had been on the line, for years. But the apparent pomposity suggested the kind of rift that would grow between the SCLC and the SNCC.

To them, King seemed more pragmatically than philosophically committed to nonviolence, more concerned with fundraising than with fomenting a mass movement. Yet King's speeches inspired those who

organized the SNCC, including Ezell Blair and John Lewis, and King himself was an enthusiastic advocate of the student activism. He expressed
that enthusiasm in a letter to a black pastor in Philadelphia who had written him about the student movement: "The students of our generation
have now come of age, and they are manifesting a maturity far beyond
their years. The most significant aspect of this student movement is that
the young people will knock some of the oldsters out of their state of
apathy and complacency." Then, writing of the student movement for
the *Progressive*, he praised the "young veterans," who had given the "first
surge of power to the post civil rights movement," and the students who
had put their bodies on the line in the struggle for school desegregation
in the face of the "moral danger presented by mob resistance." In combining direct action with nonviolence, the students had imparted to the
movement the "extraordinary power and discipline which every thinking
person observes."

Meanwhile, the SCLC was being reorganized under the leadership of a
Virginia pastor and organizer, Wyatt T. Walker, who wanted to install a
kind of military-like discipline into the freewheelingly chaotic organization. Walker was a longtime committed activist, a former member of the
Young Communist League who had in his earlier years listened to radical
speeches in New York's Union Square: "The question nobody wants to
say, or has not said, or doesn't know *how* to say, is that the people around
Dr. King, and Dr. King himself—we were all left-wingers," he later
reflected. In the Deep South, an educator and organizer named Septima
Clark worked in the SCLC's Citizenship project, educating people in the
low country and on the Sea Islands off the coast of Georgia and South
Carolina. In Atlanta, students from all five of Atlanta's black colleges
and universities called attention to broader exclusion from government;
retarding social, economic, and political progress; educational inequalities; and police brutality. Movement leaders issued comprehensive indict-
ments of black political and economic exclusion.

As sit-ins, kneel-ins, pray-ins, and other forms of direct action spread
across the South in 1960, King and the SCLC sought to capitalize on that
energy and momentum. They directed a campaign in King's home town
and new residence of Atlanta, allegedly a city "too busy to hate," to
target. In October 1960, King and over fifty others were taken to jail for
"trespassing" at Rich's department store in downtown Atlanta. King felt
called to join students in the growing sit-in movement, which had come
to Atlanta. King was still under probation for his earlier traffic violation
(something that only had come to his attention a few days before). Despite
having a skillful legal team and character witnesses such as Morehouse
president Benjamin Mays, the DeKalb county judge sentenced him to four
months. That time would be served in a prison far away from Atlanta, at

Reidsville, in a notoriously violent county. He was taken from the Atlanta jail at four in the morning and transported as just another common criminal. "They had me chained all the way down," he remembered. Stanley Levison remembers that on another occasion King had told him, "Solitary was the hardest thing for him. When he was cut off from people, he really went into a depression . . . when he was cut off . . . he worried . . . he brooded, he felt bewildered. He told me one time that he broke down completely in solitary."

In that Georgia case, King suffered emotionally while in the dingy jail, far from friends and family. He later spoke of the dread that overcame him while there, despite the brave letters he wrote to Coretta. Andrew Young later remembered that King responded badly to imprisonment, becoming short-tempered and difficult to be around. That certainly would have made sense in this case in particular, stuck in this brutal and remote part of rural Georgia, in a cell barely fit for habitation.

News of King's harsh sentence in Atlanta spread nationally; Mayor Hartsfield of Atlanta tried to dissociate himself from it, insisting it was a stupid decision that came from the DeKalb county court and not from the city. When word reached Harris Wofford, an aide to presidential candidate Kennedy and later a close associate and advisor to King, those in Kennedy's circle convinced him to make a phone call to Coretta Scott King to express his concern. Kennedy suggested he would do what he could to spring King from his unjust imprisonment. Robert Kennedy, John's brother and soon-to-be attorney general, subsequently phoned the governor of Georgia and the judge, who agreed to release him. The reason had nothing to do with the gross injustice of the case but instead with this particular segregationist judge's political ambitions. The backroom political sausage-making just so happened to fall in King's favor this time. The judge, a diehard segregationist but also an aspirant for a federal judgeship, agreed to release him on a $2,000 bail bond—this for a supposed traffic offense. Kennedy's opponent Richard Nixon remained quiet; some of his aides drafted letters and telegrams of support for him to sign, but other aides squelched the effort, and Nixon publicly said nothing. King was furious, calling Nixon a "moral coward." Nixon had solicited his advice, but when the real moment of truth came, "it was like he had never heard of me."

"Daddy" King threw his support to Kennedy, and Kennedy's aides capitalized on the political triumph by blanketing black churches with flyers. "I've got all my votes, and I've got a suitcase, and I'm going to take them up there and dump them in his [Kennedy's] lap," Daddy King reportedly said. And he did. Northern black voters mobilized as well. Kennedy won the election—barely. He emerged victorious for a number of reasons. The last-minute swing of the mostly northern black vote surely was one of them (ironically, white Democratic votes that helped him hold most of the solid South was another). Martin Luther King Jr. was now, both by intention and by accident, a force in national politics. More to the point, he determined to leverage the movement and the key role of black voters in the election to compel Kennedy to act more forcefully on civil rights, to fulfill the promises he had made in the campaign.

The entire episode taught King a lesson in how to combine the moral force of nonviolent civil disobedience with the cold-eyed strategy involved in accomplishing the objectives of the movement. During the next years of campaigns throughout the South, he sought to combine the two. He remained philosophically committed to nonviolence and demonstrations against injustice, but he learned it was just as important to know when to stop or to turn around and retreat. For that, he took a lot of heat from younger colleagues in the movement, but it was a strategy that worked effectively in a couple of the crucial campaigns. King never retreated on using moral ends to achieve moral means, but he also understood the role that moral means played in intervening at the key pressure points in a political process that involved deal-making and scratching each other's backs. His balance between idealism and *realpolitik* worked well for a time, as did his alliances with Kennedy-era white liberals. Later in the 1960s, those alliances failed or turned against him. Over time, his idealism moved him in directions that those invested in political calculations simply could not understand.

Speaking at Spelman College, King further articulated the ideals of the movement going into the 1960s. African Americans were not just struggling to free themselves but also "struggling to save the soul of America. We are struggling to save America in this very important decisive hour of her history." The students, with their determination and moral crusade, had taken up the "deep groans of the century," the "passionate longings of the ages and filtered them in their own souls and fashioned a creative protest. It is one of the glowing epics of the time and I predict that it will win . . . because this demand is a basic American demand." King and civil rights leaders put forward their demands for joint platform proposals for Democratic Party platform of 1960: "We demand that this convention and its candidates take a clear moral stand against colonialism and racism of all kinds, everywhere, and especially in Africa where apartheid has led to the massacre of hundreds of people seeking only to live in freedom and in their own land." That proposal had no chance of making it through the Dixiecrat-influenced platform committee, but it suggested the clarity of the internationalist vision of the movement.

Fresh from his jail time and its impact on the presidential election, King debated the segregationist thought leader James J. Kilpatrick on television in November 1960. The fact that Kilpatrick, a firm believer in the superiority of white civilization, appeared so often on television as a "voice" in the "debates," and how he remade himself into just another "conservative," suggests how much racism was deeply normalized in the media environment. King was not at his sharpest in this episode. Kilpatrick himself had been one of the theorists of "interposition"—that is, a state interposing itself between its citizens and the federal government, which King wrote about contemptuously for years, culminating in a memorable passage in "Letter from a Birmingham Jail."

King's performance disappointed some observers. They wrote to give him advice on parrying Kilpatrick's skeptical questioning. Kilpatrick's most effective thrusts were those challenging King's right to decide which laws to obey (or not), based on his own sense of morality. But before getting there, Kilpatrick put his white supremacist views front and center: "We believe it is an affirmatively good thing to preserve the predominant racial characteristics that have contributed to Western civilization over the past two thousand years, and we do not believe that the way to preserve them lies in fostering any intimate race mixing by which these principles and characteristics inevitably must be destroyed." He believed in public policies promoting racial segregation to forestall a "breakdown, especially among young people, of those ethnic lines that seem to us important." Like most segregationists, behind Kilpatrick's alleged philosophical or political positions lay a visceral horror of interracial sex, the violation of blood lines that would forever contaminate his vision of a treasured "western civilization."

King replied with his usual lines about looking at whether laws were moral. He needed a better answer. Suggestions poured in, including an incisive one from a University of Wisconsin student that King quickly adapted into his addresses. King developed those thoughts further for an NAACP rally in Los Angeles. States have rights, he argued, but not the right to defy federal law. Georgia politicians were threatening to close schools rather than integrate them (as had been done in Virginia), and in those cases "the national government has a moral and practical responsibility to *federalize* the schools" and ensure equal education.

King and the movement sought to tie the freedom struggle to the cause of labor. The SCLC's labor strategy in the early 1960s involved emphasizing the common needs of black and white workers, seeking support from organized labor in exchange for promises of a mobilized black electorate. King also hoped to catalyze a growing liberal energy that would come with the new administration. Speaking to the AFL-CIO in 1961, he noted that, whether it involved right-wing Birchers or the military-industrial complex, or an alliance of Dixiecrats and northern reactionaries, "these menaces now threaten everything decent and fair in American life. As we struggle to make racial and economic justice a reality, let us maintain faith in the future. At times we confront difficult and frustrating moments in the struggle to make justice a reality, but we must believe somehow that these problems can be solved."

As with most civil rights leaders of the time, King had been disappointed in the weaknesses of previous civil rights legislation. He had been disappointed because so much was omitted and did not address the issue of integration or voter registration or included provisions that were easily circumvented or thwarted. Ultimately the federal government "should set forth a uniform pattern of registration and voting, so that no citizen will have a problem at this point," he said. Likewise, along with many others in the movement, Kennedy disappointed King in failing to issue the kinds of executive orders that presidents had the authority to proclaim (including banning segregation in interstate travel and federally subsidized housing). Kennedy had said he could do so at the stroke of a pen, but as CORE activist James Farmer sarcastically noted, apparently that pen had run dry. For such reasons, in 1962 King published a scathing essay, "Fumbling on the New Frontier," blasting the relative inaction of the Kennedy administration.

King also continued to adjudicate conflicts between the NAACP and the SCLC (and later between the SCLC and the SNCC). He carried on a correspondence with baseball hero Jackie Robinson, who had broken the color line of America's game in 1947 for the Brooklyn Dodgers. Robinson remained active in Republican politics and in the NAACP and was concerned about some harsh words he had heard from SCLC activists toward the NAACP. King responded that if anyone in the SCLC spoke harshly about the NAACP, that represented only a personal view. More important, as he put, he agreed with Robinson that "we cannot afford any division at this time and we cannot afford any conflict. . . . I have no Messiah complex, and I know that we need many leaders to do the job."

King took the public stance of denying any disunity between the organizations. That was simply not true, but he felt he had no choice. Saying otherwise would feed the enemy. King wrote off the apparent public discord as understandable difference over tactics, not over ultimate aims. He acknowledged that some thought him not militant enough and that there could be some difference over the means to achieve the ends of the movement. King privately had written of the importance of projecting a sense of unity within the movement, which is why he sometimes would not respond to NAACP-inspired allegations against the SCLC. But in this public address at Cornell, it was all about uniformity and the way his religious background had brought him to his philosophy: "The whole spirit of nonviolence came to me from Jesus of Nazareth. Its central idea is that you counteract an unjust system through direct action and love your opponents at the same time. You implement the philosophy through sit-ins and boycotts. You hope to be able to bring an end to your opponent's self-defeating massacre and that he will change his attitude."

Just how to implement that philosophy was never easily determined. King faced one of his greatest challenges, and learned some of his hardest lessons, in the small city of Albany, Georgia. There young SNCC organizers Charles Sherrod (a seminary student involved with a group called Student Interracial Ministry) and Cordell Reagon sought to organize ordinary black folk of this southwest Georgia town in the heart of the most viciously racist part of the state. They started with broad goals, to attack segregation at every level, a decided change from the limited and circumscribed goals with which other campaigns began. Protest marches and sit-ins began late in 1961, and a local Baptist minister, Reverend William Anderson, invited King to come and rally the nonviolent troops.

King had no intention of staying or making this a campaign, but after his speech on December 15, 1961, to a crowd roused by spirited singing of freedom songs, he felt he had to stay. King and Ralph Abernathy were arrested for parading without a permit and briefly jailed. Police chief Laurie Pritchett could see what was coming and wanted no part of it. King and Abernathy were released from jail, on the presumed deal that the city would follow the ICC (Interstate Commerce Commission) order to desegregate places of public transportation and that hundreds of people jailed in the initial protest would be released on bail.

King believed Pritchett to be a decent man at heart, but one unable to actually honor the so-called agreement that had been made. City officials refused to implement it, and protests continued. King returned in July 1962 to appear in court and serve his time for the original offense. Given the choice of paying a fine of $178 or serving a month and a half in jail, King and his associates chose the latter. He announced, "We chose to serve our time because we feel so deeply about the plight of more than 700 others who have yet to be tried. . . . We have experienced the racist tactics of attempting to bankrupt the movement in the South through excessive bail and extended court fights. The time has now come when we must practice civil disobedience in a true sense or delay our freedom thrust for long years." But the time had not come. Pritchett concocted a fiction about how a "well-dressed black man" had bailed them out, a distraction hiding the maneuverings of city officials to sap the movement's moral energies. King and the movement also faced internal divisions; SNCC members resented that King had shown up to capitalize on the hard work of local protest organizers, who sought to have local people make their own decisions. Wyatt T. Walker of the SCLC, meanwhile, said that the SNCC had gotten in "over its head."

In short, in Albany the divisions between "mobilizing" (King's strategy of dramatizing segregation through massive and short-lived demonstrations) and "organizing" (the SNCC's faith that the patient organizing of local people would allow them better to control their own destiny, without needing "leaders" created by press coverage to fly in as saving heroes) became clear and sometimes bitter. Finally, King withdrew from Albany in late summer 1962, achieving none of the original objectives. The local movement continued, but without the press coverage that had followed the entrance of King. "Our protest was so vague we got nothing," he later said in reflecting on the apparent failure of the Albany campaign. Meanwhile, Laurie Pritchett emerged as the kind of local police official best avoided, as he know both how to defuse protest sentiment and how to outsource the brutal repression of ordinary black folk and everyday protesters to far-away jails. There, they could be treated with customary brutality without fearing the coverage of the cameras.

The national press treated Albany as a defeat—a justifiable (if oversimplified) postmortem. Before Birmingham, Emory Jackson, an editor of a black newspaper, wondered whether King's oratory was just that—words without action. Another wondered whether King "has been losing since he left Montgomery. . . . And I think eventually that more Negroes and more white Americans will become disillusioned with him and find that he after all is only another preacher who can talk well." King looked for a more effective place to stage a campaign of mass nonviolent civil disobedience. He understood more that specific objectives would have to be defined, and a place with police officials reliably inept in the arts of media management would have to be found. This was Birmingham—"Bombingham"—Alabama.

Reverend Fred Shuttlesworth persuaded King to stage a major campaign in that brutally racist working-class town. Electrified by the *Brown* decision and his sense of God's hand moving in history, Shuttlesworth's civil rights career blossomed in the 1950s. He felt divinely inspired to defy a response to the banning of the NAACP in Alabama imposed by the state authorities. Resisting more senior ministers who urged moderation, Shuttlesworth and his followers organized the Alabama Christian Movement for Human Rights (ACMHR), effectively carrying on the work of the NAACP under a different name. Repeated attempts on his life only enhanced his personal authority and charisma.

Birmingham proved an inspired choice, and the lessons learned from Albany informed the movement's campaign there. Even so, the successes there were a very close call and depended on some lucky breaks as well as audacious choices made along the way. The campaign starting around Easter 1963 got off to a slow start, with a disappointing turnout of those willing to go to jail. Eventually King determined he would do so himself, while the SCLC's organizers, partly in desperation, drew up a plan to enlist young local black schoolchildren in the movement. That strategy worked, in the short run, to near perfection, as students left school to attend demonstrations and were set upon by the infamous dogs and fire hoses. Sometimes that happened not to protesters but to bystanders or simply those who were curious, drawing unexpected numbers to fulfill the SCLC's strategy of filling the jails and attracting international media attention. As Jonathan Rieder puts it, the movement in Birmingham enacted the themes enunciated by King in his sermons: "the need for the oppressed to free themselves; the morality of breaking unjust laws like the injunction and segregation statutes; the urgency of rejecting patience; the sacredness of sacrifice; and the exceptional spirit of black people contained in the Letter's avowal."

Besides the "dream" speech, King's best-known public document, "Letter from a Birmingham Jail," arose directly from the Birmingham campaign. Like much else that spring and summer, King's letter came out of a series of circumstances both masterfully created and almost divinely fortuitous. The actual drafting of the letter itself bears some, but only some, relationship to the mythology that quickly grew up around (and was deliberately fostered and promoted about) it. King supposedly began scratching it out on some matchbook covers while in jail, and he later managed to smuggle some papers in and out. That part is true, but it bears mentioning as well how much King drew from a ready well of his addresses that he had given for years, often enunciating the precise themes of the "Letter," and how much King's editing and ghostwriting team assisted in the production. The triumphant result of the letter, as well as of the campaign, depended on a fragile but essential combination of intuitive genius, incredible personal commitment and bravery, religious faith, and carefully orchestrated media manipulation to produce the desired effect.

The letter was addressed to seven white clergyman and one rabbi in Birmingham. They had produced earlier that year the "Good Friday Statement," a plea for working out local conflicts without public disorder or demonstrations. Their public letter reflected a common sentiment of the times that the problems in Birmingham could be managed through goodwill and negotiations. "We agree rather with certain local negro leadership which has called for honest and open negotiations of racial issues in our area," they said. Demonstrations were "unwise and untimely." And indeed, local black businessmen had advocated for the same.

Martin Luther King seized the opportunity of his arrest during the Birmingham campaign to cast himself as Paul in prison, writing a letter to American Christians. It was a brilliant ploy, one he had contemplated for some time. He already had preached sermons using this biblical rhetorical device. The local authorities in Birmingham played perfectly into his hands.

Ironically, about six years earlier, King himself had expressed hope that moderate white southern leadership, exactly of the kind represented by the eight signatories to the Good Friday statement, could lead the South to a better day. Over the next years, he came to feel differently, and later in 1963 the tragic bombing of the Sixteenth Street Baptist Church in Birmingham suggested the depths to which southern segregationism still depended on the exercise of violence and brutality. Many of the eight signatories themselves knew that; some of them had been victims of the kinds of late-night harassing telephone calls and threats of personal harm that also dogged civil rights leaders. Still, they kept to the hope that King had expressed in earlier years, unable yet to make the leap of recognition that King himself had made and subsequently explained in his letter.

King's masterpiece moved from hope to anger, from a seemingly friendly opening to prophetic wrath. Along the way, it devastated, one by one, the arguments put up by good white people against King's philosophy. Likewise, the Birmingham campaign showed the wisdom contained in King's letter, summarized aptly here by Jonathan Rieder: "The limits of moral appeal by itself to secure deliverance; the selfish immorality of privileged groups; the need for blacks to rely on themselves, even as they welcomed the aid of friend, and the power of spectacle to galvanize the state to act on behalf of the suffering." The letter's marriage of religious imagery with political protest, of invocations of American civil religion together with chastisement of American hypocrisy, of heart-rending stories of the questions King's own children asked him together with lethal rhetorical questions aimed at those who kept urging blacks to "wait," all worked as a perfectly constructed symphony, each movement serving its purpose to reach the conclusion.

King also knew the effect the campaign could have on critical national negotiations on the civil rights bill. During the Birmingham crusade, he suggested again the necessity of struggle. The rights won thus far would not have been granted "without your presenting your bodies and your very lives before the dogs and the tanks and the water hoses of this city." Kennedy, he said, was battling for hearts and minds of Africans and Asians, and they "won't respect the United States if it takes away basic rights of people. Mr. Kennedy *knows* that." By the end, King felt that he was on the verge of a "significant breakthrough," with the greatest weapon being one of taking mass demonstrations national. He and his aides publicly discussed the possibility of a huge interracial march on Washington. In his publication from that time *Why We Can't Wait*, he noted that Birmingham had been one step to equality, not a miracle but one step of inspirational progress. The segregationists would fight on, the political struggles continued, and yet these only served to dramatize that segregation already was on its deathbed. "The only imponderable," King reflected, "is the question of how costly they will make the funeral."

As the Birmingham crusade wound down, King sought to keep up the pressure; he sensed he had the administration on the ropes in terms of having to produce something legislatively substantive for civil rights. The March on Washington was designed precisely for that purpose. It had long been the dream of venerated black labor organizer A. Philip Randolph, who had threatened something similar in the summer of 1941. That pressure had compelled Franklin Delano Roosevelt to sign Executive Order 8802, banning discrimination in hiring in the defense industries. Organizers of the 1963 march had something even bigger mind: a march for jobs and justice, combining King's emphasis on nonviolence and the move toward economic justice as fundamental.

That part of the march is no longer well known. Neither is the fact that at the march were 150 FBI agents, watching every move of the organizers, with a microphone on the podium rigged to be turned off remotely if a speaker got too radical. King's FBI surveillance increased after the march, with agents high up in the force calling King "demagogic" and "the most dangerous . . . to the Nation . . . from the standpoint . . . of national security." What seemed a moment of national triumph was, for federal investigators, a signal to double down on their efforts to destroy King and undermine the movement.

What remains in public memory is "I Have a Dream," the capstone, in public coverage of King's addresses, a soaring oration to the 250,000 gathered that day. Later, Coretta King remembered the triumphant day of the march: "At that moment it seemed as if the Kingdom of God appeared. But it only lasted for a moment." But discussions of the speech often ignore the bulk of the address, which was precisely focused on economic issues. Much of the speech portrays blacks occupying a "lonely island of poverty in the midst of a vast ocean of material prosperity." One hundred years after emancipation, the black American "is still languished in the corners of American society and finds himself in exile in his own land." The American founders had signed a "promissory note" for all Americans, but America had defaulted on it, had given black Americans a "bad check. . . . And so we've come to cash this check, a check that will give us upon demand the riches of freedom and the security of justice." The colorblind interpretation normally given to King's address ignores King's statements in favor of compensatory mechanisms to redress centuries of white exploitation and that it was part of a larger utopian vision. King depicted 1963 as "not an end, but a beginning," with blacks no longer content to return to "business as usual." There would be no return to the "tranquilizing drug of gradualism."

The time to judge men simply on character will be, King implies, on the day foretold by Isaiah, when there would be an apocalyptic leveling of all creation before God. Until then, the realities of where people were positioned in society would be paramount. Then, with some urging from gospel singer Mahalia Jackson, who had performed prior to his address, he concluded with the famous passages about the dream, a theme he had worked over for years in his addresses. Sources for "the dream" are legion, including everything from Archibald Carey's address at the 1952 Republican convention to King's talk at a high school in North Carolina in 1962 to the invocation of "I have a dream" by SNCC activist Prathia Hall in September 1962, commemorating the burning of a church in Terrell County, Georgia (just after the winding down of the SCLC's part of the Albany campaign). Hall's address moved King, and perhaps pushed the image to the front of his mind, but it was a rhetorical device that had long since been a part of his repertoire.

The march affirmed economic demands going beyond the Kennedy civil rights bill. Movement organizers wanted to extend promises to combat employment discrimination, unemployment, and disfranchisement. The speech also articulated one of King's major emphases through the 1960s—the need for compensatory mechanisms to address the historic injustices faced by African Americans. Still, at the end of the day, it was the dream that was remembered; the measures advocated to achieve that dream quickly were forgotten. In subsequent years, King himself recognized this and acknowledged the truth of Malcolm X's criticism that the dream was for many black Americans a daily nightmare. Meanwhile, FBI officials viewed King's address as "demagogic." They set their sights on him more intently.

Ironically, the capstone speech of King's career, the one cited and quoted out of context in yearly King celebrations, was followed by one of King's tersest statements of the requirements for achieving racial justice. It had nothing do with symphonies of brotherhood or the content of one's character but with the original theme of the march: jobs, justice, and the ballot. Brutality came not just from the actions of the George Wallaces or Bull Connors of the world; ultimately history would sweep them away. Meanwhile, "unemployment is a form of brutality, especially violence for those who live on the edge of poverty."

The exaltation of the March on Washington in August 1963 was followed by the bombing of the Sixteenth Street Baptist Church in Birmingham less than a month later. The bombings, moreover, were followed by an evening of police brutality in restive black neighborhoods of Birmingham, with one person shot dead and a teenager injured by the police. For his part, Bull Connor suggested the bombing had been some kind of inside job perpetrated by the movement to make whites look bad—what we would now refer to as the false flag insinuation.

King's dream of democracy and justice contrasts painfully with the last march on Washington: the one on January 6, 2021. On that day, a mob intent on overthrowing a free and fair election recorded on cellphones their dark vision of political strongman authoritarianism and racially targeted disfranchisement achieved through force. And yet King would not have been surprised; he knew full well the potential of this sort of fascism to rise—King's intellectual mentor Howard Thurman, after all, had written in 1946 an essay on "The Fascist Masquerade," ruminating on precisely this subject. And King often deployed the language of fascism to describe the political machinations of his most virulent white supremacist opponents.

King continued to develop and disseminate his ideas of nonviolence set within the context of justice. As he explained in the *Saturday Evening Post* in 1964, nonviolence as a philosophy and practice had been created precisely within the black freedom struggle in America, but now white leaders had developed a distorted understanding of its practice and theory: "They failed to perceive that nonviolence can exist only in a context of justice. When the white power structure calls upon the Negro to reject violence but does not impose upon itself the task of creating necessary social change, it is in fact asking for submission to injustice. Nothing in the theory of nonviolence counsels this suicidal course. . . . It is the effort of the power structure to benefit from nonviolence without yielding meaningful change that is responsible for the rise of elements who would discredit it." The answer was a "grand alliance of Negro and white," with the objective of addressing social evils that afflicted both groups. But it had its subtle and hidden forms, and it existed in three areas: employment discrimination, housing discrimination, and de facto segregation in the public schools. De facto segregation was a bad as segregation by law— even worse, as it was harder to highlight and legislate out of existence.

Not long after the March on Washington, King's address "The Negro and the American Dream," given to the North Carolina NAACP, suggested much about his developing historical narrative. "Ever since the founding fathers of our nation dreamed this dream, America has manifested a schizophrenic personality," he said. It was torn between a "self" of democracy and an opposite self, its antithesis: "Slavery and segregation have been strange paradoxes in a nation founded on the principle that all men are created equal." It was the paradox that historians were in the process of exploring; like them, King arrived at the conclusion that the "paradox" was explicable when seeing that freedom for whites was defined precisely as the lack of freedom for others. Freedom and slavery were locked in an embrace, one depending on the other. The key to realizing the dream of liberty and equality was to unlock that embrace, to free whites from seeing their freedom as dependent on the degradation of others.

This was a theme that had interested King since his teenage years. In one interview, King remembered his high school competition where he gave one of his inaugural public addresses on "The Negro and the Constitution," as well as the anger that consumed him when ordered to give up his seat and he and his friends being called "black sons of bitches." "That night will never leave my memory. It was the angriest I have ever been in my life." King reflected on some mistakes the movement had made, including in Albany, where, as he put it, "the mistake I made there was to protest against segregation generally rather than against a single and distinct facet of it," making that movement so vague that the energy fueling it dissipated. Since then, as he put it, "we have never since scattered our efforts in a general attack on segregation, but have focused upon specific, symbolic objectives." Moreover, he now recognized his mistake in thinking that the moral conscience of the white South would rise: "I felt that white ministers would take our cause to the white power structures. I ended up, of course, chastened and disillusioned. As our movement unfolded, and direct appeals were made to white ministers, most folded their hands—and some even took stands *against* us." As southern blacks rose to protest their conditions, white churchmen mostly offered only "pious irrelevancies and sanctimonious trivialities," claiming that gospel was not concerned with "social issues." King said he himself was not concerned about losing his faith but, instead, about the fact that he met "young people of all races whose disenchantment with the church has soured into outright disgust."

King referred to himself as "militantly nonviolent," suggesting that strong leaders had to be as much militant as moderate, as much realists as idealists, able to use nonviolence as both a "powerful" and a "just" weapon. Nonviolence empowered individuals to be someone bigger than themselves, to be free people. It was a "weapon fabricated of love," one that did not create tensions but surfaced tensions that already existed.

King held the white establishment "as responsible as anyone" for riots tearing apart cities in the 1960s, precisely because they had ignored the conditions that caused the riots in the first place: "The deep frustration, the seething desperation of the Negro today is a product of slum housing, chronic poverty, woefully inadequate education and substandard schools. The Negro is trapped in a long and desolate corridor with no exit sign, caught in a vicious socioeconomic vise." The legislative answer was clear, and there were "ample precedents" for it—the GI Bill of Rights, for example, a set of programs costing in fact far more than a policy of "preferential treatment" (an early term for affirmative action) to "rehabilitate the traditionally disadvantaged Negro." King advocated for a national full employment program (one that would address the automation of unemployment that hit white and black workers alike) and housing policies that would address systemic inequalities built into America's segregated housing markets, once enforced by law and now enforced by the practices of the real estate industry.

King's reflections on the 1964 election signaled his acutely perceptive reading of the national political climate. During the election, Barry Goldwater had opposed the 1964 Civil Rights Act, arguing on allegedly nonracist grounds that it extended federal authority further than the Constitution permitted. King would have none of that. Until his defeat at the hands of Lyndon Baines Johnson, King reflected, "Goldwater was the most dangerous man in America. He talked soft and nice, but he gave aid and comfort to the most vicious racists and the most extreme rightists in America. He gave respectability to views totally alien to the democratic process." As for another contender for the presidency (one who would make his impact felt most in 1968), George Wallace of Alabama, King saw him as symbolic of "many of the evils that were alive in Hitler's Germany. He is a merchant of racism, peddling hate under the guise of states' rights." Intriguingly, King speculated that perhaps Wallace did not really believe in the poison that he peddled, but "he is artful enough to convince others that he does." (He certainly convinced one drifter named James Earl Ray, King's future assassin and an admirer of Wallace's.) Referring to the Supreme Court decision banning mandatory school prayer (a decision that King approved, reasoning that the state had no business dictating a prayer of any kind), King felt assured that he was right in his view when he saw George Wallace travel to Washington to testify against the Supreme Court dictate.

By that time, King could claim as a triumph the Civil Rights Act of 1964, a legislative act that fundamentally remade American society and opened countless doors of economic opportunity. King and the movement had popularized many of the major ideas contained in the original bill. A late addition to the bill, forbidding discrimination against women, was supposed to be a "poison pill" that would kill the act and prevent its passage; it did not work. As it turned out, its enactment was even more revolutionary than King might have anticipated, since it provided the fundamental foundation for legal feminism, the work that Ruth Bader Ginsburg carried on in the 1970s and 1980s. The movement that had come from so many places, organizations, and people, the movement that had propelled King to the center stage of American life, had claimed one of its greatest accomplishments, one unthinkable just a few years before.

King's triumphs always came at a personal cost. "I often feel that I am forever *giving*," he told an interviewer, "never pausing to take in. I feel urgently the need for even an hour of time to get away, to withdraw, to refuel. I need more time to think through what is being done, to take time out from the mechanics of the movement, to reflect on the *meaning* of the movement." King would have no such time in the subsequent few short years of his life. The personal costs of his devotion to movement causes proved enormous. The movement had indeed "swallowed" him, as Howard Thurman warned in 1958.

The maelstrom that seemed always to engulf him was reflected in his drinking, smoking a pack a day, and bouts of depression and exhaustion. His continued liaisons with women, practically an addiction of its own, seemed to have stemmed from this. Or maybe King explained it best when he told his friends (tape-recorded by FBI surveillance), "fucking's a form of anxiety reduction." King's self-justificatory explanation in part represented the sexism of the era. It also married his tendency to bandy psychological terms freely with his own self-analysis of someone who struggled with a deep anger that surfaced as depression and with the crude street language that his SCLC colleagues and he freely deployed in private. Eventually, as biographer Peter Ling has written, the chaos and nonstop activity of his public life "seemed to deepen his need for sexual encounters to such an extent that he was prepared to jeopardize everything he loved for the pleasure and solace they offered."

The most important point for the historian is less the details of his sex life and more the mere fact that so much is known about it. And that is only because of this obsessive stalking by government agents. The bitter irony was that the same government King had to rely on to accomplish his legislative and political aims was the government that sought to undermine him. J. Edgar Hoover's prurient style of Presbyterianism, his self-image as an upright defender of "Christian Renewal" against "Soviet Rule," turned him from a spiritual Cold Warrior to a domestic stalker.

As historian David Garrow first uncovered through his research in the 1980s, Edgar Hoover and the FBI began its spying on King in the 1950s, often in cooperation with local and state authorities. At one point, King stayed at the home of a friend, Clarence Jones, in New York and while there spoke with his advisor and friend Stanley Levison on the phone. Levison earlier had been in some contact with communist-affiliated organizations; this caught the FBI's attention immediately. The bureau tricked Jones's wife into "replacing" some phone lines going into her house.

From there, the surveillance tightened. The FBI at first was determined to find evidence of King's supposed communism. That proved to be difficult, especially since King often explained clearly and plainly in his speeches the precise problems he found with communism—its denial of God and freedom and its relationship with totalitarian political societies. Hoover's first lieutenant, devout Catholic William Sullivan, thoroughly investigated the matter from 1962 to 1964, concluding finally that communism had no influence at all in the civil rights movement. That was the wrong answer, as far as Hoover was concerned. Imbued with a spirit of Cold War Presbyterianism that saw the civil rights movement as a threat to western Christian civilization, Hoover decreed otherwise, and Sullivan obeyed. The combination of Hoover's rigid anti-communism and his obsession with the sexuality of black men simply dictated the facts of the case for him, regardless of the evidence.

While bugging King mostly so they could track Stanley Levison and other suspicious advisors, government agents discovered evidence of King's private sexual affairs. From there, Hoover became King's most avidly prurient stalker. He saw this as an opportunity to destroy the moral credibility of a moral leader. Hoover's obedient servant Sullivan wrote to his boss that "it's clear that Martin Luther King is the most dangerous Negro in America, and we must use every resource at our disposal to destroy him."

On December 1, 1964, just as King was about to receive the Nobel Prize, King and Hoover met, in Hoover's palatial office. King tried to assure the self-righteously driven director that he was no threat to American national security; Hoover, for his part, delivered a long monologue to King about the crucial nature of FBI work; had not the FBI infiltrated the Klan, after all? Filmed while leaving, King gingerly offered some unconvincing diplomatic platitudes about having a constructive exchange. But while they were meeting, an FBI associate in an adjoining room was offering "dirt" on King to an awaiting newsman, and Hoover only two weeks before had called King the "most notorious liar in America."

While King received the Nobel Peace Prize, Hoover's deputy William Sullivan had a tape mailed from Miami to Coretta King. The package came under the pseudonym of a supposed fellow black Baptist minister, bearing a tape of Martin (presumably) with other women and a note addressed directly to the civil rights leader: "You are done. There is but one way out for you. You better take it before your filthy abnormal fraudulent self is bared to the nation." Coretta waved it off, but King's paranoia about being discovered haunted him over the next few years.

Hoover's men, writes historian Lerone Martin in his astonishing study of the FBI's deployment of ministers in its various campaigns of internal security, "pursued their campaign against King as a cosmic struggle of dueling faiths: A Christian republic defending itself against the virus of King's godless religion of social revolution." The sex tapes, it turns out, were not the main show. Instead, they were incidental to Hoover's larger enterprise of thwarting King's intended American revolution. They were useful to Hoover primarily for combatting a radicalism that he perceived to be undermining America.

As King once said in a sermon, "Each of us is two selves," and the burden was to keep "higher self in command." That pressure proved unbearable for King; it cost him, dearly, physically and psychologically. King's extramarital sexual life also deepened the guilt he suffered, perhaps (so speculates biographer David Garrow) throwing him back into that very chaos from which he sought solace. If so, it was a vicious circle that could have destroyed him (and, at times, nearly did). As scholar and minister Michael Eric Dyson puts it, the sexist culture in which King had been raised, and from which he never escaped, meant that when he most needed it, he missed the "intimacy that might have been replenished had he torn loose from his punishing presumptions about women." King was very much a man of his times in relation to women in spite of transcending his own era in so many ways. He saw clearly what he called the triple evils of his era; he never fully saw or understood the culture of sexism that had so profoundly shaped him.

King reached the peak of his career in 1963 and 1964. The capstone, for King, was being awarded the Nobel Prize in late 1964. He accepted the award with misgivings, as he represented a "movement which has not won the very peace and brotherhood which is the essence of the Nobel Prize," but he accepted it as a "profound recognition that nonviolence is the answer to the crucial political and moral question of our time—the need for man to overcome oppression and violence without resorting to violence and oppression." Eventually, such a method would have to extend beyond blacks in America or the Gandhian campaign earlier in India: "Man must evolve for all human conflict a method which rejects revenge, aggression, and retaliation. The foundation of such a method is love." King projected his vision "that unarmed truth and unconditional love will have the final word in reality. . . . I believe that wounded justice, lying prostrate on the blood-flowing streets of our nations, can be lifted from this dust of shame to reign supreme among the children of men."

Of the Nobel trip, King said, "I am a minister of the gospel, not a political leader." But he was both. King had not yet reached the point of alienation from national political figures (Johnson in particular) that he would soon face as he turned against the Vietnam War. He still felt that Johnson would remain a strong force for civil rights and that, although the "concept of [white] supremacy is so imbedded in the white society," there was still a prospect of a "thoroughly integrated society." King concluded on how he subjected himself to frequent self-questioning and soul searching, to test whether he was "maintaining my sense of purpose" and holding to his ideas. But still he felt called to accept the task of helping to make this nation and this world a place where justice would flow forth like mighty waters. King's alliance with liberalism had yielded substantive benefits.

He also knew what its limitations were. As his vision grew larger and more radically questioning of the basic precepts of American civil religion, his opposition, internal and external, grew stronger.

6

✝

Struggling in Selma and Chicago

I still have a dream that one day all of God's children will have food and clothing and material well-being for their bodies, culture and education for their minds, and freedom for their spirits.

—Martin Luther King Jr., sermon at Ebenezer Baptist Church,
July 4, 1965

Public accommodations did not cost the nation anything; the right to vote did not cost the nation anything. Now we are grappling with basic class issues between the privileged and the underprivileged.

—Martin Luther King Jr., speech at Howard University,
November 6, 1966

King's triumphs in 1964 were all the more astonishing for how unexpected they were and how much turmoil they came from. The pace of events was relentless. The seeming triumph of the March on Washington had been followed less than a month later by the deaths in Birmingham, and two months later by the assassination of John F. Kennedy. The swirl of events would not stop spinning. And even the triumph of the March on Washington did not have the effect intended, as the Civil Rights Bill stalled in Congress. Kennedy had seemed more interested in advancing the cause of civil rights in the summer of 1963, when he had given an eloquent national address. But that same night, June 12, 1963, NAACP leader Medgar Evers was gunned down by a Mississippi white supremacist assassin. Meanwhile, the Kennedys authorized J. Edgar Hoover's investigation of King's associates and the taping of King's strategy conversations with movement leaders and his private liaisons with women—as did Lyndon Johnson, John F. Kennedy's successor.

Following the March on Washington and the deaths of four children in Birmingham, the SCLC set itself again on a course of finding a campaign to dramatize injustice. Other civil rights groups brought their own ideas, such as the SNCC's campaign in Mississippi during Freedom Summer. King knew that the Civil Rights Bill, for all its accomplishments, had not addressed the problem of political power or the right to vote for many disfranchised African Americans.

By the end of 1965, King was moving on from social gospel liberalism to larger visions of social transformation. He saw the wisdom of what Ella Baker had said in 1960: the struggle was about more than a hamburger. In some sense, that always had been his philosophy. Now, he was willing to put it out in the open. Martin Luther King Jr. once described Norman Thomas, the long-time American socialist, as the "Bravest Man I Ever Met," the title of his article about Thomas in 1965. King recounted how Thomas had worked for peace and racial equality of all the world's minorities and for social justice everywhere, including the Soviet Union. He mentioned Thomas's activism when Thomas had discovered discrimination in the WPA (Works Progress Administration). He had heard southern whites saying they were content with less pay provided they were paid more than blacks, a classic example of the wages of whiteness. King was moving in Thomas's direction.

And he placed the struggle in an internationalist light. In a sermon he gave to his Atlanta congregation in 1965, King spoke on Jawaharlal Nehru, Gandhi's successor and first prime minister of an independent India. The genius of imperialism historically, King said, was to delude people into thinking it was civilizing savages while it exploited real human beings: "*Satyagraha* made the myth transparent as it revealed the oppressed to be the truly civilized party. They rejected violence but maintained resistance, while the oppressor knew nothing but the use of violence." African Americans found that "*satyagraha* applied in the U.S. to our oppressors also clarified who was right and who was wrong."

King tapped into a global language of human rights. He was one of a group of church leaders who brought a new dimension to human rights discourse in global Christianity in the 1950s and 1960s. King's last southern campaign, in Selma, Alabama, in 1965, culminated in the apparent triumph of the Voting Rights Act. The next year, his attempt to bring the movement North, to Chicago, taught a number of painful lessons about the workings of political power and patronage in major metropolitan settings. King saw and understood better how racism was embedded into housing financing, school systems, highway construction plans, environmental policies, and policing tactics. He brooded over those lessons as his aim and goals reached toward a more radical restructuring of American society.

This King, willing to risk his former alliances with establishment fig- ures in order to address deeper issues of injustice, remains the figure who is least known to Americans today. History did not stop with his announcing the dream. He saw nightmares around him over the next years and struggled for strategies to address them. He did so even while alienating former friends and allies. He tried to build a broad multiracial coalition of poor and working-class people. That did not happen then, and it has not happened since, suggesting the audacity and difficulty of what he took upon himself to accomplish.

King's career as a published author also took off during the 1960s; it was for him a central part of fashioning his image as a preacher of renown and as a social thinker and moral philosopher. Earlier, one of the Harper & Row editors for *Stride Toward Freedom* had told King, "I learned what the enemies of freedom and liberalism can do. Therefore, I made—and am now making—every attempt to see that not even a single sentence can be lifted out of context and quoted against the book and the author." In particular, he toned down or removed King's strongest statements about colonialism, the capitalistic economic system, and critiques of militarism. He wanted a King who would challenge segregation on the basis of the treasured tenets of American civil religion. That would be the case with subsequent books as well. King spoke more openly to black and labor union audiences on these themes; for the widely distributed books, his prose was honed to meet different demands and to appeal to the broad- est language of American civil religion. As always, he played the racial diplomat for the mainstream audience. It was convincing in large part because he believed it; it wasn't an act.

King's central message was still there; some of the style of the presenta- tion changed. The passages most potentially biting or offensive to white readers dropped out, while a more generally spiritual message of that same point remained. King consented to the editorial changes; he saw how they had made his book *Stride Toward Freedom* successful, and he was intent on crafting the best public image possible. Meanwhile, those passages trimmed from the book remained in his sermons and some- times in his talk with labor unions and groups devoted to peace and civil rights. King had learned to modulate his message, to continue playing the racial diplomat, to be what a historian of that era called the "conservative militant."

The last few years of his life saw more of those self-imposed restrictions come off. This was true particularly in his last work *Where Do We Go from Here: Chaos or Community?*, King's most bracingly political work. In his earlier work and public sermons, King had muted his references to "labor trampled over by capitalistic power." Later, though, he took dead aim. Revising his sermons for religious and middle-class readers, King said, "Our unswerving devotion to monopolistic capitalism makes us more concerned about the economic security of the captains of industry than for the laboring men whose sweat and skills keep industry functioning."

King also spoke more frequently to the rising tides of black nationalism represented by Malcolm X. One brief meeting and respectful dialogue between Malcolm and Martin occurred on March 26, 1964; both were in Washington, DC, to support passage of what became the Civil Rights Act. As the scholar Peniel Joseph has written, the accidental summit "represented a culmination of two political leaders whose search for black citizenship and dignity found them converging at an unlikely location on the road to a shared rendezvous with destiny." King recognized the convergence between Malcolm's struggle for radical black dignity and his own quest for radical black citizenship. He wrote for the *Saturday Review* that year that "We are happy to know that our struggle in Selma has gone far beyond the issue of the right to vote and has focused the attention of the nation on the pivotal issue of equality in human rights." Ultimately, argues Joseph, Malcolm X's impact on King's evolving thinking was enormous, as King developed his vision from civil rights to human rights. As Joseph explains, for King "human rights encompassed more than formal legal and legislative breakthroughs. It required both the elimination of racial prejudice and economic injustice and the guarantee of justice in every aspect of black life in America. It required nothing less than a revolution." In many ways, King always had believed that, but it was now more central to his public rhetoric. He learned lessons from Malcolm X and others of speaking more forthrightly.

Earlier, Malcolm had said that while King "was having a dream, the rest of us Negroes are having a nightmare." That was a language that King would use in the coming years, speaking to those who were not from the southern church. Meanwhile, Malcolm had broken from the Nation of Islam, in part to throw his energies into the civil rights struggle as well. Their trajectories would never intersect, but they were converging.

King continued to pursue his internationalist vision, speaking forcefully for example against the apartheid regime in South Africa and other similar white supremacist governments around the world (including those in the states of the American South). In December 1964 in London, on his way to receive the Nobel Prize, he spoke about Nelson Mandela and others in prison, the torture inflicted upon them, and the militant opposition that was silenced by a prosperous police state. King compared and contrasted the struggle in the American South with that in South Africa, where, as he put it,

even the mildest form of nonviolent resistance meets with years of imprisonment, and leaders over many years have been restricted and silenced
and imprisoned. We can understand how in that situation people felt so
desperate that they turned to other methods, such as sabotage. Today, great
leaders, like Nelson Mandela . . . are among the many hundreds wasting
away in Robben Island prison. Against a massive, armed and ruthless state,
which uses torture and sadistic forms of interrogation to crush human beings
. . . the militant opposition inside South Africa seems for the moment to be
silenced.

The answer, he argued, was for a massive withdrawal of economic
resources from the South African state, to bring it to its economic knees.
Such a divestment campaign was in fact resurrected in the 1980s and
became an essential part of ending the apartheid regime. In the 1960s,
though, despite its brutality, South Africa remained a close American ally,
largely due to its role as a faithful servant of American Cold War foreign
policy. Many scholars historically have depicted the Cold War as an ally
of the civil rights movement, and sometimes it was. But the limitations of
that alliance were evident and glaring to King in the mid-1960s.

Not surprisingly, King's attempt to visit South Africa was denied when
the embassy would not issue him a visa. At Hunter College in 1965, in a
benefit speech for the protest movement against apartheid, King made
his feelings clear about who was civilized and who was not: "Africa does
have spectacular savages and brutes today, but they are not black. They
are the sophisticated white rulers of South Africa who profess to be cul-
tured, religious, and civilized, but whose conduct and philosophy stamp
them unmistakably as modern-day barbarians."

King had been influenced by the drama of Freedom Summer in Mississippi in 1964, when large groups of northern students organized by
the CORE and the SNCC had gone to Mississippi to register voters. The
Kennedy administration first, and then Lyndon Johnson, had suggested
repeatedly to King that the movement focus itself on "safer" projects,
such as voter registration, and avoid staging public demonstrations that
invited chaos and violence. That's in fact exactly what Freedom Summer
volunteers proposed to do. But they were to do it in the most violently
cruel southern state, where just two years before white students rioted
against the admission of black student James Meredith, and Governor
Ross Barnett led a huge rally at the Ole Miss football stadium, preaching his gospel of segregation amid a sea of Confederate flags. Three of
the first to arrive in June 1964 for Freedom Summer—Andrew Goodman
and Michael Schwerner, both white men from the North, and James
Chaney, a black native of Mississippi—had been murdered, their bodies
dumped into an earthen dam outside of the city of Philadelphia, Mississippi. Through the summer, whites bombed churches and SNCC offices,

attacked civil rights workers, pursued them on highways to intimidate drivers, and investigated the project under the state-level miniature of the FBI, the Mississippi Sovereignty Commission.

The summer was a turning point for many students, who came to doubt whether the philosophy of nonviolence was workable in practice given the brutality and violence that underlay the apartheid regime of Mississippi. Two years later, King gave a speech in Philadelphia, Mississippi, commemorating the death of James Chaney. The experience was harrowing. King spoke while standing alongside Cecil Ray Price—the sheriff of Neshoba County, Mississippi, and a Klan member—who had been part of the clique that had assassinated the civil rights workers. King addressed Price directly, saying, "You're the one who had Schwerner and those fellows in jail." As whites nearby heckled him, King announced, "I believe in my heart that the murderers are somewhere around me at this moment." Price said, "You're damn right, they're right behind you right now." King shot back, "They ought to search their hearts . . . I want them to know that we are not afraid. If they kill three of us, they will have to kill all of us. I am not afraid of any man."

After his address, King and others from the ceremony were set upon by a mob of young white men; only when some of the black marchers fought back did policemen intervene, seeming to prove the point of the Black Power advocates who were a key part of the March Against Fear that summer in Mississippi. "There is a complete reign of terror here," a shaken King said of Neshoba County just afterward. The following year, Price himself was arrested, and eventually served four and one half years in a penitentiary in Minnesota, later to be released to live out his days back in Neshoba County. Nonviolence for King was the most courageous act of all, and here that was evident to all. But advocates of violence when necessary for self-defense also seemed to have made their point.

King and the SCLC led an abortive campaign in the tourist city of St. Augustine, Florida, in 1964. Violent reprisals against black civil rights demonstrations perhaps aided the passage of the Civil Rights Bill but did little to change conditions for blacks in the city or region. Again, as in Albany, King had learned the lesson of selecting his targets wisely and winnowing down the objectives of a local movement carefully so that particular victories could be achieved. The SCLC chose as its next target the city of Selma, located in Dallas County, Alabama, about fifty-five miles west of Montgomery. SNCC workers had been in Selma since 1963, braving beatings by local policemen and constant threats to their safety as they tried to register voters. They had little success in doing so. That local organizing could not alter the fact that whites constituted 99 percent of Selma's voters even though they were less than half of the population. A legislative remedy was necessary. Press coverage, many believed, would dramatize the need for voting rights legislation, and the SCLC specialized in attracting that attention. The SCLC's part of the campaign began very early in 1965, as King came and led a mass meeting to call attention to the gross injustice so evident in Dallas County. King spoke with president Lyndon Johnson that January, and the two agreed that Selma would be the spot that could engineer pressure on Congress to pass voting rights legislation.

The Selma campaign, like Birmingham a little less than two years before, offered up some of the most indelible footage of the southern civil rights campaigns. What Bull Connor's dogs and firehoses were in Birmingham, sheriff Jim Clark's clubs and horseback-riding police vigilantes were for Selma. Selma also represented King's attempt to produce a media masterpiece, a story that could be told visually and powerfully, particularly on television. No plan for that worked better than the beating of a group or marchers, including John Lewis and others, who had crossed the Edmund Pettis Bridge on March 7, 1965, intending to march to Montgomery. The day was soon dubbed "Bloody Sunday." They were set upon by Clark's men and brutally beaten, some almost killed. That night, footage of the event interrupted a network broadcast of the television program *Judgement at Nuremberg*. Two years of violence visited upon civil rights workers in and around Selma had gained no attention at all. Bloody Sunday, by contrast, riveted a nation. As King said afterward, "we will no longer let [whites] use their clubs on us in dark corners. We are going to make them do it in the glaring light of television."

The previous month, in a protest meeting at Selma's Brown Chapel, Malcolm X came to visit; he sat next to Coretta and made it clear that he was ready to bring his philosophy of "by any means necessary" to bear on the situation. Privately, though, he told Coretta King that he had not come to make her husband's job "more difficult," but he "thought that if the white people understood what the alternative was that they would be willing to listen to Dr. King." Shortly thereafter, Malcolm X died in a hail of bullets from his internal enemies in the Nation of Islam organization. Like King, he had lived the last part of his life harried, constantly under surveillance (both by the government and by his enemies), and predicting his own untimely death. By that time, the two nationally known figures, who had been pitted as enemies, were de facto allies in the pursuit of what the scholar Peniel Joseph has termed "radical black citizenship" (King's idea) and "radical black dignity" (Malcolm's). King had come to understand and sympathize with Malcolm's expressions of black pride, while Malcolm had come to see what role he could play in advancing the freedom struggle (even if only as a foil, as he suggested to Coretta). The two were never going to agree philosophically on nonviolence, but in many other areas, their trajectories were converging.

The melee at the Edmund Pettus Bridge pleased some in the SCLC, who understood these were the mini-dramas that were ready-made for television. Others in the student movement felt disgusted and used almost as props; it was their bodies that were on the line, after all. To them, nonviolence seemed as much a cynical tactic as a Gandhian-derived philosophy (here, they ignored how much Gandhi also relied on provocations to produce publicity for his movement). Internal movement tensions were not eased when on March 9, two days after Bloody Sunday, King privately agreed to a plan to follow a court-ordered injunction against the planned march to Montgomery. He would lead the demonstrators to the bridge, pray and turn around, having made his point without having another episode of violent attack on a civil rights crowd. (King and the SCLC believed the judge would later lift the injunction and allow the march, as indeed turned out to be the case.) Because King had not made his intensions clear and offered inconsistent explanations for his decisions, his critics felt that the song "Ain't Gonna Let Nobody Turn Me Around" now had a bitterly ironic meaning. The tensions within civil rights groups were increasingly evident after this "Turnaround Tuesday" and would grow subsequently.

The irony of King's compromise at the bridge grew even more painful when, at the end of the aborted march on the 9th, white thugs set upon James Reeb, a Unitarian Universalist minister from the North who had come to support the Selma movement. They clubbed him in the head; he died two days later in a Birmingham hospital. Members of the gang who attacked Reeb later were acquitted of the murder. His slaying became one of four that led the grim commemorative toll of Selma.

After the dramatic events in March, King believed the key was to look for a good exit strategy. The people of Selma were "tired," he thought; carrying on a movement in their circumstances was incredibly difficult, and he needed to release locals from the burdens they had borne. Selma began with one tragic death: Jimmie Lee Jackson, a young black man killed at the end of a civil rights protest in nearby Marion, Alabama, on February 18. It ended with another: Viola Liuzzo, a Detroit housewife and peace activist, who had come, along with a number of other whites, shocked by the television footage of the Edmund Pettus Bridge incident. A gang of whites shot Jackson in a café in the nearby town of Marion; he had gone there to protect his mother and grandmother from the rampaging whites. A group of three self-appointed vigilantes murdered Liuzzo in her car outside of town; she had been driving two black civil rights workers from Selma to Montgomery. Police made arrests in both cases, but no one was ever convicted, despite the presence of an FBI informant in the car of the assassins. FBI agents afterward spread disinformation that Liuzzo was a Communist who was interested in having sex with African American men in the movement.

The coverage of the Edmund Pettus Bridge and later of the martyrs of the campaign produced action in Congress, just as SCLC organizers had hoped. The result was the Voting Rights Act of 1965, signed into law on August, 16, 1965. In arguing for it, King had pointed out that blacks were instrumental to a Democratic victory in 1964 "that repudiated a Republican party which had allowed itself to be captured by racism and reaction," thereby proving that "voting is more than a badge of citizenship and dignity—it is an effective tool for change." And not only would the power of the ballot work for the benefit of blacks, but all would "benefit from a color-blind land of plenty that provides for the nourishment of each man's body, mind and spirit." The need for the protection of voting rights with federal power had been made evident in the Selma campaign, when southern sheriffs straight from central casting (but all too real in their practice of police brutality in defense of white supremacy) had their practices exposed for the world to see. The nation had learned what the movement had tried to teach, that "any real change in the status quo depends on continued creative action to sharpen the conscience of the nation and establish a climate in which even the most recalcitrant elements are forced to admit that change is necessary."

By 1965, King had decided his greatest levers of power lay in mobilizing poor black people in their communities against specific forms of concentrated poverty, institutional racism, and disempowerment. His advisors and associates in the struggle, including Bayard Rustin, A. Philip Randolph, Michael Harrington, Walter Reuther, and others, had joined the Ad Hoc Committee on the Triple Revolution. King was putting together his thoughts on what national policies would have to be pursued to combat unemployment. He had thought about this for many years, sprinkled it into his sermons, but he took a much more targeted message to his public audiences from 1965 forward, even more so than in the March on Washington's reference to the uncashed check. He spoke of how "the unshackling of men from the bonds of unfulfilling labor frees them to become citizens, to make themselves and to make their own history." The paradox was not just of poverty amid plenty. It was, rather, how American abundance structured black poverty. "An economic depression rages today" in black neighborhoods. That depression was not a coincidence; it had been deliberately created. As he told his congregation in Atlanta on July 4, 1965, "I still have a dream that one day all of God's children will have food and clothing and material well-being for their bodies, culture and education for their minds, and freedom for their spirits. . . . One day men will no longer walk the streets in search for jobs that did not exist . . .

one day the rat-infested slums of our nation will be plowed into the junk heaps of history."

In January 1965, at a meeting called by A. Philip Randolph on "The State of the Race," King and other African American leaders debated the future of where the movement should go. A. Philip Randolph advocated for fundamental structural change, the stance King was moving toward, while Roy Wilkins of the NAACP insisted that enforcement of the Civil Rights Act and other laws would bring the economic change required. King's close advisor Stanley Levison also doubted that Americans would "change their society to free the Negro," and he worried about the future of the SCLC's funding if it moved too far beyond its previous stances and carefully calibrated demonstrations. Others, including SNCC representatives, questioned the wisdom of the movement's aims of assimilating blacks into mainstream American economic life at all. Meanwhile, King and others soon saw that Selma and its aftermath showed the interdependence of political rights and economic security.

Many in the movement were not ready for the Selma campaign to end when it did. Some sought a major economic boycott. That desire fueled a resolve to double down in the North and address issues of structural racism, segregated housing, and schools. King's thoughts turned northward. His goal was to address issues of race and justice at a national level. Most of King's later radicalism was established by late 1964, before the escalation of the Vietnam War, Black Power, and the Chicago Freedom Movement. He and Malcolm were converging on solutions to poverty that invoked the mechanisms of the state and the self-help tradition of African Americans. King came to share Malcolm's description of the American nightmare, especially disillusionment with the liberal state. He always returned to the need for jobs and income for all poor Americans as essential preconditions to full African American economic emancipation. King turned to the "legion of the deprived" as a force for change. By 1966, King's posture of critical support for the War on Poverty had turned negative; he thought the alleged "war" was just a skirmish, lacking the resources and the political will to wage the battle necessary. He also faced the reality that his hoped-for coalition of blacks and labor would be difficult to create.

A subsequent television interview with King in August 1966 found him already reflecting on the shortcomings and failures of what had seemed to be the legislative triumphs of the movement in 1964–1965. The "extravagant promises made a year ago in connection with the voting rights bills have now become a shattered mockery," he said, pointing to the numbers of southern communities where the dearth of federal registrars ensured the continuance of "outright patterns of discrimination." He felt that southern political pressure exerted on the Johnson administration had prevented federal registrars from working in the areas of Georgia where voter suppression was still a reality. King also lamented the lack of enforcement of the Voting Rights Act, the gerrymandering of districts to dilute black political influence, and the continued discouragement of voters by local election officials. He may have been too critical here; over the years, the Voting Rights Act did transform the South politically, just as its authors and supporters hoped. However, that progress is under threat now. If King had been around to see the measures enacted (and later struck down) in North Carolina in the 2010s—those "surgically targeted" to reduce black voting—and similar proposals in numerous state legislatures after the 2020 election, he would have seen exactly the same thing that he had criticized in his day. The disfranchisement and voter suppression carried on openly before the Voting Rights Act now continues, with the subterfuge of "fraud" as its cover.

In an interview conducted with Alex Haley (who had also done the interviews that became the book *The Autobiography of Malcolm X*), a grimly serious King discussed his mistakes and his plans going forward. He should not have been bailed out of jail in Montgomery, he said, and the Albany campaign of 1961–1962 should have focused more clearly on specific objectives rather than attacking "segregation-in-general." He had also come to see that he had overestimated the spiritual integrity of white ministers. "The projection of a social gospel, in my opinion, is the true witness of a Christian life." His anger showed in the conversation. He asked, "Why do white people seem to find it so difficult to understand that the Negro is sick and tired of having reluctantly parceled out to him those rights and privileges which all others receive upon birth or entry in America? I never cease to wonder at the amazing presumption of much of white society, assuming that they have the right to bargain with the Negro for his freedom. This continued arrogant ladling out of pieces of the rights of citizenship has begun to generate a *fury* in the Negro."

The urban uprising in Watts, Los Angeles, in mid-August 1965, a conflagration that took the lives of thirty-four people and caused hundreds of millions of dollars in property damages, amplified King's efforts to turn the civil rights movement into human rights movement. The urban explosion in Los Angeles, after all, coincided in timing almost exactly with the signing of the Voting Rights Act, with Johnson telling Congress, "And we shall overcome."

Meanwhile, King's working alliance with the Johnson administration's liberals frayed as the Vietnam War sucked the oxygen out of the air. In Los Angeles, investigating the conditions that had caused the Watts riot, King left with a heightened sense of police brutality. The public understood police brutality in evidence against nonviolent civil rights demonstrators to be "an atypical incident of excessive conduct," when in fact that kind of state-sanctioned violence was a "daily experience" for Negroes who lived within a police state set within a democratic republic. By 1965, he had decided that the greatest levers of power lay in mobilizing poor black people in their communities against specific forms of concentrated poverty, institutional racism, and disempowerment. Speaking at Howard University at that time, he said, "Public accommodations did not cost the nation anything; the right to vote did not cost the nation anything. Now we are grappling with basic class issues between the privileged and the underprivileged. In order to solve this problem, not only will it mean the restructuring of the architecture of American society, but it will cost the nation something. . . . If you want to call it the human rights struggle, that's all right with me."

In 1966, defending nonviolence against its increasing number of critics, King noted that he had "talked with many persons in the ghettos of the North who argue eloquently for the use of violence. But I observed none of them in the mobs that rioted in Chicago," and in Harlem and Chicago, "in spite of the bitterness preached and the hatred espoused, none of them has ever been able to start a riot. So far, only the police through the fears and prejudice have goaded our people to riot. And once the riots start, only the police or the National Guard have been able to put an end to them." What this showed, King believed, was that these were unplanned eruptions "brought on by long-neglected poverty, humiliation, oppression and exploitation." But while King had sympathy for those involved, he had no patience for the strategy invoked: "All the sound and fury seems but the posturing of cowards whose bold talk produces no action and signifies nothing."

King spoke to the triple forces of race, poverty, and misery entrapping blacks in conditions of inadequate employment, housing, and education. "It is paradoxical but fair to say that Negro terrorism is incited less on ghetto street corners than in the halls of Congress," King said. In his analysis, nonviolence would be effective only when it had "achieved the massive dimensions, the disciplined planning, and the intense commitment of a sustained, direct-action movement of civil disobedience on the national scale." King saw that the "hard cold facts of racial life in the world today indicate that the hope of the people of color in the world may well rest on the American Negro and his ability to reform the structures of racist imperialism from within and thereby turn the technology and wealth of the West to the task of liberating the world from want." The call was for a "tactical program which will bring the Negro into the mainstream of American life as quickly as possible. So far, this has only been offered by the nonviolent movement." The racial revolution ultimately was one to join, not overthrow, the system—to make proper education, housing, and opportunity available for the average black man or woman.

By this time, King had a fully developed critique of poverty as a structural pillar of capitalist society:

> Slums with hundreds of thousands of living units are not eradicated as easily as lunch counters or buses are integrated. Jobs are harder to create than voting rolls. . . . It is easy to conceive of a plan to raise the minimum wage and thus in a single stroke extract millions of people from poverty. But between the conception and the realization there lies a formidable wall. Someone has been profiting from the low wages of Negroes. Depressed living standards are a structural part of the economy. . . A hardening of opposition to the satisfaction of Negro needs must be anticipated as the movement presses against financial privilege.

But intensified calls for full employment and an end to slums through targeted federal spending met with resistance. Vietnam occupied the energies of the left and the nation, and civil rights activism had to swim against a rising tide of the national convulsions in the later 1960s.

King's sympathies were with a European-style social democracy, but one achieved through reform rather than revolution. He called for a Bill of Rights for the Disadvantaged and a guaranteed annual income that would provide a livable floor for all Americans, modeled on the GI Bill of the World War II era. He attacked white moderates but positioned himself as the alternative to radical black rage. He condemned violence on the streets of American cities but always added that any condemnation of violence was empty "without understanding the daily violence which our society inflicts upon many of its members. The violence of poverty and humiliation hurts as intensely as the violence of a club." He sympathized with the Black Power movement but criticized it for offering no program to achieve the black pride which it preached. He remained the conservative militant, pushing moderate whites one direction, and blacks to his left in another.

King determined to test these theories with an audacious but risky campaign in Chicago in 1966. His campaign quickly demonstrated how difficult it would be to attack the structural racism which he had so keenly dissected and analyzed in his addresses of the era. He hoped to mobilize white middle-class churches as well as Chicago's black community, and to use the city as a kind of testing ground for his proposal of a "Marshall Plan" to reconstruct urban America. He hoped to mobilize labor, civil rights, and church forces. King attacked the problem of slums, noting how they had been perpetuated by a toxic combination of interests between real estate agents, bankers, and governments at all levels. On July 10, 1966, he mimicked the original Martin Luther in nailing his demands to the door of Chicago City Hall; his version called for enforcement of nondiscrimination in the housing industry, within unions, and in private businesses. Cannily, Mayor Richard Daley immediately agreed to some (including a call for enforcement of the 1964 Civil Rights Act). Meanwhile, King grew increasingly concerned that rioting had eroded white support as well as black faith in nonviolence as a redemptive method of social change. Riots, he saw, garnered attention that his own methods sometimes failed to provoke.

Along the way, he met the formidable political machine of mayor Richard Daley. Daley saw Chicago as a "city of neighborhoods," and that historically had been both its strength for white ethnic communities and its weakness for the black migrants who had moved there in huge numbers from the World War I era to the 1960s. Black Chicagoans lived in a small north-south corridor of crowded neighborhoods on the South Side, in areas segregated from the white ethnic neighborhoods to their north and west. The freeway construction projects of the Eisenhower era had placed what is now the Dan Ryan Expressway right along the historic dividing line of white and black Chicago. The real estate industry was also a key to maintaining the "integrity" of neighborhoods; in fact, by law they were required to do so. Any attempts to breach de facto residential segregation usually met with hostility from neighbors determined to protect their turf. Mayor Daley oversaw the system with the majority of black ministers in the city as his allies. They were protected members of his political machine.

King addressed the criticisms that immediately greeted him—that he should stay in his lane, a southern minister addressing the problems of his region. King responded that Chicago's problems were symptomatic of the national disease of institutionalized racism. A doctor, he said, does not cause cancer when he finds it; instead, he diagnoses it. He proposed to do the same. "Our humble marches have revealed a cancer," he said. King understood Daley within a Niebuhrian framework—that the mayor saw everything through the lens of "individual intent, rather than as a societal sin."

Very little went as planned during the Chicago Freedom Movement, and most went as feared by King's advisors who had tried to dissuade him from the project. Daley defused King's efforts to highlight neighborhood problems by swiftly cleaning up apartment buildings and other sites where King hoped to dramatize problems faced by black residents. He employed the ministers in his machine to deny cooperation to the SCLC. Marches led by SCLC activists in nearby white neighborhoods such as Gage Park and Marquette Park produced fearful scenes of thousands of whites on sidewalks, jeering and throwing objects at the marchers, once felling King with a stone that caught him on the head. King later commented that he had "never seen anything so hostile and hateful" as he had seen on the streets of Chicago's suburbs. The movement's attempts to march in Cicero created another situation of tense confrontations between marchers and onlookers. "We can walk in outer space, but we can't walk the streets of Cicero without the National Guard," King said of the impenetrable small city just to the west of downtown Chicago.

The Chicago campaign ended with a "Summit Agreement" that in theory would open housing opportunities to blacks, something the real estate industry fought fiercely. But of course relatively few African Americans had the means to shop for housing in those areas. Meanwhile, Daley cemented his political power, as he had appeared to negotiate openly and fairly and to have addressed King's concerns. Daley and his political machine in the huge northern industrial center were more than up to the challenge of defusing the SCLC's protests.

This only reinforced King's philosophy of attacking segregation nationally. At a November 11, 1966, SCLC meeting, King again called for social democracy in America. He was sharing his economic radicalism in a safe space where he would not be red baited. He compared the United States to Sweden and other parts of Europe where poverty and inequality were far less obviously destructive than in North America. He spoke of how a guaranteed income would free up creative energies, and he quoted the nineteenth-century social philosopher Henry George in envisioning a more just system of remunerative work. One could imagine, he noted, a program of paying civil rights workers to spend a year "meeting people and shaking hands, and talking with them about their problems." The political mobilization of the poor remained a necessity.

The Chicago crusade taught King painful lessons that influenced his approaches to race, poverty, and power. His radicalism grew out of an interaction between analytical perspectives and policy advice offered by his social democratic advisers with the lessons learned on the ground. He deepened his analysis of political and economic power, engaging in dialogues with critics around him. As King himself put it, "I choose to identify with the poor. I choose to give my life for the hungry and those who have been left out of the sunlight of opportunity." But restructuring, he knew, would be costly, and he had come to understand racism as more deeply entrenched than he had earlier believed. He denounced the "triple ghetto" of poverty, race, and human misery. "I cannot see," he said in defending his faith in integration, "how the Negro will be totally liberated from the crushing weight of poor education, squalid housing and economic strangulation until he is integrated, with power, into every level of American life. . . . In the struggle for national independence, one can talk about liberation now and integration later, but in the struggle for racial justice in a multiracial society where the oppressor and the oppressed are both at home, liberation must come through integration." At the same time, the language of black radicalism came more easily to him after examining the intertwined roots of race, urban politics, and poverty in Chicago: "The problems of racial injustice and economic injustice cannot be solved without a radical redistribution of political and economic power." That would be his call to the end of his life.

After the struggles in St. Augustine, Selma, and Chicago, King searched for some time away to reflect and regroup. He knew he needed it. During all these struggles, King's enemies tape-recorded many of his conversations, often informal strategy sessions with his colleagues in the SCLC. The material surreptitiously collected has provided historians with a rich pool of sources for better understanding the personality of King when he was with friends, away from the cameras and the spotlight. In private, King was often gregarious and playful, a lover of banter, raunchy jokes, and preacher humor. He enjoyed needling his colleagues. King loved to deliver mock funeral sermons for his friends, parodying them at their weakest points. In preaching such a funeral for Andrew Young, known for being a sort of unofficial SCLC ambassador to talk to whites, King "eulogized" his colleague with a wickedly funny sermon on how white Americans would mourn Young's death. Nobody ever loved white people more than Andy Young, King screamed, to the delighted of the assembled "congregants." His colleagues later remembered King as the stand-up comic of the movement, whose wickedly acid humor could defuse tense situations.

King clearly needed those episodes to escape the strain of being *Martin Luther King Jr.* all the time in public. It's hardly a surprise that someone whose house was bombed, who was randomly stabbed by a mentally deranged person and on multiple occasions physically assaulted by neo-Nazis, and who was bugged and harassed by all levels of government, searched for outlets. The sheer manic nature of his life in the movement was unbearable otherwise.

In 1967, King planned a vacation to Jamaica for a time of recuperation. That was not to be. His own advisor James Bevel abruptly flew there, on his own sense of a God-given mission that the SCLC should devote itself to the growing protest movement against the Vietnam War. King had no plans to abandon the SCLC's historic emphases, but he needed little convincing to make his public stand against the war. On the way to Jamaica, he leafed through a magazine that showed pictures of Vietnamese children burned from American bombs. "Nothing will taste any good for me until I do everything I can to end that war," he told SCLC colleague Bernard Lee, who had asked him why he had shoved away a plate of food.

Moderation about the war now seemed as obstructively evil as white "moderation" about segregation in Birmingham. He knew he would be subject to a torrent of media criticism, but again he felt the call of God and duty. "The thing is I am to stay in my place and I am a Negro leader, and I should not stray from a position of moderation. I can't do that," he told his wary long-time advisor and confidant Stanley Levison. The press loved him when he said they should be nonviolent to Bull Connor, he noted, but now the same people "curse you and damn you when you say be nonviolent toward little brown Vietnamese Children." He also, in moments of despair, wondered whether the tragic course of human violence and alienation were inevitable. Meanwhile, his own vision grew more radical, more ambitious, and (in his view) more necessary—but also more unachievable.

7

✝

Shot Rings Out in the Memphis Sky

The problems of racial injustice and economic injustice cannot be solved without a radical redistribution of political and economic power.

—Martin Luther King Jr., in Chicago, August 31, 1967

If death had to come, I am sure there was no greater cause to die for than fighting to get a just wage for garbage collectors.

—Benjamin Mays, speaking of Martin Luther King Jr.

By late 1967, Martin Luther King Jr. was, one observer remembered, "dark, gaunt, and tired. He felt that his time was up. He said he knew they were going to get him." He reminded his best friend Ralph Abernathy, "We live in a sick nation." He had said the same to Coretta years earlier, following the bombings in Birmingham and the assassination of John F. Kennedy, but he felt it even more deeply now. He carried the weight of the world and felt guilty when he fell short of the hopes of his admirers. The movement for a time seemed to be an irresistible force, but he now constantly ran into seemingly immovable objects: the obstacles of local politics, internal fighting and ego wars within the SCLC, a distrust bordering on hatred for him coming from the Johnson administration, and an ambitious program of attacking poverty through a multiracial coalition of the poor that looked increasingly impossible to realize. He drank more and indulged in sexual liaisons even as the government stepped up its surveillance; "It seems almost as if he was courting exposure—as if he would welcome the fall," biographer Peter Ling plausibly concludes.

Perhaps it was an unconscious psychological wish to free himself of the burdens he had accepted.

"We see so many tragic interruptions these days," he preached in January 1968, in one of his darker sermons. "They have come to transform the buoyance of hope to the fatigue of despair. The lights have gone out in so many of our lives." He fought irritably with those around him and with advisors on the phone. His long-time advisor Michael Harrington, who strongly shared King's democratic socialist sentiments, described King in January 1968 as a different person from the "ebullient, relaxed, even exuberant" man he had known; he seemed instead to be in "almost despairing mood," perhaps because even advisors such as Harrington stood in opposition to King's initial ambitiously confrontational plans for the Poor People's Campaign.

They advised him that going smaller and securing a victory on a specific issue would be a better course to follow than to engage in a massive demonstration without a clearly aimed objective. King resisted that idea—ironically turning against the lessons he claimed to have learned from the Albany campaign. "We've got to go for broke this time," he told an advisor. "We've gone for broke before, but not in the way we're doing this time, because if necessary, I'm going to stay in jail six months." Most of all, he felt personally inadequate to carry the burdens he felt had been involuntarily placed upon him, while feeling the God-given call to carry those burdens and most especially to represent the poor and disfranchised. In "Nonviolence and Social Change," for the posthumously published *Trumpet of Conscience,* he had asked, "Can a program of nonviolence . . . realistically expect to deal with such an enormous, entrenched evil? . . . Many people feel that nonviolence as a strategy for social change was cremated in the flames of the urban riots of the last two years. They tell us that Negroes have only now begun to find their true manhood in violence." King had another answer. He intended to show that "nonviolence will be effective, but not until it has achieved the massive dimensions, the disciplined planning, and the intense commitment of a sustained, direct-action movement of civil disobedience on the national scale." As he saw it, "The dispossessed of this nation—the poor, both white and Negro—live in a cruelly unjust society. They must organize a revolution against that injustice . . . against the structures through which the society is refusing . . . to lift the load of poverty." He proposed, against the advice of many around him, to be at the front of that revolution. Instead, his death augured a meaner era of racialized resentments and white backlash.

The major struggles of the last two years of King's life—his opposition to the Vietnam War, his dream of a Poor People's Campaign, and his support of the garbage workers' strike in Memphis—framed a period when

King self-consciously identified with the struggles of the black working class and with larger anti-imperialist movements. He further developed his anti-colonial and economically radical thought within his Christian nonviolent framework. Vietnam and Memphis represent the continued evolution of King's thought, the struggles he faced in confronting deeply entrenched norms of inequality, and his determination to be an increasingly prophetic voice in the context of a disintegrating consensus in the late 1960s.

King often cast himself as the suffering Jesus, ready to lay down his life; later, he increasingly cast himself as an Old Testament prophet, who expressed the wrath of God for the sins of a society. As resistance grew to his calls for economic justice, argues scholar Richard Lischer, King sounded more like his radical black predecessors of the past—Henry Highland Garnet, David Walker, Frederick Douglass, Henry McNeal Turner, and others—and he embraced "the more dangerous function of prophecy, namely, the exercise of speech that is received directly from God and hurled against God's opponents." Like those prophets, he experienced the loneliness of pinpointing the deep flaws of a society. His close friendship with and admiration of Rabbi Abraham Joshua Heschel, who had marched with him in Selma, deepened his understanding of the connection between African American and Jewish suffering; the two admired and learned from each other. In "My Jewish Brother," published in the *New York Amsterdam News* in February 1966, he had written, "We particularly need the Hebrew prophets because they taught that to love God was to love justice; that each human being has an inescapable obligation to denounce evil where he sees it and to defy a ruler who commands him to break the covenant."

King cast himself as an Old Testament prophet now, and perhaps that contributed to his angry streak as well. His normal stew of ideas—from neoorthodoxy, the social gospel, evangelical piety, political liberalism, and Gandhian nonviolent resistance—increasingly turned toward the radical black Christianity in which he had been steeped. This was the era of the development of what came to be called black theology, particularly with the writings of James Cone and Vincent Harding. King never self-consciously identified with that; his vision was universalist. He still wanted to hear that symphony of brotherhood. But he increasingly expressed sympathy with black nationalism. While he heard that symphony, he also preached that black was beautiful. Blackness should be a point of pride rather than self-hate.

Through much of his career, King had a unique ability, writes Michael Eric Dyson in his illuminating study *I May Not Get There with You*, to "extend the public witness of radical black Christianity throughout the nation. King used the language of civic piety to express the goals of black religion and radical democracy." Late in his life, his views on white racism darkened. He came to understand systemic racism and unconscious bias. He believed that such healing could occur only after an acknowledgment of the way racism was written into America's DNA.

This is the King who too often is forgotten in the saccharine yearly memorials of our day. As scholar Peniel Joseph puts it in his study *The Sword and the Shield*, a look at the growing convergence between King and Malcolm X in the 1960s:

> This radical King, who gathered an army of poor to descend upon the nation's capital in defiance of critics, is airbrushed from history. The risk-taking King, who defied a sitting president to protest war, is missing from our popular memory. The revolutionary King, who marched shoulder to shoulder with garbage workers, locked arms with Black Power militants, and lived in Chicago ghettos in an effort to stimulate social change, is forgotten. The King who proclaimed that America's greatness remained "the right to protest for right" has all but vanished, replaced by generic platitudes about freedom and justice. . . . The most important legacy is his conception that radical black citizenship as not simply the absence of racial oppression but the beneficial good found in a living wage, decent housing, safe neighborhoods, health care, and racially integrated public schools and communities.

King's late-life emphases on the triple evils of militarism, racism, and unbounded capitalist exploitation grew from his lifelong concerns but extended them to new areas. Over time, the language of public black radicalism came more easily to him. As he put it, "The problems of racial injustice and economic injustice cannot be solved without a radical redistribution of political and economic power. . . . The ghetto is a domestic colony. Black people must develop programs that will aid in the transfer of power and wealth into the hands of residents of the ghetto." His expansive determination to end poverty and his agenda for distribution across class lines were more radical than the rhetoric of most Black Power advocates.

In addition, King's radical internationalism arose earlier than most assume. His critiques of militarism and imperialism, and his identification with anti-colonial movements, were longstanding. He saw the hypocrisy of blacks fighting for American society. The urban riots of the era amplified his desire to transform a movement for civil rights into one for human rights that would involve a reimagination of American democracy. That effort frayed his relations with many white liberals and infuriated Lyndon Johnson, who once lashed out to his aides about "that goddamned nigger preacher." King's analysis of how the Vietnam War consumed and stole resources from the War on Poverty defied Johnson's "guns and butter" mythologies. But beyond that, King saw that the fostering of violence through foreign policy was part of the same process by which violence against African Americans and others was fostered at home. The Vietnam War and the war on poor people could not be separated; they were part of the same state-sanctioned violence. Black Americans were caught up in the same sense as black and yellow brothers abroad. "Racism can well be that corrosive evil that will bring down the curtain on western civilization," he concluded.

During these years, to his congregants in Atlanta and to national audiences, King offered his most comprehensive and radical definition of black citizenship. He fused themes of racial integration, black empowerment, and economic justice, and saw the Vietnam War as the chief enemy of his vision. Part of that vision was expressed in his support for compensatory action to make up for centuries of oppression, and in universalist programs such as a guaranteed annual income.

King articulated his economic emphases forcefully in numerous talks to labor unions through this era. To the New York Trades Council in 1967, he noted that African Americans had learned what labor had learned many decades ago—that having some theoretical rights in law meant nothing. Rights only counted once gained through social struggle. Passivity would only lead to abuse. He told them also about the limitations he had discovered of white liberalism, the kind of view that balked at obvious physical abuse but drew the line at equality. King advocated a solution that would aid all poor people and therefore help blacks most of all: a guaranteed annual income. The rising tide never lifted all boats, so that no matter how dynamically economy expands, it does not eliminate poverty. Deliberate redistributive measures would be necessary. To his skeptical colleagues, he insisted on using the slogan "jobs or income," a morally potent simplification useful for movement demands. It was something so "possible, so achievable, so pure, so simple that even the backlash can't do much to deny it, and yet so non-token and so basic to life that even the black nationalists can't disagree with it that much. Now that's jobs or income." In recent years, economists and social thinkers of various political stripes have taken up and re-proposed this idea as an effective remedy to persistent poverty. Here, King was at his best in marrying a prophetic vision with a means of protest and concrete proposals.

In his presidential address to the SCLC, August 1967, King emphasized the economic development of what were effectively colonized areas of American cities. "America is going to hell if she doesn't use her wealth . . . her vast resources of wealth to end poverty," he cried. "Scavengers" in ghettoes had deprived black Americans of decent housing and health care. They had created food deserts (a term that postdates King, but one he described perfectly) and profit centers for scammers and exploiters. King urged his colleagues to draw up plans to integrate the most isolated and deprived black Americans into the mainstream of American life. Black nationalists and Black Power advocates demanded this rhetorically but had no concrete plans to achieve it. So far, King said, it had only been offered by the nonviolent movement. The civil rights movement had accomplished much, but now was the time to "make real the promises of democracy." It was time to achieve an adequate income for all, time to protest against substandard schools, rapacious politicians, and poorly paying or nonexistent jobs.

To another labor group in New York, he advanced one of his favorite themes of his later addresses: the fact that through American history there had been a system of socialism for the wealthy and raw capitalism for the poor. Nowadays, we would call this socializing risk but privatizing wealth. Historically, while the government extended the Homestead Act of the nineteenth century, land-grant colleges, and other forms of help to white farmers, the freed people after the Civil War were given "nothing but freedom." Without boots, they had to lift themselves up by their bootstraps. Most poor people lacked the means to function in the mainstream economic life of the country, King pointed out, and even the very fact of being poor was expensive. Poor people without better options relied on loan sharks, emergency rooms for health care, and long hours on buses commuting to temporary jobs lacking benefits. Hospital workers and other laborers in essential services were often not organized, for example. But in fact the janitor in the hospital was as significant as the physician; both were necessary to make it run. That did not mean that their incomes would be the same, but rather that the janitor's income would not be so low as to make it impossible to live decently. Most of society was more concerned with tranquility and the status quo than about justice, humanity, and equality. Riots were a brutally effective way to communicate anger about this situation—hence his famous phrase "a riot is the language of the unheard." And what is it that America has failed to hear? "It has failed to hear that the plight of the Negro poor has worsened . . . that promises of justice and freedom have not been met."

At the SCLC's 1967 meeting, King returned to "America as beacon" rhetoric. God had allowed America to be a melting pot of peoples, meaning that if the United States could not figure out how people could live together peacefully, then the world was in trouble. He urged shifting resources from militarism to domestic and global conquest of poverty. "Violence at home and abroad, actual power and powerlessness, relative deprivation, and violations of law and justice lay at the core of the ongoing urban crisis," he said. His longtime advisor Bayard Rustin pushed him toward more engagement with the ordinary political process; he said he would rather have a "job program for blacks than a psychoanalysis of whites." Actually King had both, and more, but this point lay at the heart of their increasing disagreements over strategy and philosophy. Rustin wanted legislative victories, one piece at a time; King looked toward more fundamental transformations.

King returned to his experiences with the nonviolent movement. Whatever challenges had arisen from it, from Black Power advocates or other skeptics, he maintained his faith in its ability to empower a movement to achieve the ends of justice through moral means. Fires—both literal and metaphorical—were raging through black and poor communities, as "disinherited people all over the world are bleeding to death from deep social and economic wounds." Massive movements of nonviolent civil disobedience could dramatize these injustices, as it had done in the South. King understood why skeptics doubted the ability of a new nonviolent movement, as well as those who felt that urban blacks had found their "manhood" in acts of violence, rather than kneeling down before those who were the perpetrators of violence.

Through the mid-1960s, King felt an urge to come out against the war. He did so in some more private addresses and sermons. But he was conflicted: the success of the civil rights movement, legislatively, now depended on the same administration that dialed up the prosecution of the Vietnam War in 1965. Meanwhile, Coretta Scott King, who had strong interests in international peace movements, urged her husband to take stronger stands against war. "She educated me," King later said. He felt convicted and knew he had to say something in a more public way. He could not remain "silent about an issue that is destroying the soul of our nation." Soon thereafter, Mennonite minister and civil rights activist Vincent Harding drafted a speech for him.

This speech, King's most important late-life address, happened at Riverside Church in New York City. It was April 1967, exactly one year before his death. King's statement on the war alienated the presidential administration of Lyndon Johnson and numerous centrist allies. But King had moved beyond that kind of consensus politics. As a seminary student and young pastor, he had spoken out against imperialism and the violence of state-sanctioned political domination. In that sense, his address "A Time to Break Silence" was not necessarily new.

The difference now was that he was *Martin Luther King Jr.*, the Nobel Prize winner and African American celebrity; he was not just a Negro preacher or even just a regional civil rights leader—rather, he stood as a primary voice of the American liberal left. He acknowledged the difficulty of opposing governmental policy, "especially in time of war," when people wanted to rally around the troops. He likewise acknowledged the difficulty and uncertainty of this particular conflict but insisted that one could not be paralyzed by complexity, for the moral issue was paramount. Most important, the times were "revolutionary," for "all over the globe men are revolting against old systems of exploitation and oppression and out of the wombs of a frail world new systems of justice and equality are being born." He continued, "we are confronted with the fierce urgency of now," with the immediate choice of "nonviolent coexistence or violent co-annihilation."

King knew well all the critiques he faced. The critics thought that "peace and civil rights don't mix." But those who so spoke knew nothing of "my commitment or my calling." And that was a commitment that encompassed peace and justice at home and abroad, a peace that could not be won through violence directed against African Americans at home or Vietnamese abroad. The war in Vietnam was the violence of American state power and white supremacy made manifest. That war abroad destroyed the hopes of a war on poverty that so far had amounted to little more than a "skirmish." The demographics of the actual war fighting symbolized the same inequality, as young black men bore a disproportionate share of fighting in a war for a society that already had crippled them, a war to "guarantee liberties in Southeast Asia which they had not found in southwest Georgia or East Harlem."

King also knew that the war confronted him with an unanswerable question coming from angry residents of ghettos. He had tried to insist on the efficacy of nonviolence, but they had an unanswerable counter— "what about Vietnam?" They asked why our own nation was "using massive doses of violence to solve its problems, to bring about the changes it wanted. . . . I knew that I could never again raise my voice against the violence of the oppressed in the ghettos without having first spoken clearly to the greatest purveyor of violence in the world today—my own government." The unfree of America would not be freed by the violence of the wars abroad. On the contrary, "if America's soul becomes totally poisoned, part of the autopsy must read Vietnam." For King, his calling was to "speak for the weak, for the voiceless, for victims of our nation and for those it calls enemy, for no document from human hands can make these humans any less our brothers."

The church's role was clear: to raise its voice "if our nation persists in its perverse ways in Vietnam." The church had to speak against the "far deeper malady within the American spirit," one represented by the unjust exercise of American power in Latin America, Southeast Asia, and South Africa. The nation had assumed the role "of those who make peaceful revolution impossible by refusing to give up the privileges and the pleasures that come from the immense profits of overseas investment." Without a "radical revolution of values," the nation would remain beholden to the "giant triplets of racism, materialism, and militarism," for a "nation that continues year after year to spend more money on military defense than on programs of social uplift is approaching spiritual death." The only thing preventing such a revolution of values was a "tragic death wish." A reflexive anti-communism, one unable to act with "wise restraint and calm reasonableness," would not take positive action for justice, or extirpate the very conditions of poverty and injustice which provided the seed grounds for communism in the first place. For King, the hope was to "go out into a sometimes hostile world declaring eternal hostility to poverty, racism, and militarism."

King likened anti–Vietnam War dissent to Abraham Lincoln's opposition to the Mexican-American war and other acts of moral opposition in the American past. "I speak for those whose land is being laid waste," he preached, "whose homes are being destroyed, whose culture is being subverted. I speak for the poor in America who are paying the double price of smashed hopes at home and death and corruption in Vietnam. . . . The great initiative of the war is ours. The initiative to stop it must be ours."

Conservatives and liberals alike blasted the Riverside speech. An editorial in the *New York Times* argued against the exact point King was making, linking the civil rights and antiwar movements: "This is a fusing of two public problems that are distinct and separate. By drawing them together, Dr. King has done a disservice to both. The moral issues in Vietnam are less clear-cut than he suggests; the political strategy of uniting the peace movement and the civil rights movement could very well be disastrous for both causes." Afterward, King reserved talk of economic imperialism for sympathetic left audiences, but he argued the same points that the *Times* had criticized. "Racism and its perennial ally—economic exploitation—provide the key to understanding most of the international complications of this generation," he insisted.

In a July 1967 interview, King was challenged on why he had spent as much time as he had speaking about the Vietnam War. He responded that this was a misconception, that he had been a clergyman first and a civil rights leader second, "and when I was ordained to the Christian ministry, I accepted that as a commission to constantly and forever bring the ethical insights of our Judeo-Christian heritage to bear on the social evils of our day," notably including war. Beyond that, as he pointed out, he could not divide up moral concerns, because "justice is indivisible," while injustice could be found as much in Mississippi as in Vietnam. King remained the profound advocator of the social gospel he always had been. For him, there was no dramatic shift; he was simply applying the same principles to new situations and to broader contexts.

The causalities of the war in Vietnam were not just those killed or maimed on any side but also those at home. The "triplets" of racism, militarism, and exploitation worked in an evil concert together with the war. "Genuine power is the right use of strength," King had said, but if not used rightly, it led to arrogance and doom. He was disappointed in the failure to "deal positively and forthrightly with the triple evils of racism, extreme materialism, and militarism" and wanted advocates of demobilization to spread a "propaganda of peace" just as the war hawks spread their venom. The peace movement and the civil rights movement were natural allies. They would have to combine forces against the injustices they both confronted.

During the final months of his life, King met Rosa Parks again in Grosse Pointe, Michigan. Parks by then was working as an aide for congressman John Conyers, and King came as part of his campaign to address conditions facing African Americans in the North: substandard housing, de facto school segregation, and abusive policing in black communities. King blasted liberals and northern city leaders for their own inequalities, but expressed his concern that urban unrest, while understandable, intensified rather than addressed the problems at hand: "I'm absolutely convinced that a riot merely intensifies the fears of the white community while relieving the guilt." However, it was not enough to condemn the riots without also condemning the conditions inciting them. Media outlets recently had "discovered the interlocking issues of racism, poverty, and state violence" as something new, "when in fact they hadn't been listening before." At a press conference before the Poor People's Campaign in December 1967, he pointed to the government's responsibility for "low minimum wages, for a degrading system of inadequate welfare, for subsidies to the rich and unemployment and underemployment of the poor." King announced, "Consider the spectacle of cities burning while the national government speaks of repression instead of rehabilitation. Or think of children starving in Mississippi while prosperous farmers are rewarded for not producing food. . . . Or the awesome bombardment [of Vietnam] while political power brokers de-escalate and very nearly disarm a timid action against poverty. Or a nation gorged on money while millions of its citizens are denied a good education, adequate health services, decent housing, meaningful employment, and even respect, and are then told to be responsible."

The King of 1967–1968 saw the necessity of radical overhaul of beliefs and values of whites. He told author and reporter David Halberstam he had thought to work within institutions of society, to seek some change here and there, but now felt very differently: "I think you've got to have a reconstruction of the entire society, a revolution of values." King tied in his understanding of history, the longevity of white supremacy and its effect on more than African Americans. "Our nation was born in genocide when it embraced the doctrine that the original American, the Indian, was an inferior race," he proclaimed. "From the sixteenth century forward, blood flowed in battles over racial supremacy. We are perhaps the only nation which tried as a matter of national policy to wipe out its indigenous population." American history depended on the violent suppression of untouchables, and, combined with the Vietnam War, this made America the "greatest purveyor of violence in the world today." King's statements presaged works of history that would come over the next generation. Meanwhile, the backlash against his words forecast the resistance to understanding American history this way.

King also developed his own personal historiography of white supremacy in a late-life reflection on the great black intellectual W. E. B. Du Bois, published in *Freedomways* and delivered as an address also at Carnegie Hall in New York in February 1968. Du Bois still had not made it into the canon of American universities, and his work from 1935, *Black Reconstruction in America*, although well known for decades to black scholars, was only then in the early stages of being recovered by white scholars. Du Bois, King said, had "shredded the army of white propagandists—the myth-makers of Negro history." An irrationally obsessive anti-communism had left Du Bois exiled by the end of his life (he died in Ghana on the eve of the March on Washington address) and had led the country into too many quagmires. Du Bois "confronted this powerful structure of historical distortion and dismantled it." Before anyone else, he "demolished the lies about Negroes in their most important and creative period of history." Du Bois knew that to "lose one's history is to lose one's self-understanding of and with it the roots for pride." He revealed truth about Reconstruction, the only period of true interracial democracy in American history. He confronted the establishment as a "model of militant manhood and integrity" but knew also that one "must organize and unite people so that their anger becomes a transforming force." Were Du Bois still alive, King said in 1968, he would join the peace movement. Du Bois's greatest quality, King concluded was his "divine dissatisfaction with all forms of injustice" and his "committed empathy with all the oppressed." Like Du Bois, a misunderstood prophet, King also was coming to feel that his numerous late-life critics had never known him.

As King spoke during these years, President Lyndon Johnson fumed privately about his political activities (FBI agents tried unsuccessfully to interest Johnson in the sex tapes, but Johnson found them amusingly ribald and nothing else; he only cared about King's political affairs). King had attended the ceremony for the signing of the Voting Rights Act of 1965 and even teared up a little when he had seen Johnson addressing Congress on behalf of the bill, saying, "and we shall overcome." Many of King's colleagues already had grown distrustful of the Johnson administration, in spite of the legislative triumphs of 1965. But King wandered outside the corral of some part of the liberal establishment, and that made its exponents angry.

King traversed the country in the last two years prior to his assassination. The message of nonviolence remained paramount, ever more so set within the context of the violence of Vietnam abroad, the Cold War conflict, and the continued brutalities of poverty and racism black Americans faced at home. For him, the problems abroad and at home always had been connected; he wrote about them in his graduate school papers and in his earliest sermonic messages. He had not changed his tune so much as amplified it for the huge audiences that now followed him. For him, the central concept that "we are all caught in an inescapable network of mutuality, tied into a single garment of destiny" was still a salvific one, and the only way to preserve and extend peace. So was the imperative of using just means toward just ends. We could never have peace, he insisted, until "men everywhere recognize that ends are not cut off from means, because the means represent the ideal in making, and the end in process . . . the means represent the seed, and the end represents the tree." He pushed his message on the "nonviolent affirmation of the sacredness of all human life."

King's latter years, too, were those of talking about nightmares as much as dreams. The dream he preached on that epic day in August 1963, he remembered in a Christmas Eve address in 1967, had turned into a nightmare just a few weeks later at the Sixteenth Street Baptist Church in Birmingham. He had seen the dream "turn into a nightmare as I moved through the ghettos of the nation and saw my black brothers and sisters perishing on a lonely island of poverty in the midst of a vast ocean of material prosperity." The same was true of the war in Vietnam, the urban riots, and the retreat away from the ballyhooed war on poverty. "Yes, I am personally the victim of deferred dreams, of blasted hopes," he said—and yet he still had that same dream from 1963. The dream had a specific substance to it, as he envisioned a day when "brotherhood will be more than a few words at the end of a prayer, but rather the first order of business on every legislative agenda." One day, he dreamed late in 1965, "men will no longer walk the streets in search for jobs that did not exist . . . one day the rat-infested slums of our nation will be plowed into the junk heaps of history."

King's last few sermons replayed older classics, such as "The Drum Major Instinct," a favorite of his that he preached at Ebenezer Baptist, exactly two months before his assassination. He had taken the sermon from the mid-century white Methodist minister J. Wallace Hamilton but as always adapted for his own purposes. In this case, King reflected on his own life, before his congregation in Ebenezer in February 1968. The theme was the desire of humans for recognition, "to be important, to surpass others, to achieve distinction, to lead the parade," a damaging tendency if not harnessed properly. King mentioned a man in Mississippi who said that God was a "charter member" of the White Citizens' Council, pointing out that "so God being the charter member means that everybody who's in that has a kind of divinity, a kind of superiority." He continued with an oft-told story of his time in a jail in Birmingham. "I always try to do a little converting when I'm in jail," he joked. And so was the case with his conversations with wardens in Birmingham, who expressed the typical obsessions with interracial marriage and black sexuality. They were unable to see that the grand scheme of white supremacy had entrapped them. They could not understand that the same forces that oppressed them, that made it difficult for them to pay the bills, were those facing all of the working class—"and all you are living on is the satisfaction of your skin being white, and the drum major instinct of thinking that you are somebody big because you are white."

This part of the drum major instinct was King's way of explaining what Du Bois had meant by the "wages of whiteness," the psychological wage of white skin that locked down the American racial system in separating people whose basic human and economic interests should have united them. The same went for the contest for supremacy between nations, which had set the world on a suicidal course.

King famously finished the address with thoughts on how he would want to be remembered—a life devoted to others, to love, to combatting war and poverty. And so "if you want to say that I was a drum major, say that I was a drum major for justice; say that I was a drum major for peace; I was a drum major for righteousness. And all of the other shallow things will not matter. . . . I just want to leave a committed life behind." That particular passage is now often replayed on King's holiday, but the preceding paragraphs, his ruminations on the way white supremacist attitudes had ensnared and entrapped ordinary whites in a system that paid them the false wages of whiteness rather than the real wages of justice, are omitted.

Where Do We Go from Here: Chaos or Community?, King's last book, came out in a chaotic period of his life, and against the advice and wishes of some of his closest advisors and counselors. One of them, Stanley Levison, urged him to tone down his speeches and writings. Levison, the northerner and former Communist ally, tried (but after 1965 usually failed) to exercise a moderating influence on King's public presentations. Levison pushed King to advance the objectives of the movement within the political system. King, though, was moving in the other direction. The irony is stunning: the FBI's surveillance of King originated in fact because they wanted to track and follow Levison, for his supposed possibly radicalizing influence on King. In truth, Levison's advice consistently pushed King in more conservative directions. But in his last years, King often chose to follow his own instincts.

King preached his last sermon on March 31 at the National Cathedral in Washington. He addressed the points that consumed his thinking and public speaking in his last years—the combination of a techno-logical revolution, a revolution in warfare and armaments, and a human rights revolution worldwide. The three worked together; the world had become a "neighborhood," ensuring that men would have to learn to live together. And yet, King warned, "racial injustice is still the black man's burden and the white man's shame," with racism, "spoken and unspo-ken, acknowledged and denied, subtle and sometimes not so subtle," still being a disease that "poisons a whole body politic." Time would not heal the wound, for progress came only through struggle and work. And the presumed means of ascension of blacks on the ladder of success ignored the particular historical circumstances that challenged this narrative of progress.

The problem was not wealth in and of itself; the story of Jesus telling the rich man to sell all his goods was not meant as a universal prescription but as an individual counsel for a rich ruler. The question for America was not its wealth per se, but whether it would have the will to address the national crisis of poverty that King had personally witnessed in places as diverse as rural Marks, Mississippi, and in Newark, New Jersey, and in Harlem, New York. King used his address to prepare the audience for the coming Poor People's Campaign, a plan to bring a multiracial coalition of people to Washington to dramatize and demand action on the problem of poverty and inequality. Commissions, meetings, and recommendations had been made and sat on shelves ignored. And so, for King, "nothing will be done until people of good will put their bodies and their souls in motion," with a "soul force" that would compel America to make good on its promissory note it once had signed.

King raised his voice as well against the war in Vietnam, still seeking to arouse a national conscience in spite of criticisms that had confronted him at every turn. As he responded, he determined his moral crusades not on the budget of the SCLC or by conducting polls but simply by ask-ing the question—is it right? "There comes a time," he said, "when one must take the position that it is neither safe nor politic nor popular, but he must do it because conscience tells him it is right." Later he concluded that the struggle would be successful "because both the sacred heritage of our nation and the eternal will of the almighty God are embodied in our echoing demands." The more his former allies moved away from him or warned him against his more ambitious visions, the more he felt compelled to follow them.

King's last essay, published posthumously, considered the state of civil rights and gave—for a larger audience who did not originally hear his addresses pitched to SCLC-organized meetings, labor conventions, and church meetings—his extended reflections on the state of civil rights in the United States.

King considered the roots of the black rebellion, an uprising he considered "not only inevitable but eminently desirable." Without it, he thought, "the old evasions and procrastinations would have continued indefinitely. Black men have slammed the door shut on a past of deadening passivity. Except for the Reconstruction years, they have never in their long history on American soil struggled with such creativity and courage for their freedom." But King knew what barriers remained. He asked why equality was so difficult to achieve in a nation so professedly democratic, so manifestly wealthy, and so astonishingly productive of goods and ideas. His response: "The problem is so tenacious because, despite its virtues and attributes, America is deeply racist and its democracy is flawed both economically and socially. All too many Americans believe justice will unfold painlessly or that its absence for black people will be tolerated tranquilly." Indeed, without "radical changes in the structure of our society," true justice simply could not be achieved. While America fought unjust wars abroad, perpetuated racism at home, and tolerated material inequality shocking to any who dared to look carefully, it was clear that "our moral values and our spiritual confidence sink, even as our material wealth ascends." The black struggle for freedom had confronted the nation with the flaws that had been a part of its very founding, flaws that were all tied together—"racism, poverty, militarism, and materialism." The struggle had exposed flaws interwoven within the most basic structures of American society, flaws that were "systemic rather than superficial."

King acknowledged the existence of good white people who had allied themselves with the struggle for rights and dignity, but he also knew that the "largest portion of white America is still poisoned by racism, which is as native to our soil as pine trees, sagebrush, and buffalo grass." Even whites who acknowledged the necessity of equal access and voting rights could not see that "we do not intend to remain in the basement of the economic structure." They remained beholden to a limited vision of "civil rights," one that made no room for any fundamental change. And some well-intentioned whites joined in the struggle, thinking it would be short and easy, "with a kind of messianic faith that they were going to save the Negro and solve all of his problems very quickly." They had, to use more recent terminology, a white savior complex. And in doing so, they overshadowed local African Americans who lacked the same privileges and elite training and came to resent the feeling of white paternalism.

Moreover, nearly everyone overestimated the achievements made from 1955 to 1965 and underestimated both black rage and potential violence and white bigotry barely beneath the surface. The answer was a cold look at what would be necessary in the next stages of the human rights struggle: "For much of the fervent idealism of the white liberals has been supplemented recently by a dispassionate recognition of some of the cold realities of the struggle for that justice." Justice required resources, not just rhetoric.

One of those realities, one fundamental to the future of the struggle, was a real sharing of power—not a "romantic mixing of colors," but a sharing of "power and responsibility" in a manner that would be difficult for a people systematically brutalized and devalued. Yet King, echoing Du Bois's *Souls of Black Folk*, also felt that "Negroes bring a special spiritual and moral contribution to American life," which would be fundamental to American survival. King continued in this Du Boisian vein in hoping that black Americans could serve as a bridge between white westerners and nonwhites elsewhere, precisely because black Americans had roots in both: "Spiritually, Negroes identify understandably with Africa, an identification that is rooted largely in our color; but all of us are a part of the white American world, too. . . . Our very bloodlines are a mixture. I hope and feel that out of the universality of our experience, we can help make peace and harmony in the world more possible."

King acknowledged the changes that had come with the civil rights struggle. Political structures had moved. The "sociological fossils" of Lester Maddox and of George Wallace were still there, but black citizenship rights had been expanded. Those changes were basically in social and political opportunities, while the reality of economic inequality remained intractable.

Black Power advocates justified rioting from the idea, drawn from Franz Fanon, that "violence has a certain cleansing effect," or that acts of public rage were acts against fear. But the problem remained, power structures intact, grievances unmet. And as King saw it, "the aura of paramilitarism among the black militant groups speaks much more of fear than it does of confidence." King reflected on his own experience of giving up guns he had kept for self-protection: "ultimately, one's sense of manhood must come from within him."

Black Power advocates tried to claim the mantle of manhood against what some implied was a kind of feminized nonviolence. This meant fighting back when attacked rather than taking what was coming. King, by contrast, inverted the associations, suggesting that lobbing bromides from ghettos solves nothing: "They cannot solve the problems they face because they have offered not challenge but only a call to arms, which they themselves are unwilling to lead, knowing that doom would be its reward." Conservatives and radicals alike shared an equal helplessness. Further, advocates of violence actually imitated, rather than challenged, the worst aspects of American society. Their rhetoric was rooted as much in fear as in manhood. It was true that riots were the language of the unheard, but, as the scholar Jonathan Walton has said of King's philosophy, "nonviolence is the language of justice—a clear and coherent alliance of love and power speaking truth to justice."

Meanwhile, the root causes of the problems that easily exploded into riots remained, and those problems were economic. The lack of "*meaningful* work" created a situation of "social dynamite." And the poisonous relations of policemen with African American communities spurred distrust and hatred. Police would have to stop "being occupation troops in the ghetto and start protecting its residents." Moreover, the very way American cities were structured embedded racist policies into the framework of everyday lives. Transportation systems, for example, exiled black neighborhoods to bus and subway deserts, while middle-class suburbanites, safe in districts historically segregated through real estate practices, enjoyed easy access to jobs downtown. "There is only one possible explanation for this situation," King concluded, "and that is the racist blindness of city planners." And yet it was a "paradox that those Negroes who have given up on America are doing more to improve it than are its professional patriots. They are stirring the mass of smug, somnolent citizens, who are neither evil nor good, to an awareness of crisis." It was true that "habitual white discrimination" had been transformed into "white backlash," but those lies were losing their grip, as commitment to reform emerged just as it had in past movements from abolitionism to the New Deal. And in this way, just as Jesus owned nothing but transformed the world, so the "poor and despised of the twentieth century will revolutionize this era." With the cooperation of white allies, black America would "shake the prison walls until they fall."

In his final address to the SCLC, "Where Do We Go from Here?" (published posthumously), King tied together his lifelong work toward justice together with his more recently developed emphases on "arousing manhood within a people." By the 1960s, he was attuned to the discourse of racism, the way racist practices emerged from the very structures of common English language usage. Further, King reflected on the uses of power, noting the falseness of separating the concepts of love and power, "so that love is identified with a resignation of power, and power with a denial of love." What had not been understood, he said, was that "power without love is reckless and abusive, and love without power is sentimental and anemic. Power at its best is love implementing the demands of justice and justice at its best is power correcting everything that stands against love." The way toward that end involved the uses of political power to achieve the ends of love and justice. King connected this to his ideas for a guaranteed annual income to offset the inequitable workings of the pure market.

King returned again to the indispensable role of nonviolence. Thinking over the riots of recent years, he found in them a "desire for self-destruction, a kind of suicidal longing." It was nihilism of pure rage with no end directed to justice. And it was an impractical strategy, regardless of its philosophical shortcomings, simply because any black revolution depending on violence would win no support from whites, and not even much from blacks. "This is a time for action," he said, not for "romantic illusions and empty philosophical debates about freedom." Only the nonviolent movement offered a practical strategy for change and action, as well as a philosophical standpoint that did not end up defeating itself: "Darkness cannot put out darkness. Only light can do that."

King returned here to a theme based on his reading of Howard Thurman and other theological diagnosticians of the psychological roots, and effects, of hate. When he saw hate on the faces of Klansmen, policemen, or supposedly upstanding members of the White Citizens' Council, he could only see that "hate is too great a burden to bear"; it crippled those who bore its burdens, while love held the key to unlocking the "meaning of ultimate reality."

That would be a love that produced justice, which would require facing the "question of restructuring the whole of American society." And that would require seeing the "problem of racism, the problem of economic exploitation, and the problem of war" as all tied together, the "triple evils" that marched together and would have to be defeated together. Jesus had looked at Nicodemus and said, "you must be born again," by which he meant, "your whole structure must be changed." And Jesus said the same to a nation dependent on the triple evils of racism, militarism, and inequality. The more his liberal allies, the *New York Times*, and mainstream liberals of the day fought that insight, the more King preached it. A certain lessening of the coarsest acts of brutality did not by itself signify the "presence of justice. To stay murder is not the same thing as to ordain brotherhood."

King's last work provided a penetrating analysis of the historic alliance of racism in the South with reactionary politics in the North. The migration of white southerners had seeded racism elsewhere, and reactionaries nationally pressed their ideology. This explained, King thought, why the United States lagged so far behind most of Western Europe in providing for measures of security. By attacking southern racism, a guardian of this ideology, southern blacks already had improved the rest of the nation. That being said, African Americans had, at best, "established a foothold, no more"; the hard work of equality lay ahead. Equality with whites would not solve the problems of either whites or Negroes if it meant equality in a world society stricken by poverty and in a universe doomed to extinction by war.

King pushed his internationalist analysis of civil rights aims as well. The American civil rights movement was part of broader world developments. "These are revolutionary times," King wrote, and "all over the globe men are revolting against old systems of exploitation and oppression. . . . We in the West must support these revolutions." But because of a complacent attachment to the status quo and a "morbid fear of communism, and our proneness to adjust to injustice, the Western nations that initiated so much of the revolutionary spirit of the modern world have now become the arch counter-revolutionaries." King likewise analyzed the rise of youthful revolt against the norms of society, concluding they had grown up with "evils enough to send reason reeling," enough to engender the alienation which they evidenced in their personal war with conventional societal values.

King marched with James Meredith and Stokely Carmichael in the heart of Mississippi in 1966. Chants of "Black Power" drew crowds frustrated by the slowness of progress. This had shown King the transition of a movement into a new phase. King recounted his conversation with Carmichael and others about their "unfortunate choice of words for a slogan."

Contrary to how the press portrayed it at the time, King in fact had a friendly relationship with his young critics; he saw them moving toward the same goal, albeit with a different style. King told Carmichael that it was a question of semantics, that "Black Power" as a slogan had been associated, rightly or wrongly, with violence, and that the press had attached that meaning to the phrase. For Carmichael, however, the question really was about power, the "only thing respected in the world, and we must get it at any cost." King thought it advisable to use the phrase "black consciousness" or "black equality," but Carmichael understood the potential of "Black Power" as the organizing theme. And so it entered national life. It was, King concluded, a "cry of daily hurt and persistent pain," one that quite logically rose from the brutalizing state of Mississippi. Carmichael suggested that he was going to use King as a kind of foil; they could play off each other in the press. "I have been used before. One more time won't hurt," King ruefully replied. He understood Carmichael's use of press coverage to advance various movement agendas.

King insisted that the nonviolent movement ultimately was the most effective way to achieve power. King saw that he had come to be seen as the apostle of love and nonviolence, but, in fact, that was with the understanding that love came with a "resignation of power and power with a denial of love." Black Power had come from the cries of those who sought to assert selfhood and manhood; it was a "psychological reaction to the psychological indoctrination that led to the creation of the perfect slave." Black Power was a cry against that drive to erase blacks from history; it was a "self-affirmation" of the "black man's need made compelling by the white man's crimes against him."

The despair from which Black Power emerged was real, but a true revolution, King continued, could not be "sustained by despair," because hope, not despair, kept revolutions alive: "When hope dies, a revolution degenerates into an undiscriminating catchall for evanescent and futile gestures." A slogan was a start, but a slogan that could not produce a tangible program was a dead end.

King returned repeatedly to the fact that American politics depended on coalition building, and how much this could be the ally for African Americans in the next phase of the freedom struggle. There were more poor whites than poor blacks, and "their need for a war on poverty is no less desperate than the Negro's," King wrote. Racial division had prevented political coalition, and thus poor whites, in a struggle to preserve the wages of their whiteness, had fought against themselves. But there seemed to be some hope, as evidence from recent elections suggested that interracial coalitions might be possible in a de facto sense. And this gave King hope as well, because "the ability of Negroes to enter alliances is a mark of our growing strength, not of our weakness." It showed that blacks could be equal political partners.

And this reinforced the fatal weakness of Black Power—it could not see that "the black man needs the white man and the white man needs the black man." The romanticization of the slogan ignored the reality that there existed "no separate black path to power and fulfillment that does not intersect white paths." And the reverse was true as well; there would be no path to power for poor whites that did not "share that power with black aspirations for freedom and human dignity. We are bound together in a single garment of destiny." American culture was a cultural mélange, "a mulatto culture, an amalgam of black and white." Hatred and violence, or even rhetorical embrace of them, only intensified white fears and shame; it served only to "deepen the brutality of the oppressor and increases the bitterness of the oppressed."

For King, the issues of poverty were moral more than material. Souls were of "infinite metaphysical value," meaning no one could rest easy with hunger, exploitation, and inequalities of wealth, health, and opportunity. Human societies were composed of interdependent men: "All life is interrelated. The agony of the poor impoverishes the rich; the betterment of the poor enriches the rich. We are inevitably our brother's keeper because we are our brother's brother."

King concluded his final book by reenvisioning the discord of the status quo of hatred, division, and exploitation into the "symphony of brotherhood" he had long envisioned. There was nothing, except a lack of vision and political will, inhibiting measures to ensure decent wages for all, including those workers most necessary but most overlooked. There was nothing preventing the guarantee of a minimum livable income for all. That is, nothing except a "tragic death wish" that blocked a reordering such that "the pursuit of peace will take precedence over the pursuit of war." And such a "revolution of values" would be the ultimate defense against communism, the ideology that thrived on the very divisions and exploitations engendered by America's unjust social systems. The choice still remained between "nonviolent coexistence or violent co-annihilation," with mankind at its last chance to "choose between chaos and community."

King strongly supported some measure of reparations, or a compensatory mechanism to make up for centuries of economic pain inflicted on African Americans. It could be, he thought, the font of a "massive program by the government of special, compensatory measures which could be regarded as a settlement in accordance with the accepted practice of common law." In such a way, historical tragedy could be transformed into present-day justice. And while he envisioned a world of justice, he also could see its opposite. As scholar Jonathan Walton emphasizes, King's final book "reminds us that the beloved thinker and activist whose last speech assured his listeners that he had seen the Promised Land had just as surely glimpsed its alternative." But at least in the "Promised Land" there was the possibility of reconciliation and redemption between former enemies; there would instead be *agape* love.

The day of his death, the BBC aired an interview with King done in February of 1968. There, King said that "we have to honestly admit that the problems in the world today, as they relate to the question of race, must be blamed on the whole doctrine of white supremacy, the whole doctrine of racism, and these doctrines came into being through the white race and the exploitation of the colored peoples of the world. . . . Now if the white world does not recognize this and does not adjust to what is to be, then we can end up in the world with a kind of race war, so it depends on the spirit and the readjusting qualities of the white people of the world, and this will avoid the kind of violent confrontation between the races if it is done properly by the white people." Likewise, in *Where Do We Go from Here*, he argued that "peace is not merely a distant goal that we seek but a means by which we arrive at that goal. We must pursue peaceful ends through peaceful means." That seemed an ever-more-distant dream as he planned the Poor People's Campaign and took an unexpected opportunity in Memphis to promote it.

King split his last months between his projected Poor People's Campaign in Washington, DC, and the garbage workers' strike in Memphis. King was in Memphis in March 1968, called there by his friend and longtime associate in the philosophy of nonviolence, James Lawson, then a local Methodist minister. In Memphis, garbage workers were angry following the terrible deaths of two of their fellow workers. They had been crushed to death in one of the garbage truck machines that had entrapped them. King intended a quick fly-in, fly-out visit, but, as had often happened in the past, he was caught up in the course of events he could not control but that he felt demanded his presence. When King arrived, he found a spirit of unity between the haves and have-nots that he had been looking for. "I've never seen a community as together as Memphis," King told Levison. Memphis lifted up a depressed King.

On behalf of the strikers, King had said in his initial foray into Memphis, "you are reminding the nation that it is a crime for people to live in this rich nation and receive starvation wages." The sanitation employees toiled in unspeakably awful conditions; some depended on welfare in spite of having full-time jobs. Quotes from the sanitation workers give some hint of what they endured: They "toted" trash on their heads, the tubs full of water, "rain, garbage, maggots, everything else running out. Back then you had to supply your own clothes, own gloves, they didn't give you anything but the tubs. If you'd get a hole in it the water'd run all out the tub down on ya. Boss would sit around drinkin' coffee, come around once or twice a day to check on the truck." The workers had no bathroom breaks and had fifteen minutes for lunch. They also had no opportunity to advance: "We didn't have no say about nothing," as one put it.

Meanwhile, in March, marches for the garbage workers' strike had spun out of control, as young people in Memphis retaliated when attacked and damaged property downtown. King and the SCLC had to retreat and regroup. King and others negotiated with local blacks, including a group of gang members known as "The Invaders," who were not sold on the nonviolent approach; they knew from past experience that violent reaction often grabbed attention while nonviolent marches could be easily defused if there were local white leaders savvy enough to know how to do that. King maintained his steadfast posture about nonviolence but knew that more instrumental arguments—how many guns do we have, and how many do they have, he asked—were necessary. Speaking to a local branch of a labor union on March 18, he praised them for highlighting economic issues: "You are going beyond purely civil rights to questions of human rights." A previous phase of the movement centered on political and constitutional rights; the next phase would be for economic equality.

J. Edgar Hoover's assistant said that blacks had taken up "general guerilla warfare," and they hoped to destroy it from within, using their plants and their bugs to stay one step ahead of the movement. They paid the SCLC's accountant for information, monitored calls, and sent out reports to the local and national press slandering King. They were busy at the same time sowing misinformation about the Poor People's Campaign, in an attempt to undermine it from within. Hoover told agents to "prevent the rise of a black messiah."

In early April 1968, still struggling to plan his new dream, the Poor People's Campaign, King returned to Memphis to support the workers, who carried signs saying "I Am a Man." The previous weeks had been chaotic and difficult, full of internal tension and division within the SCLC. Organizing for the Poor People's Campaign had proved difficult; the interracial coalition King sought was easier to envision than to enact. King's advisers pushed him to scale back his efforts to something more manageable, with a narrower and more clearly defined set of goals. King was intrinsically a radical reformer who sought resolution rather than protracted conflict. He had backed away in Birmingham and Chicago, and by the end of January 1968 he already (on the advice of numerous advisers) was dialing down his ideas of disrupting ordinary life in DC, in favor of a more conventional campaign.

Death threats followed King around everywhere, including one directed toward the plane carrying him to Memphis. Accustomed to them, King sat quietly while some of his fellow passengers sought to escape the plane. King generally refused to travel with security or use police for that purpose. He felt it distracted from the message of nonviolence, and if someone intended to kill him, they would do so, regardless of the precautions taken. The evening of April 3, exhausted from his travels, he had sent his companion Ralph Abernathy to speak to the crowd at the headquarters for the Church of God in Christ. King sought a night of respite, but the crowd demanded his presence. He made his way to Mason Temple, the home church of the nation's largest black Pentecostal denomination, with an April thunderstorm providing the dramatic backdrop for his epic oratory and protest speech improvised from bits and pieces of addresses he had delivered before, woven together with references to the local conditions in Memphis.

Toward the end, King reflected on his life, in words that electrified the crowd watching and that since have come down as legend as they eerily seemed to predict King's own mortality. King unfurled highlights from the rest of the civil rights victories achieved over the last few years before concluding with the question of what would happen if the threats against him were carried out "from some of our sick white brothers." He only knew that, regardless of what might happen, he had been to the mountaintop and had "seen the promised land" and that "we as a people will get to the promised land. And I'm happy, tonight. I'm not worried about anything. I'm not fearing any man. Mine eyes have seen the glory of the coming of the Lord." He stumbled backward off the stage, in part from exhaustion, in part from being captured by the spirit of his own oratory. It was his last public appearance.

The local and state police, the FBI, and other authorities had tracked and threatened King for years; they were so present that at times King and his fellows meeting in hotel rooms on the road would mockingly address them, knowing full well they were likely bugged at that very moment. And the police knew about a drifter named James Earl Ray (although he usually went by other aliases) as well, and they had some information about his intentions.

The psychologically obsessed Ray followed King's movements for weeks. Finally, in Memphis, he had his prey in sight. He rented a room in the New Rebel Motel with his rifle ready. The media helped him by broadcasting King's exact location, down to his room number (306) at the nearby Lorraine Motel, a black-owned establishment where King often stayed; King enjoyed the fried catfish in the restaurant there. Local police assigned to protect King had knocked off duty late that afternoon. Just before six o'clock, King stood exposed on the balcony. Ray's rifle shot tore through King's body and left him crumpled next to the balcony window, a scene made famous in photos from the era that capture the exact moment. King died about an hour later.

In the end, law enforcement authorities were skillful at the surveillance of King and completely incompetent in preventing his assassination at that moment. They simply didn't care enough to take any forceful action on it. Afterward, a vigorous investigation tracked down Ray and compiled the details of his deadly pursuit of King. It was too little, too late. In the coming next few years, government surveillance of every single black protest or civil rights organization in the country amped up. The tactics of surveillance and infiltration used in the pursuit and harassment of Martin Luther King Jr. had been perfected. They worked with the malice intended.

After the assassination, Ray fled first to Canada and then later to England, apparently hoping to end up in what was then still the British colony of Rhodesia (now Zimbabwe). Ray later tried to shift the blame to mysterious characters with whom he had been involved. It's possible that he and his brothers were accomplices, and it is almost certainly true Ray thought his actions would help the Wallace campaign. There is some evidence of a group based in St. Louis that raised funds for Ray and his brothers. Ray's post-assassination travels to Canada and England, with some vague plans to end up in Rhodesia, were remarkable, as were his different aliases and passports that he carried with him. How a man of such few resources managed such international travel remains an unsolved mystery. And it's entirely plausible that he had considerable help in his eventually aborted escape.

Ironically, Ray had been a working-class white man attracted by the 1968 campaign of George Wallace, then running as a kind of straight-talking populist who sought specifically to appeal to ordinary whites. And in that sense, Ray was exactly the kind of white man King had in mind in his final Poor People's Campaign, and the kind of white man he had dealt with as the ordinary men who worked in the jails of the South. During one of his incarcerations in Birmingham, he remembered speaking with the person who came to give him food or unlock his cell and learned that this man could barely afford to feed his family and was generally estranged from the social system. When King spoke of a campaign to unify blacks and whites who shared common economic problems, this is who he had in mind.

However, the variety of other conspiracy theories launched over the years about King's assassination have not offered much in the way of solid proof. The one theory that certainly holds up is that the government (at all levels) easily could have protected King's life but failed to do so. This was certainly the case in Memphis; the evidence for assassination attempts on King was mounting, and it would not have been difficult to protect a man apparently so marked. The evidence here points to an incompetence derived more from indifference and years of quotidian brutality than any grand conspiracy. Government agents were interested in surveilling his sex life but not in protecting his actual life. J. Edgar Hoover was certainly not distraught over King's death, but the FBI's thorough investigation of the events leading to his death still holds up.

King was gunned down by the very kind of person he had encountered time and again on the streets, in jails, in confrontations with white authorities, and from far back in his boyhood: the white man obsessed more with the possibility of justice for African Americans than for the conditions that had made his own life miserable. It was the same tragic tale that had undermined Reconstruction and the populist movement in the nineteenth century and had made southern labor organizing difficult. Much the same tale has hindered interracial political coalitions since King's time as well. And so it remains in our day. Race remains the wall that divides ordinary working and middle-class Americans who suffer from similar maladies of economic insecurity, lack of access to health care, and a political system primarily responsive to the wealthiest classes. The same things King confronted and challenged.

Early morning, April 4
Shot rings out in the Memphis sky
Free at last, they took your life,
They could not take your pride.

—U2, "Pride (In the Name of Love)," *The Unforgettable Fire* (1984)

Epilogue

The Irrelevance of Sainthood:
The Afterlives of Martin Luther King Jr.

And besides,
it is easier to build monuments
than to make a better world.

—Carl Wendell Hines Jr., "A Dead Man's Dream"

We know how King would respond to our current mean season of political unrest, racial division and state-sanctioned violence. He understood much more than the fact that "riots were the language of the unheard." He eloquently argued that the racial upheaval gripping the country during the 1960s was the direct result of white supremacy's uncanny hold on every aspect of American life, from public schools, housing and health care to criminal justice, employment and domestic and foreign policy. What would Martin Luther King Jr. do in our time? . . . He would find our age of racial division, white denial and spreading wealth inequality and violence an all too familiar artifact of his own time.

—Historian Peniel E. Joseph in the *Washington Post*, June 2020

King ended his life much as he lived it through the 1960s: an unpopular man, one surveilled and harassed by governmental authorities, one tormented by his own failures and inadequacies as a man and as a movement leader, but one imbued always with a religious vision of transcending the circumstances of the movement to reach toward the beloved community. In a 1966 Gallup Poll, 72 percent of white Americans had an unfavorable opinion of him, and 85 percent said that demonstrations had hurt the cause of civil rights—just after Selma. After the assassination, the FBI and other agencies continued surveilling Coretta Scott King; they worried that she would tie the anti–Vietnam War movement to the civil rights movement (as she already had done for years). In a speech in Central Park on April 27, 1968, one that Martin was supposed to have given, Coretta King called on the power of women to "heal the broken community now so shattered by war and poverty and racism." Surveillance continued during the Nixon administration.

The fate of martyrs is to be made into saints, and the fate of saints is to be made into statues, mausoleum pieces, and irrelevant national holidays. Martin Luther King Jr. was a misunderstood martyr. He was misunderstood at the time by a majority of white Americans who expressed a dislike or distrust of him. He was misperceived at times by some on the black left who failed to recognize the radicalism inherent in his philosophy.

But the real distortions started much later. The first King holiday was proposed by John Conyers, a black Democrat from Michigan, in 1968. Its acceptance took twenty years. Then, when signing it, Ronald Reagan apologized to the governor of New Hampshire, who had opposed it fiercely at home. Reagan shared the governor's reservations but said that "the perception is reality." Reagan effectively redirected anger at his budget priorities away from the historic concerns of civil rights activists and to the measures that King most criticized. Symbolism could replace substance, and King was woven indelibly into the national civil religion. On signing the act, Reagan said, "We can take pride in the knowledge that we Americans recognized a grave injustice and took action to correct it." That was a charitable interpretation of how the freedom struggle managed to compel whatever gains it had won through the 1960s.

As his image was burnished and made suitable for King holiday consumption, the tough edges were whittled down. Emptied of its content, the King holiday has been drained of its political significance. "Where the historical King aspired to transform the polis and its inhabitants," writes philosopher Paul Taylor, "the King of 'MLK Day' calls citizens, more or less as they stand, simply to serve the polis, more or less as it stands. . . . Service still floats free of any sustained reflection on the ends one serves, or the implications of serving just these ends and not others."

Over time, his status as a martyr and a saint made him useful for numerous causes, many of which he spent virtually his entire public career inveighing against. From the 1980s forward, his assimilation into a mainstream national narrative pits King against allegedly more dangerous or radical figures. In the process, "King" as a static symbol came to replace King as the constantly evolving thinker and person. Recent scholarship on the latter years of King's life has pushed back against that narrative, but this has yet to find its way into popular conceptions of King, now the smiling hero of children's books.

King's afterlives evolved in a number of distinct phases. First was the reaction to his death and the few years after. At that point, it was still safe for white supremacist politicians to direct the same venom toward him and the movement upon his death as they had during his life. Later, during the 1970s and the Reagan years, the process of sanctification was in full evidence. Ronald Reagan resisted it, suggesting darkly that whether King was a communist would have to await the full opening of King's papers and FBI files decades later. Reagan clearly played to a constituency that had not accommodated itself to the transformations wrought by King as a public figure. And yet it was the conservative Ronald Reagan, strident opponent of King in his lifetime, who signed the King national holiday legislation into law.

That opened the way for people of all political stripes to join their causes to King—including those whose causes were exactly contrary to his. "Content of their character"—King's well-known phrase, made famous in 1963 but certainly a stock in trade of other sermons and public addresses he gave—was reduced to colorblindness.

The problem with colorblindness, of course, is that America is not colorblind. King had an acute sense, from his youngest years but fully developed later, that American racism was not incidental but systemic. It was baked into the system and was the hellhound on the trail of every black American. Certainly he envisioned a world beyond color, but he also understood what it would take to get there. That would be a revolution in American social, economic, and political institutions.

Many who condemned him during his life continued doing so right after his death. After hearing of King's death, Strom Thurmond, the legendary racist senatorial leader from South Carolina, portrayed King as an outside agitator "bent on stirring people up, making everyone dissatisfied." King had just "pretended to be nonviolent." King had received his just deserts when he was killed.

For that reason, others at the time prepared for a possible armed conflict. The year 1968 was tumultuous for many reasons—the assassinations, the turmoil over the Vietnam War, the contested Democratic convention in Chicago—and some African Americans believed, with good reason, that they were, or would soon be, under attack. Late in his life, King expressed the notion that "there must be somebody to communicate to the two worlds." He sought to build a coalition of conscience, drawing together Black Power advocates and mainstream civil rights activists; he wanted a "militant middle." But that looked increasingly difficult to achieve.

What immediately became clear was the love of the black community for King. While white liberals had criticized what they perceived as his turn to radicalism and focus on foreign policy issues such as the Vietnam War, black workers expressed love and admiration for their fallen hero.

Sanitation workers vowed to carry on with their struggle in Memphis; they knew that King sympathized with their plight. "Dr. King died on the case," his SCLC associate James Bevel said. Of King coming to Memphis, as one expressed it, "it was just like Jesus was coming into my life. I was full of joy and determination. Wherever Dr. King was, I wanted to be there." They held a silent march for him. At his funeral, James Baldwin wrote, "The atmosphere was black with a tension indescribable—as though something, perhaps the heavens, perhaps the earth, might crack." Carried by mules, King's coffin, another said, "symbolized what he lived for and what he died for." For those on the black left, King's evolution had been striking. As one put it, King had been able to tell "white Americans that they're wrong for being over there in . . . Vietnam killing those Vietnamese . . . I was diggin' on what he was saying."

Meanwhile, the response of whites stood in striking contrast. Only 42 percent of whites showed an emotional response when asked about his death. As the historian Jason Sokol has written, "King's assassination was not a tragedy to wrestle with—much less an event that would affect their lives or their outlook. It was just another inconvenience to navigate." Only one southern congressman attended the funeral; the primary reaction consisted of a few polite statements of regret. Some felt that the hatred of King among whites had in effect empowered the assassin. One observer noted that "The assassin heard enough condemnation of King and of Negroes to feel that he had public support." One housewife told the reporter David Halberstam, "I wish you had spit in his face for me." Ronald Reagan, governor of California, thought the assassination and all the disorder of that time started when "we began compromising with law and order, and people started choosing which laws they'd break." Even in eulogizing King, he took a swipe at him. Meanwhile, white workers in a Ford plant in Nashville protested the lowering of the American flag, expressing anger toward the United Auto Workers; the same would not have been done for Billy Graham, they said. These were the kinds of workers then being energized by the political campaign of George Wallace, the Alabama segregationist whose star was on the rise nationally as he ran a right-wing populist campaign that drew considerable working-class support. King's vision, that the labor struggle and the freedom struggle shared common goals and common enemies, was fading from view.

Prior to his death, King had warned that "our national government is playing Russian roulette with riots; it gambles with another summer of disaster." The assassination "changed the whole dynamic of the country," wrote Kathleen Cleaver. It was the "single most significant event in terms of how the Panthers were perceived by the black community." The critiques black radicals had made of American society seemed to have been confirmed in the most painful way possible.

Some sympathy was noted in the white community. Samuel DuBois Cook, the only African American on the Duke University faculty, thought initially that King's death would not be redemptive but only worsen divisions. But in the days after his death, he saw a silent student vigil, picket lines on behalf of black workers, and support for cafeteria employees. The movement energy evident in the vigil made the pain of the death more bearable and seemed to represent an awakening of the Duke student body. Likewise, a story from Memphis gave some of King's associates heart. Jerred Blanchard was a lawyer originally from Missouri who had moved to Memphis as a teenager, received his education elsewhere, served in World War II, and then returned to Memphis and became an ally of mayor Henry Loeb on the city council. During the sanitation workers' strike, he did his best to be a peacemaker, and in the process, this formerly conservative anti-labor lawyer learned from listening to the grievances of the garbage collectors and eventually ended up participating in protest marches. Reflecting on people like Blanchard, Andrew Young later wrote, "Martin Luther King's death was something of a turning point, of white people suddenly being willing to come around. I think a lot happened in white America that's never been recorded, in the wake of [his] death . . . I sensed then that whites wanted to help, but didn't know how." There seemed, at times, some hope still for King's vision.

In the next campaign, King had told Bernard Lafayette, "we'll have to institutionalize nonviolence and take it international." And King was already an international celebrity; he was known as a partner and ally in global anti-colonial struggles. King had spoken eloquently on that since the 1950s, defended African independence movements, and was an early critic of South African apartheid. And his European visits had let him see that world opinion would be an ally in the struggle. The Congo created a postage stamp in homage to King, and such commemorative pieces flourished throughout the Third World. In India, Indira Gandhi called King's murder "a setback to mankind's search for light."

King's image was shaped in West Germany to fit aims of both government and student radicals, who saw him as standing with their revolutionary struggle. But in Great Britain, right-wing populists and anti-immigrant forces were gaining strength. A famous speech titled "Rivers of Blood" from the conservative politician Enoch Powell presaged a darker age of politics and race relations to come. "We must be mad, literally mad," he said, "as a nation to be permitting the annual inflow of some 50,000 dependants. . . . It is like watching a nation busily engaged in heaping up its own funeral pyre." Many politicians, including some Tories, were uncomfortable with the venom of Powell's speech, but Powell was bombarded with letters of support, and one letter writer to the *London Times* suggested, "Mr. Powell's crime is to have said what

every Englishman thinks." Another dockworker, involved in a spontaneous strike to protest Powell's removal from the cabinet, said, "We think
there are too many bloody coons coming into the country." Rising tides of
white populist nationalism in the United States, England, and elsewhere
suggested that King's dream would recede from rather than emerge into
view.

The night of King's assassination, Bobby Kennedy was in Indianapolis,
running in the primary for the nomination of the Democratic Party to run
for president. Kennedy was stunned by the news, which reached him as
he was addressing the crowd. He delivered a short, unscripted address,
expressing the anguish of many and asking people to "make an effort, as
Martin Luther King did, to understand, and to comprehend, and replace
that violence, that stain of bloodshed that has spread across our land, with
an effort to understand, compassion, and love." Kennedy clearly touched
the crowd with his unvarnished emotion—"I saw it, he felt it man, he
cried," one African American in attendance later said. Robert Kennedy's
transformation was remarkable and might have presaged a political coalition to carry forward movement aims. That did not turn out to be the case.
Two months later, Robert Kennedy was assassinated.

The closest student of the legacy of King's death, Jason Sokol, writes,
"Americans were able to so admire King because they picked and chose
which parts of his career they wanted to embrace. They scrubbed his
message and blunted his meaning. Eventually, the historical King—a
courageous dissident who unsettled the powerful—would be replaced
by a mythical one." He points out that King was consistent; he appealed
to a yearning that whites and blacks could live together equally. Whites
"began to appropriate King's legacy and wield it in their own causes."
Later, for whites to adopt King as a national hero, "his message would
need to be shaped into something simpler and less threatening." That
process started not long after his death, and it has continued since.

By 1971, Martin Luther King Jr. Day was a state holiday in nine states,
and in 1973, Illinois became the first state to declare it a paid state holiday.
In other states, though, bitter words about King stanched such efforts.
The governor of New Hampshire, for example, in arguing against the
appointment of Andrew Young to the United Nations, wrote that "I heart-
ily agree with the appraisal of Dr. Martin Luther King by the late J. Edgar
Hoover and believe that King did a great harm to the American Way of
Life through his association with communist inspired organizations." A
few years later, as some momentum began to build to make King Day
national, that kind of opposition frequently arose. The holiday, an Ohio
political leader announced, would simply give the false idea that King
was a great man, and not someone who sought "not to work through
the law but around it, with contempt and violence." Meanwhile, King's

own opponent, the unrepentant segregationist and right-wing columnist James J. Kilpatrick, thought that King's political views were "naïve" and "sophomoric" and that King's Riverside Church address against the Vietnam War was unforgivable. Kilpatrick, like many other white Americans, was unrepentant; indeed, he felt vindicated.

King holiday legislation took a winding path, once almost being killed by its opponents turning it into a unpaid Sunday non-holiday holiday. President Reagan remained opposed to it early in 1983, even as some Republicans, seeing an opportunity to pick up some black votes, began to advocate it even as they opposed the extension of the Voting Rights Act and other key civil rights measures. Its fiercest opponent remained Jesse Helms of North Carolina, who still referred to the freedom struggle as the "so-called civil rights movement." King's speeches, he said, contained "the crackle of anarchy and the threat of violence," and King's work in Memphis had created the atmosphere that led to his assassination (or, in other words, King was responsible for his own murder). Helms conducted a filibuster against the legislation leading to the holiday, attempting to compel an investigation into King's supposed ties to Communists. But momentum kept growing, and Reagan decided finally to cut his losses and sign the bill into law.

King's transformation into a plaster saint took off from there. By the mid-1980s, the majority of whites saw him as a national hero of some sort, even if they disagreed on exactly why. For black radicals, he was a hero of the battle against international colonialism. For many whites, he was a minister who breathed life into Christian concepts and renewed America's constitution. For white progressives, he was a champion of federal power used toward progressive ends. For reformists, he showed that change was possible within the system. And for conservatives, he was a champion of individual character over skin color and an example of an individualist hero who had forged his own path.

King was all of those and more; and thus King could appeal to many constituencies, each of which could pick and choose what they wanted to from his life. And he had a universal appeal, imagining a society in which people would live as equals.

The conservative refashioning of King into its own image occurred with breathtaking rapidity. On the first King holiday, in January 1986, Reagan claimed his mantle, portraying King as an individualist hero. Roger Wilkins of the NAACP was disgusted. Reagan and King stood for almost exactly contrary policies, he noted; Reagan was "pretending to adhere to ideals that his policies clearly indicate he opposes." Meanwhile, the Reagan administration opposed sanctioning the South African apartheid regime and seemed more interested in retaining the apartheid government as an anti-communist ally than in moving against the most explicitly racist regime left in the world. Reagan's attorney general, Edwin Meese, attempted to eliminate anti-racist hiring practices in federal contracts, saying that he was "trying to carry out the original intent of the civil rights movement." He was moving, he said, toward the "colorblind society" of which King had dreamed.

In fact, this was explicitly contrary to King's vision of achieving equality in a society that had spent hundreds of years denying it. Society had worked against the Negro, and now it had to work for him, King had said. King also endorsed compensatory mechanisms, by which he meant a kind of GI Bill program that in particular would benefit African Americans. Nonetheless, numerous politicians, such as the governor of Louisiana, continued to say that "I can't find anywhere in his writings that he wanted reverse discrimination"; obviously they never tried to look, since the evidence is abundant of his support for compensatory measures. King's speeches from that era almost exactly mirror words taken from BLM protests.

As has been emphasized throughout this book, King was always a "profound advocator of the social gospel," as he described himself as a twenty-year-old man. Over time, he fully developed a program that could be best described (and as he described it himself) as social democracy, more or less along the lines of a European social democratic state. He also supported reparations for African Americans; believed quotas in hiring would be a good first step in dealing with the problem of employment discrimination; called for a massive Marshall Plan–style program of aid to America's urban areas; blasted the Vietnam War as evidence of the connection of militarism, colonialism, and racism; and condemned conservative politicians of both parties, everyone from George Wallace to Barry Goldwater, as being propagators of a reactionary politics aimed equally at blacks and labor.

The appropriation of King for every cause imaginable came also because King's near universal popularity by the 2000s meant that his mantle *had* to be claimed. As the vigorous protest movement Black Lives Matter arose in the 2010s in response to police violence against African Americans, white Americans expressed shock that BLM would dare to claim the King mantle. The movement, one commentator claimed, "encourages violence through irresponsible rhetoric." Another conservative politician declared, "Dr. King would not participate in a Black Lives Matter protest," while a former vice presidential candidate suggested that BLM was "the antithesis of Martin Luther King's Message." Thus, politicians and pundits reduce King's message to a slogan, insisting that he "stood for" measures that he in fact did not stand for and that he was or would be opposed to policies that in fact he vigorously supported.

Criticisms of the contemporary protest movements in fact replay exactly what King's critics said about him during his life. They accused him of fomenting disorder and violence, of fostering disunity and vision, and of promoting un-American and unpatriotic ideals. Moderate critics urged him to wait until the political system had better leaders in place, or to call off protests and instead create commissions and task forces to resolve issues. People accused him of being a publicity seeker or of having a messiah or martyr complex; of undermining the stability of southern and American society; of cavorting with communists and promoting radicalism; and of messing in problems (such as the Vietnam War) where he had no business.

Even more than Black Lives Matter, one contemporary movement has claimed, accurately and eloquently, the King mantle: the Moral Mondays movement led by the Reverend William Barber of North Carolina. Barber rose to prominence in the 2010s as he led a series of protests at the state capitol of North Carolina (every Monday for some time, hence the name). Under a legislative regime determined to roll back voting and civil rights protections, the state implemented an egregiously inegalitarian set of voting districts designed to reduce the impact of black votes and put in place voting eligibility requirements that were intentionally and maliciously directed at African Americans: "Although the new provisions target African Americans with almost surgical precision, they constitute inapt remedies for the problems assertedly justifying them and, in fact, impose cures for problems that did not exist," a circuit court unanimously decided.

As president of the North Carolina chapter of the NAACP, William Barber celebrated the decision. Over the next years, the Moral Mondays movement continued its quest to bring to public light the ways the North Carolina legislature deliberately set to roll back the gains so painfully won through the King years. As Barber explained his philosophy, "the gospel is clear that there's no separation between Jesus and justice, there's no separation between Jesus and caring about the least of these and challenging the systems, whether that system be racism or economic exploitation, or ecological devastation, or the war economy, or false religious nationalism—the gospel is a critique of all of it." Barber also emphasized that King's quest for economic justice, taken up most explicitly toward the end of his life, remained the paramount concern. And that quest was not a "civil rights" issue affecting African Americans but a moral and human rights issue equally affecting ordinary white and black Americans struggling with economic inequalities, job insecurity, and lack of access to basic health care.

Here, Barber clearly takes up King's theme: the relationship of moral means to the moral ends of civil rights and economic justice. In that sense, Barber clearly carries on the King legacy. Through the country, local leaders do the same, on issues ranging from environmental justice to systemic racialized inequalities in the health care system to mass incarceration disproportionately affecting black men. There, far more than in the typically vacuous words of politicians, celebrities, newspaper editors, and university presidents on King's annual birthday celebration, his legacy lives.

The contemporary rise of a white nationalist alt-right—including those who stormed the Capitol building on January 6, 2021, egged on by the then-president as well as by an entire ecosystem of disinformation that had been peddled to them for months and years previously—now rejects the King legacy of a "symphony of brotherhood" altogether. They have unapologetically returned to the white supremacist playbook of King's enemies. In a sense, those living in this particular present-day bubble of the white nationalist right actually may have a much more accurate interpretation of King than the various other distortions we are surveying here. It's just that they fundamentally reject that vision.

King said that one could hew a stone of hope out of a mountain of despair. And such may be the case here. The justice envisioned by King was substantive, not merely rhetorical. There is time to refresh King's vision, to free it from the plaster sainthood where it has been entombed. There is time to recapture the morally clarifying force of his vision of a government devoted to equality and justice, and not one that would simply repeat empty mantras of "unity." That time is now.

Bibliographic Essay

PROLOGUE

This book is based largely on the writings and oratory—sermons, speeches, letters, notes, videos, interviews, etc.—of Martin Luther King Jr. The sources are discussed at length in the next section ("Primary Sources"). I have also been influenced by a number of secondary texts in particular. When these authors are quoted in the text, I have tried to make that clear, so readers may easily follow up on their thoughts, even without having formal endnotes to the chapter.

Here are the most important secondary works (presented in alphabetical order) I have used and, on a few occasions, quoted from. Fuller discussions of their ideas, methods and approaches are in the bibliographic essay below: Lewis V. Baldwin, *The Voice of Conscience: The Church in the Mind of Martin Luther King, Jr.* (New York: Oxford University Press, 2010); Gary Dorrien, *Breaking White Supremacy: Martin Luther King Jr. and the Black Social Gospel* (New Haven, CT: Yale University Press, 2018); Michael Dyson, *I May Not Get There with You: The True Martin Luther King, Jr.* (New York: Simon & Schuster, 2000); David Garrow, *Bearing the Cross: Martin Luther King, Jr., and the Southern Christian Leadership Conference* (New York: William Morrow, 1986); Michael Honey, *To the Promised Land: Martin Luther King and the Fight for Economic Justice* (New York: Norton, 2018); Thomas Jackson, *From Civil Rights to Human Rights: Martin Luther King, Jr., and the Struggle for Economic Justice* (Philadelphia: University of Pennsylvania Press, 2007); Peniel Joseph, *The Sword and the Shield: The Revolutionary Lives of Malcolm X and Martin Luther King, Jr.* (New York:

Basic, 2020); Peter Ling, *Martin Luther King, Jr.*, 2nd ed. (London: Routledge, 2015); Richard Lischer, *The Preacher King: Martin Luther King, Jr. and the Word That Moved America* (New York: Oxford University Press, 1995); Lerone Martin, "Bureau Clergyman: How the FBI Colluded with an African American Televangelist to Destroy Dr. Martin Luther King, Jr.," *Religion and American Culture* 28, no.1 (2018): 1–51; Keith D. Miller, *Voice of Deliverance: The Language of Martin Luther King, Jr., and Its Sources* (Athens: University of Georgia Press, 1992); Patrick Parr, *The Seminarian: Martin Luther King Jr. Comes of Age* (Chicago: Lawrence Hill Books, 2018); Jonathan Rieder, *The Word of the Lord Is upon Me: The Righteous Performance of Martin Luther King, Jr.* (Cambridge, MA: Harvard University Press, 2008); and *Gospel of Freedom: Martin Luther King, Jr.'s Letter from Birmingham Jail and the Struggle That Changed a Nation* (New York: Bloomsbury, 2013); Tommie Shelby and Brandon Terry, eds., *To Shape a New World: Essays on the Political Philosophy of Martin Luther King, Jr.* (Cambridge, MA: Harvard University Press, 2018); Jason Sokol, *The Heavens Might Crack: The Death and Legacy of Martin Luther King Jr.* (New York: Basic, 2018); Douglas Sturm, "Martin Luther King, Jr., as Democratic Socialist," *Journal of Religious Ethics* 18, no. 2 (Fall 1990): 79–105; Brandon M. Terry, "MLK Now," *Boston Review*, September 10, 2018, at http://bostonreview.net/forum/brandon-m-terry-mlk-now; and Jeanne Theoharis, *A More Beautiful and Terrible History: The Uses and Misuses of Civil Rights History* (Boston: Beacon, 2018).

PRIMARY SOURCES

The volume of material written by Martin Luther King Jr., and written *about* him, is enormous. I have endeavored to read everything published by him, and unpublished as available now in the seven printed volumes and online material of *The Papers of Martin Luther King, Jr.* I also read as many biographical, theological, critical, historical, and polemical studies of his life and work as I possibly could, in the preparation of this volume—but certainly not all of them. Here, in this short bibliographic essay, I hope to direct attention to the most important and pertinent of the primary and secondary literature, as well as to easily available books and articles.

Since the 1990s, Clayborne Carson (now emeritus professor at Stanford) has directed the Martin Luther King, Jr. Papers Project, with a projected goal of publishing a definitive set of the papers of King over fourteen volumes. So far, seven volumes have been published. They are the basis of all serious writing and scholarship about King. The currently published volumes (noted here just under the general editorship of Clayborne Carson;

each individual volume has a varied set of associate editors) include Clayborne Carson et al., eds., *The Papers of Martin Luther King, Jr. Volume I: Called to Serve, 1929–June 1951* (Berkeley: University of California Press, 1992); *The Papers of Martin Luther King, Jr. Volume II: Rediscovering Precious Values, July 1951–November 1955* (Berkeley: University of California Press, 1994); *The Papers of Martin Luther King, Jr. Volume III: Birth of a New Age, December 1955–December 1956* (Berkeley: University of California Press, 1997); *The Papers of Martin Luther King, Jr. Volume IV: Symbol of the Movement, January 1957–December 1958* (Berkeley: University of California Press, 2000); *The Papers of Martin Luther King, Jr. Volume V: Threshold of a New Decade: January 1959–December 1960* (Berkeley: University of California Press, 2005); *The Papers of Martin Luther King, Jr. Volume VI: Advocate of the Social Gospel, September 1948–March 1963* (Berkeley: University of California Press, 2007); *The Papers of Martin Luther King, Jr. Volume VII: To Save The Soul of America, January 1961–August 1962* (Berkeley: University of California Press, 2014).

All of the volumes are of immeasurable historical significance but. for my purposes, I found particularly crucial volumes I, II, and VI. Volume I reproduces documents from King's early life, including his teenage years, up to his entrance as a PhD candidate at Boston University. Volume II produces the documents from King's doctoral study (including a full footnoting and accounting for the plagiarism evident in his PhD dissertation) and from his first months at the Dexter Avenue Baptist Church in Montgomery. Finally, volume VI produces the original typescripts and manuscripts, prior to editing, of many of King's published books. Through the painstaking work of the editors, we can see what changes King's published work went through prior to publication. In this way, we sense more clearly what King's initial unfiltered thoughts were before they were smoothed and sanded down (with his assent and cooperation) for a wider public consumption.

King's writings and speeches are now readily available in a number of texts that reproduce them. First, of course, are King's own books, including *Stride Toward Freedom: The Montgomery Story* (New York: Harper & Row, 1958); *Strength to Love* (New York: Harper & Row, 1963); *Why We Can't Wait* (New York: Harper & Row, 1964); *Where Do We Go From Here: Chaos or Community?* (New York: Harper & Row, 1967); *The Trumpet of Conscience* (published posthumously, New York: Harper & Row, 1968).

The first, and still the most important, anthology, came out in the 1980s, edited by the black religious history scholar James Melvin Washington: *A Testament of Hope: The Essential Writings and Speeches of Martin Luther King, Jr.* (New York: HarperOne, 1986). In more recent years, Beacon Press has done scholars and the public the great service of publishing a series of "King Legacy" works, reproducing his essays and speeches that in many cases were recovered from tape-recorded versions or from lesser-known articles in the black press and in black religious periodicals. These now form an instrumental part of the King corpus. The first focuses on King's relationship with the labor movement and his tying together of the progressive forces in labor and the black freedom struggle; the second reproduces addresses featuring King as a visionary of a system of global justice and a critic of the Vietnam War and all instances of colonialism abroad; and the third is a compendium of King's addresses focused most directly on systems of exploitation, power, and inequality in American society. Collectively, these volumes have added an immeasurable depth to the original work of James Melvin Washington in putting together the first collection, *A Testament of Hope* in the 1980s. See Lewis V. Baldwin, ed., *"In a Single Garment of Destiny": A Global Vision of Justice* (Boston: Beacon, 2012); Michael K. Honey, ed., *All Labor Has Dignity* (Boston: Beacon, 2011); and Cornel West, ed., *The Radical King* (Boston: Beacon, 2015). A very useful volume contrasting and comparing speeches of King and Malcolm X may be found in David Howard-Pitney, *Martin Luther King Jr., Malcolm X, and the Civil Rights Struggle of the 1950s and 1960s: A Brief History with Documents* (Boston: Bedford/St. Martin's, 2004). Other useful anthologies include Clayborne Carson and Peter Holloran, eds., *A Knock at Midnight: Inspiration from the Great Sermons of Reverend Martin Luther King, Jr.* (London: Abacus, 2000); Clayborne Carson, ed., *The Autobiography of Martin Luther King, Jr.* (New York: Intellectual Properties Management, 2009); and Clayborne Carson et al., eds., *A Call to Conscience: The Landmark Speeches of Dr. Martin Luther King, Jr.* (New York: Intellectual Properties Management in association with Grand Central Publishing, 2002).

Memoirs, autobiographies, and other works by King's family members, relatives, professional colleagues, and associates add much to the literature, even if some are not especially reliable on matters of detail. I have consulted Ralph David Abernathy, *And The Walls Came Tumbling Down: An Autobiography* (New York: Harper & Row, 1989); James Farmer, *Lay Bare the Heart: An Autobiography of the Civil Rights Movement* (New York: Arbor House, 1985); Robert S. Graetz, *Montgomery: A White Preacher's Memoir* (Minneapolis: Fortress, 1991); John Lewis, *Walking with the Wind: A Memoir of the Movement* (repr. paperback ed.; New York: Simon & Schuster, 2015); Kathryn Johnson, *My Time with the Kings: A Reporter's Recollections of Martin, Coretta and the Civil Rights Movement* (New York: RossettaBooks, 2016); Dexter Scott King, *Growing Up King: An Intimate Memoir* (New York: Warner, 2004); Coretta Scott King, *My Life with Martin Luther King, Jr.* (New York: Holt, Rinehart & Winston, 1969); Coretta Scott King and Rev. Dr. Barbara A. Reynolds, *My Life, My Love, My Legacy* (New York: Henry Holt, 2017); Mary King, *Freedom Song: A Personal Story of the 1960s Civil Rights Movement* (New York: William Morrow, 1987); Rev. Martin Luther

King Sr., *Daddy King: An Autobiography* (New York: William Morrow, 1980); Benjamin Mays, *Born to Rebel: An Autobiography* (Athens: University of Georgia Press, 1987); L. D. Reddick, *Crusader Without Violence: A Biography of Martin Luther King, Jr.* (New York: Harper, 1959); Jo Ann Gibson Robinson, *The Montgomery Bus Boycott and the Women Who Started It: The Memoir of Jo Ann Gibson Robinson*, ed. David J. Garrow (Knoxville: University of Tennessee Press, 1987); Pat Watters, *Down to Now: Reflections on the Southern Civil Rights Movement* (New York: Pantheon, 1971); and Andrew Young, *An Easy Burden: The Civil Rights Movement and the Transformation of America* (New York: Harper Perennial, 1998).

PRIMARY SOURCES ON THE CIVIL RIGHTS MOVEMENT

There are few subjects in American history with a richer and more easily accessible primary source base for research and further study than the civil rights movement. Recently published documentary history collections are providing easy-to-access and invaluable forays into primary source research. Besides *The Papers of Martin Luther King, Jr.*, and other works of King mentioned above, other highly recommended anthologies include Milton Sernett's *African American Religious History: A Documentary Witness* (Durham, NC: Duke University Press, 1999) and a volume of essays that can be mined extensively for primary source references: Cornel West and Eddie Glaude's *African American Religious Thought: An Anthology* (Philadelphia: Westminster John Knox, 2003). Other indispensable edited collections of primary sources include Howell Raines, ed., *My Soul Is Rested: Movement Days in the Deep South Remembered* (New York: G. P. Putnam's Sons, 1977); Stewart Burns, ed., *Daybreak of Freedom: The Montgomery Bus Boycott* (Chapel Hill: University of North Carolina Press, 1997); Henry Hampton et al., eds., *Voices of Freedom: An Oral History of the Civil Rights Movement from the 1950s through the 1980s* (New York: Bantam, 1990); Faith S. Holsaert et al., eds., *Hands on the Freedom Plow: Personal Accounts by Women in SNCC* (Urbana: University of Illinois Press, 2010); and Constance Curry et al., eds., *Deep in Our Hearts: Nine White Women in the Freedom Movement* (Athens: University of Georgia Press, 2000).

The indispensable filmed documentary history source is *Eyes on the Prize* (PBS, 1987); accompanying it is a documentary history book from Henry Hampton et al., eds., *The Eyes on the Prize Civil Rights History Reader: Documents, Speeches, and Firsthand Accounts from the Black Freedom Struggle* (New York: Penguin, 1991). More recently, two massive volumes present a giant database of speeches and sermons from the civil rights era, formerly available only on reel-to-reel and cassette tape collections in archives scattered throughout the country: Davis W. Houck and David

E. Dixon, eds., *Rhetoric, Religion, and the Civil Rights Movement* (Waco, TX: Baylor University Press), with volume I from 2007 and volume II from 2014.

Digitized oral history collections are a gold mine for civil rights history research; many have just become available in the last few years and are easily keyword searchable by topic: available at https://kinginstitute.stanford.edu/king-papers/about-papers-project. Another invaluable source for more general studies of the civil rights era is the KZSU Project South Interviews, thousands of pages of interviews collected from student volunteers in 1965, now digitized at http://www.oac.cdlib.org/findaid/ark:/13030/tf7489n969/entire_text/. These interviews provide the single most valuable compilation of real-time, on-the-ground sources from that era of the thoughts, motivations, and struggles of volunteers in the movement. Another outstanding compilation lies in the oral history projected conducted by Mississippi State University over the last generation, now collected and accessible at Civil Rights History Project: https://www.loc.gov/collections/civil-rights-history-project/?fa=location%3Amississippi. The "Civil Rights Digital Library," at http://crdl.usg.edu, is particularly strong in broadcast and other media sources from the time period. The Chicago Freedom Movement of 1966 has a fine website where students may access original documents and other materials, at https://sites.middlebury.edu/chicagofreedommovement/. Finally, the older classic Southern Oral History Program, at http://sohp.org, has a collection of interviews from people who lived through the civil rights era. An excellent compilation of resources on the Student Nonviolent Coordinating Committee may be found at https://snccdigital.org/resources/gateway-conversations/.

To these can be added the website and digital history project "Veterans of the Civil Rights Movement," at http://www.crmvet.org/. A keyword search of "religion" and related terms will quickly yield a goldmine of accounts, memoirs, reminiscences, and other valuable material for the researcher. Reading all the volumes together gives a profoundly rich and complex sense of King, shorn of the myths and oversimplifications that have hampered public understanding of his life and work.

SECONDARY SOURCES AND MAJOR STUDIES

As he took his Baptist pulpit in Montgomery, Martin Luther King Jr. had no idea of the history that was about to overtake him, but long-time community activists quickly recognized the usefulness of the young doctoral candidate. The story in elaborate detail has been told most fully, and for a popular audience, in Taylor Branch's trilogy, starting with his classic work of journalistic history, *Parting the Waters: America in the King Years* (New York: Simon & Schuster, 1988). A scholarly rendition of this story in all its intricate detail may be found in David Garrow's *Bearing the Cross*. That work provided a landmark scholarly biography that everyone else has drawn from since. Peter Ling's shorter work *Martin Luther King, Jr.* is a fine, compact, strongly argued addition to the list of indispensable biographies.

More specifically focused studies of critical interest include several of the works of the scholar Lewis Baldwin, especially *The Voice of Conscience*; Richard Lischer's *The Preacher King*; and Albert Miller's *Voice of Deliverance*. These three together provide a fascinating exploration of the sources and roots of King's thought and sermons. The two works of Jonathan Rieder listed previously, *The Word of the Lord Is Upon Me* and *Gospel of Freedom*, join this august list of recent vital works for all students of King. The first work just mentioned is especially strong in arguing for the universalism of King, his status as both black and post-ethnic. Finally, Thomas Jackson's *From Civil Rights to Human Rights: Martin Luther King, Jr., and the Struggle for Economic Justice* is the most important work published on King since 2000. Jackson places King squarely in the tradition of American social democracy, and emphasizes how much his later radicalism was evident even from his earlier years in seminary and the ministry. (Full references to the above are in the first paragraph of this bibliographic essay.)

Much of the most innovative recent scholarship has studied the "long history of the civil rights movement." One groundbreaking article that set the discussion for a generation of books to come was Jacquelyn Dowd Hall, "The Long Civil Rights Movement and the Political Uses of the Past," *Journal of American History* 91, no. 4 (March 2005): 1233–1263. This work seeks to break from the "Montgomery to Memphis" paradigm, starting with the bus boycott and ending with the assassination of King. It examines the longer history of movement activism, dating at least back to the New Deal. Some have claimed a "movement" lasting roughly from Emancipation to the present. Looking forward, the "long history" advocates see contemporary issues, such as rates of incarceration, defunded public institutions, attempts to roll back the Voting Rights Act, and disproportionate effects of "The Great Recession" from 2008 forward as evidence that the civil rights movement did not fade away but simply moved on to other issues. Critics have countered that the period of the 1950s and 1960s should be seen as special for a reason. Moreover, they argue that even "local people" understood the indispensable role of public figures such as Martin Luther King Jr.; David Chappell has advanced this thesis in his important (if controversial) history *A Stone of Hope: Prophetic Religion and the Death of Jim Crow* (Chapel Hill: University of North Carolina Press, 1994).

Those looking at religion and the civil rights movement find similar debates. Certainly, black churches from Reconstruction to World War II organized NAACP chapters, educated leaders who led the struggle against American apartheid, and supported educational institutions and fraternal clubs and societies that nurtured a small but crucial black middle class. At the same time, figures such as W. E. B. Du Bois blasted the church for doing "less than nothing," and later scholars analyzed the "de-radicalization of the black church." Even during the "classic" period of the civil rights movement, a small fraction of "the black church" pursued active involvement in a freedom struggle that required sacrifice and subjected people to the danger of violence from white terrorists. At the same time, black Christians formed the rank-and-file of the movement, put their bodies on the line, filled jail cells and manned picket lines, and demonstrated the dramatic impact of black spirituality on a social movement that transformed American life.

Like many other historical topics, the historiography of the civil rights movement began with "top-down" stories, often biographies of major leaders such as Martin Luther King Jr. Then, over time, social history (or "bottom-up") approaches gradually became more prominent. Most recent scholarship has emphasized the latter, in part because participants in the civil rights movement themselves, particularly those in the Student Nonviolent Coordinating Committee, sought to "let the people decide," a point well explored in Todd Moye, *Let the People Decide: Black Freedom and White Resistance Movements in Sunflower County, Mississippi, 1945–1986* (Chapel Hill: University of North Carolina Press, 2004).

The connection between religion, civil rights, and social justice in everyday life found an especially powerful connection in the "local people" who did much of the actual work of the civil rights movement. Aldon D. Morris's *The Origins of the Civil Rights Movement: Black Communities Organizing for Change* (New York: Free, 1984) begins not with Montgomery but with an earlier boycott led by black Baptist pastor T. D. Jemison in Baton Rouge, Louisiana, in 1953, an action that set the stage for mass mobilizations to come. Morris refers to the Southern Christian Leadership Conference (SCLC) as the "decentralized arm of the black church." The argument advanced by Morris is furthered by Andrew Manis's memorable biography of Fred Shuttlesworth, *A Fire You Can't Put Out: The Civil Rights Life of Birmingham's Reverend Fred Shuttlesworth* (Tuscaloosa: University of Alabama Press, 1999), which shows the longtime Baptist pastor in Birmingham at the forefront of civil rights crusades in this most brutally racist of southern cities long before the more well-known names from the SCLC showed up in 1963. Readers will also want to consult Glenn Eskew's *But for Birmingham: The Local and National Movements in the Civil Rights Struggle* (Chapel Hill: University of North Carolina Press, 1997).

Civil rights activists such as Shuttlesworth mixed the language of evangelicalism with the tenets of American civil religion. In their minds, both the Bible and American history were full of freedom struggles. They were also inseparable in the mind of Fannie Lou Hamer, the subject of several biographies and analyses, the best of which is Maegan Parker Brooks's *A Voice That Could Stir an Army: Fannie Lou Hamer and the Rhetoric of the Black Freedom Movement* (Jackson: University Press of Mississippi, 2014). Much the same could be said for Ella Baker, the long-time NAACP organizer whose career stretched from the Harlem Renaissance of the 1920s to the SCLC and the formation of the SNCC in the early 1960s, whose life and principles of community organizing are detailed in Barbara Ransby's *Ella Baker and the Black Freedom Movement: A Radical Democratic Vision* (Chapel Hill: University of North Carolina Press, 2005). See also Katherine Mellen Charron, *Freedom's Teacher: The Life of Septima Clark* (Chapel Hill: University of North Carolina Press, 2009).

Much recent debate has concerned whether, and how much, "religion" influenced and drove the civil rights movement. Gary Dorrien's lengthy and impressive work *Breaking White Supremacy*, part of his two-volume exploration of the black social gospel from the mid-nineteenth century almost to the present, places King squarely within the black social gospel tradition, as do Vaneesa Cook in "Martin Luther King Jr. and the Long Social Gospel Movement"; Douglas Sturm in "Martin Luther King Jr. as Democratic Socialist"; Clayborne Carson in "Martin Luther King, Jr., and the African-American Social Gospel," *African-American Religion: Interpretive Essays in History and Culture*, ed. Timothy E. Fulop and Albert J. Raboteau (New York: Routledge, 1997); and Vaneesa Cook in "Martin Luther King, Jr., and the Long Social Gospel Movement," *Religion and American Culture* 26, no. 1 (2019): 74–100. Three important studies particularly focused on theologies and church organizations include James F. Findlay Jr., *Church People in the Struggle: The National Council of Churches and the Black Freedom Movement, 1950–1970* (New York: Oxford University Press, 1993); David P. Cline, *From Reconciliation to Revolution: The Student Interracial Ministry, Liberal Christianity, and the Civil Rights Movement* (Chapel Hill: University of North Carolina Press, 2016); and Charles Marsh, *God's Long Summer: Stories of Faith and Civil Rights* (Princeton, NJ: Princeton University Press, 1997).

Critically important broader studies for understanding the civil rights movement in local and national contexts, and with ample attention to the connection between local people and nationally known figures, include Charles Payne, *I've Got the Light of Freedom: The Organizing Tradition and the Mississippi Freedom Struggle* (Berkeley: University of California Press, 1995); Ansley Quiros, *God with Us: Lived Theology and the Freedom Struggle in Americus, Georgia, 1942–1976* (Chapel Hill: University of North Carolina

Press, 2018); Emilye Crosby, ed., *Civil Rights History from the Ground Up: Local Struggles, a National Movement* (Athens: University of Georgia Press, 2011); Vicki L. Crawford et al., eds., *Women in the Civil Rights Movement: Trailblazers and Torchbearers, 1941–1965* (Bloomington: Indiana University Press, 1993); and Wesley Hogan, *Many Minds, One Heart: SNCC's Dream for a New America* (Chapel Hill: University of North Carolina Press, 2007).

For the "long" history of King's influences, see the indispensable biography by Peter Eisenstadt, *Against the Hounds of Hell: A Life of Howard Thurman* (Charlottesville: University of Virginia Press, 2021), and for a compelling history of "nonviolence before King," see Anthony Siracusa, *Nonviolence Before King: The Politics of Being and the Black Freedom Struggle* (Chapel Hill: University of North Carolina Press, 2021). For a broader context seeing the movement in the long history of southern religious history, see Paul Harvey, *Redeeming the South: Religious Cultures and Racial Identities among Southern Baptists, 1865–1925* (Chapel Hill: University of North Carolina Press, 1997); *Christianity and Race in the American South: A History* (Chicago: University of Chicago Press, 2016); and *Freedom's Coming: Religious Culture and the Shaping of the South from the Civil War through the Civil Rights Era* (Chapel Hill: University of North Carolina Press, 2005).

Thomas Sugrue's *Sweet Land of Liberty: The Forgotten Struggle for Civil Rights in the North* (New York: Random House, 2008) is the indispensable study of the civil rights movement in the northern states; more specifically for Chicago, the standard work is James Ralph, *Northern Protest: Martin Luther King, Jr., Chicago, and the Civil Rights Movement* (Cambridge, MA: Harvard University Press, 1993). See also David Chappell's *Waking from the Dream: The Struggle for Civil Rights in the Shadow of Martin Luther King., Jr.* (New York: Random House, 2014) for a study of the accomplishments of the movement after King's death, especially in the area of housing.

A number of recent scholars, particularly those who focus on the student movement, dispute the centrality of religion. Southern white churches, of course, were most often either indifferent or hostile toward the movement, a story told for Mississippi in Carolyn Dupont's *Mississippi Praying: Southern White Evangelicals and the Civil Rights Movement, 1945–1975* (New York: New York University Press, 2013). She shows how much white theology underlay segregationism, as do works on the church "pray-ins" such as Stephen Haynes's *The Last Segregated Hour: The Memphis Kneel-Ins and the Campaign for Southern Church Desegregation* (New York: Oxford University Press, 2013). Jonathan Bass's *Blessed Are the Peacemakers: Martin Luther King Jr., Eight White Religious Leaders, and the "Letter from Birmingham Jail"* (25th anniversary edition; Baton Rouge: Louisiana State University Press, 2021) is a fascinating look at the white Birmingham religious leaders who provoked King's famous "Letter," providing critical context for that crucial document of civil rights history. Finally, Jane Dailey's article, "Sex, Segregation and the Sacred After *Brown," Journal of American History* 91, no. 1 (June 2004): 119–144, is a must for understanding how the phobia of interracial sex so deeply shaped the period.

A number of recent important interpretive works on King have been published, compelling especially a reexamination of his role as a political philosopher, his dialogue with Malcolm X and the Black Power movement, and his status as one of the most pursued victims of FBI surveillance in American history. On King and Malcolm X, there are a number of good works but the best of them is Peniel Joseph's *The Sword and the Shield*; I would also recommend the set of primary documents collected in *Martin Luther King Jr., Malcolm X, and the Civil Rights Struggle of the 1950s and 1960s: A Brief History with Documents*. For an excellent set of reflections by a group of historians, philosophers, and theologians on King as a political philosopher, see Shelby and Terry, eds., *To Shape a New World*, a book that has the singular virtue of taking King as a philosopher seriously and grappling with his ideas within higher realms of thought. A number of recent works, such as those by James Cobb, Timothy Tyson, and Akinyele Umoja, consider the implicit "dialogue" between proponents of violence in self-defense and proponents of the philosophy of nonviolence, as well as the very real presence of guns for self-defense in numerous black communities who knew too well that, as the title of Cobb's book puts it, "this nonviolent stuff'll get you killed." King understood their views, and himself had to be coaxed into adopting the full philosophy of nonviolence. See James E. Cobb, *This Nonviolent Stuff'll Get Your Killed: How Guns Made the Civil Rights Movement Possible* (Durham, NC: Duke University Press, 2015); Timothy B. Tyson, *Radio Free Dixie: Robert F. Williams and the Roots of Black Power* (Chapel Hill: University of North Carolina Press, 2001); and Akinyele Omowala Umoja, *We Will Shoot Back: Armed Resistance in the Mississippi Freedom Movement* (New York: New York University Press, 2013).

Finally, on the subject of FBI surveillance, the film director Sam Pollard late in 2020 released a searching and fascinating documentary which is the best place to start on this complex topic: *MLK/FBI*. Pollard's film depended on the original work of investigation on this subject, done by David J. Garrow and published originally in 1983 as *The FBI and Martin Luther King, Jr.: From "Solo" to Memphis* (New York: W. W. Norton, 1981). Since then, some new information has come to light, based largely on some documents that were misfiled in other archival papers; they were supposed to be in the FBI files, many of which are closed to researchers until 2027 (and the published ones are heavily redacted). One such misplaced document records some notes from a surveillance of a hotel room, where some sex acts occurred, with one agent scribbling a note alleging that King had been present and joking as a woman was sexually assaulted. The scholar David Garrow has argued that these notes are more reliable than many others in the FBI files; others have contended they are just as unreliable as the others simply because the agents were feeding their boss, the prurient J. Edgar Hoover, exactly what he wanted to hear to bolster his campaign to "destroy" King. As of this writing, there simply is no way to assess the allegation, based as it is on one dubiously sourced comment on a surveillance document. Presumably, after 2027 there will be updates to this story. For an objective summary of what we know, and what we don't, see David Greenberg, "How to Make Sense of the Shocking New MLK Documents," *Politico*,   https://www.politico.com/magazine/story/2019/06/04/how-to-make-sense-of-the-shocking-new-mlk-documents-227042/.

Most recently, Lerone Martin's revelatory article "Bureau Clergyman" and forthcoming book *Apostles of Justice: How J. Edgar Hoover and His F.B.I. Aided and Abetted the Religious Right* (Princeton, NJ: Princeton University Press, forthcoming) meticulously documents how the FBI cooperated with Elder Lightfoot Solomon Michaux in a campaign to discredit King politically; Martin stresses less the sexual obsessions of Hoover than Hoover's self-perceived status as a warrior in the battle of "Soviet Rule" versus "Christian Renewal."

I also recommend the very frank and extensive discussion of the topics of King's flaws as a person in Michael Eric Dyson's *I May Not Get There with You: The True Martin Luther King, Jr.* (New York: Free, 2000). Dyson concludes King's flaws do not overshadow his power as the master orator and inspiration for a movement for justice. Dyson also makes painfully clear the immense cost King paid, the damage inflicted upon him by the enormous pressures of constant work and travel, having always to be a "model" Negro, the perils of celebrityhood, the realities of government harassment and surveillance, and the psychic wounds exacted by confronting American racism directly. The unflinching look at King's personal life makes his brilliant achievements all the more astonishing.

The chapter on King's "Afterlives" in this book relies very heavily on the excellent scholarship of Jason Sokol's *The Heavens Might Crack: The Death and Legacy of Martin Luther King Jr.* (New York: Basic, 2018), an extensive examination of reactions to King's death in the immediate aftermath of his assassination and during the subsequent decades. For the events leading up to his death, see in particular Joseph Rosenbloom, *Redemption: Martin Luther King Jr.'s Last 31 Hours* (Boston: Beacon, 2018), and Michael Honey, *To the Promised Land: Martin Luther King and the Fight for Economic Justice* (New York: Norton, 2018). To that one may add a growing literature on the misuse of King and his words in history.

The best source on the misuse of civil rights history to serve various contemporary nefarious agendas is Jeanne Theoharis's *A More Beautiful and Terrible History*. A short version of this argument that explains the various categories of the "remembered" King may be found in Tom Sugrue, "Restoring King," in the periodical *Jacobin*, available at https://www.jacobinmag.com/2014/01/restoring-king/, and in Paul Harvey, "Recovering Martin Luther King's Dream of Democracy," at the Berkley Forum, https://berkleycenter.georgetown.edu/responses/recovering-martin-luther-king-s-dream-of-democracy. Most recently, a series of essays, headed up by Harvard political philosopher Brandon Terry, may be found at Brandon M. Terry, "MLK Now," *Boston Review*, September 10, 2018, http://www.bostonreview.net/forum/brandon-m-terry-mlk-now. A number of other authors and scholars, including Barbara Ransby and Elizabeth Hinton, respond to Terry's essay.

Finally, an extensive examination of the details of King's death, James Earl Ray, and the entire assassination controversy may be found in Gerald Posner, *Killing the Dream: James Earl Ray and the Assassination of Martin Luther King, Jr.* (New York: Random House, 1998). Posner concludes that Ray acted alone. For a contrary view, which sees the assassination as a plot involving the FBI, organized crime, the CIA, and local enemies of King in Memphis, see William Pepper, *An Act of State: The Execution of Martin Luther King* (updated edition; New York: Verso, 2008). From there, a quick Google search will yield an entire sub-universe of King assassination plot conspiracy theories and polemics for and against Posner's book.

Index

CPSIA information can be obtained
at www.ICGtesting.com
Printed in the USA
BVHW081916210921
617160BV00002B/4

9 781538 115923